FC

A GAMBLER

ON THE

MISSISSIPPI

FORTY YEARS

A GAMBLER

ON THE

MISSISSIPPI

BY

GEORGE H. DEVOL.

A CABIN BOY IN 1839; COULD STEAL CARDS AND CHEAT THE BOYS
AT ELEVEN; STOCK A DECK AT FOURTEEN; BESTED SOLDIERS ON
THE RIO GRANDE DURING THE MEXICAN WAR; WON HUNDREDS
OF THOUSANDS FROM PAYMASTERS, COTTON BUYERS, DEFAULT-
ERS, AND THIEVES; FOUGHT MORE ROUGH-AND-TUMBLE FIGHTS
THAN ANY MAN IN AMERICA, AND WAS THE MOST DARING GAM-
BLER IN THE WORLD.

ILLUSTRATED.

FACSIMILE EDITION

APPLEWOOD BOOKS
BEDFORD, MASSACHUSETTS

Forty Years a Gambler on the Mississippi was first published by Devol & Haines of Cincinnati in 1887.

ISBN 1-55709-110-2

Thank you for purchasing an Applewood book. Applewood reprints America's lively classics—books from the past that are of interest to modern readers. For a free copy of our current catalog, write to:

Applewood Books
PO Box 365
Bedford, MA 01730

Library of Congress Cataloging-in-Publication Data:
Devol, George H., b. 1829.
    Forty years a gambler on the Mississippi / by George H. Devol. – Facsim. ed.
        p.   cm.
Originally published: Cincinnati: Devol & Haines, 1887.
    ISBN 1-55709-110-2
    1. Devol, George H., b. 1829. 2. Gambling – Mississippi River – History – 19th Century. 3. Mississippi River – Description and travel. 4. Frontier and pioneer life – Mississippi River. 5. Gamblers – Mississippi River – Biography.
I. Title.
F353.D49 1955
977'.02'092–dc20
[B]   95-36846
                                              CIP

FORTY YEARS

A GAMBLER

ON THE

MISSISSIPPI

PREFACE.

THE author of this book has written the stories as they would recur to his memory, and no effort has been made at classification. They are not fictitious; many of the persons named are now living, and they can and will testify that the stories are founded on facts.

He belongs to the celebrated Devol family of Marietta. His grandfather, Jonathan Devol, was an officer in the Revolutionary War, and was well known to the pioneer history of Ohio. He was one of the passengers on the *Mayflower*, which he constructed for the use of the first company of emigrants to Ohio. He erected a house on the Campus Martius in 1788, and was joined by his wife and six children in December of that year. He was one of the committee to explore the country in search of suitable places for mills and farming settlements. In 1791 he repaired to Belpre with his family. He succeeded in clearing a patch of land, and built a log cabin not far below the house of Captain William Dorce. The news of the Big Bottom massacre reached him while attending court at Marietta, and he hurried home. Mrs. Devol, hearing that the Indians were on the war-path, ordered the children to lie down with their clothes on, ready for the danger signal. He became famous by building the floating mill. In 1792 he built a twelve-oared barge of twenty-five tons burden for Captain Putnam. The author's father was Barker Devol, who died at Carrollton, Ky., on the 8th day of March, 1871, at the age of 85. He was a ship-builder, and worked with his father at Marietta. He left a widow and six children, who are all living, except one, the youngest being George H. Devol.

THE AUTHOR.

CONTENTS.

CONTENTS.

CONTENTS.

CONTENTS.

Forty Years a Gambler on the Mississippi.

BOYHOOD DAYS.

"I'll serve his youth, for youth must have his course,
For being restrained it makes him ten times worse;
His pride, his riot, all that may be named,
Time may recall, and all his madness tamed."

My DEAR READER: I first saw the light of day in a little town called Marietta, at the mouth of the Muskingum River in the State of Ohio, on the first day of August, 1829. I was the youngest of six children, and was the pet of the family. My father was a ship carpenter, and worked at boat-building in the beginning of the present century. I had good opportunities to secure an early education, as we had good schools in the West at that time. I had very little liking for books, and much less for school. When my parents thought me at school, I was playing "hookey" with other boys, running about the river, kicking foot-ball, playing "shinny on your own side," and having a fight nearly every day. I hardly ever went home that I did not have my face all scratched up from having been in a fight, which innocent amusement I loved much better than school. When I was hardly ten years of age, I would carry stones in my pocket and tackle the school teachers if they attempted to whip me. My father was away from home at his work most of the time, and my mother (God bless her dear old soul) could not manage me. She has often called in some passer-by to help her punish me. I can now see I richly deserved all the punishment I ever received, and more too. When there was company at our house, and my mother would be busy preparing a meal, I would get my bow and arrows and shoot the cups off from the table, and then run away. I guess I was about the worst boy of my age west of the Allegheny Mountains that was born of good Christian parents. I have often heard the good old church members say. "That boy will be hung if he lives to be twenty years old." But I have fooled them, and am still on the turf, although I have had some pretty close calls, as you will see by reading this book.

LEAVING HOME.

In the year 1839, while at the river one day, I saw a steamer lying at the wharf-boat by the name of *Wacousta*. The first steward said I could ship as a cabin boy at $4 per month. I thought this a great opportunity, so when the boat backed out I was on board without saying anything to my parents or any one else. My first duty was to scour knives. I knew they would stand no foolishness, so at it I went, and worked like a little trooper, and by so doing I gained the good will of the steward. At night I was told to get a mattress and sleep on the floor of the cabin; this I was very glad to do, as I was tired.

About four o'clock in the morning the second steward came up to me and gave me a pretty hard kick in the side that hurt me, and called out: "Get up here, and put your mattress away." I did get up and put away my bed, and then I went to the steward who kicked me and said: "Look here! Don't kick me that way again, for you hurt me." He let go and hit me a slap in the face that made my ears ring; so into him I pitched. I was a big boy for only ten years old; but I struck the wrong man that time, for he hit me another lick in the nose that came very near sending me to grass, but I rallied and came again. This time I had a piece of stone coal that I grabbed out of a bucket; I let it fly, and it caught him on the side of the head and brought him to his knees. By this time the passengers were getting up to see what was the matter; the pilot and first steward soon put a stop to the fight. I told my story to the boss, and he took sides with me. He told the officers of the boat that I was the best boy to work that he had; so they discharged the second steward at Cincinnati, and you can bet I was glad. I remained on the *Wacousta* for some time, and thought myself a good steamboat man. I knew it all, for I had been there.

The next boat I shipped on was the *Walnut Hills*, at $7 per month. You could hear her " scape " (whistle) for a distance of twenty miles of a clear day or night. I would get up early in the morning and make some " five-cent pieces " (there were no nickels in those days) by blacking boots.

PUT ASHORE FOR FIGHTING.

I quit the *Walnut Hills* after three months, and shipped with Captain Patterson on the *Cicero*, bound for Nashville. The first trip up the Cumberland River the boat was full of passengers, and I had a fight with the pantryman. The Captain said I should go ashore. They brought me up to the office, and the clerk was told to pay me my wages, which amounted to the large sum of one dollar and fifty cents. I was told to get my baggage; but as two blue cotton shirts and what I had on my back was all I possessed, it did not take me long to pack. My trunk was a piece of brown paper with a pin lock. They landed me at a point where the bank was about one hundred feet high, and so steep that a goat could not climb it. They commenced to pull in the plank, when the steward yelled out to the Captain, " that he could not get along without that boy," and asked him to let me go as far as Nashville. I was told to come aboard, which I did, and I remained on that boat for one year, during which time I learned to play " seven-up," and to " steal card," so that I could cheat the boys, and I felt as if I was fixed for life. I quit the *Cicero*, and shipped with Captain Mason on the steamer *Tiago*. Bill Campbell, afterward the first captain of the *Robert E. Lee*, was a cabin boy on the same boat. He is now a captain in the Vicksburg Packet Line. During the time I was on the *Tiago* the Mexican War broke out.

WAR WITH MEXICO.

"Land intersected by a narrow frith
    Abhor each other. Mountains interposed
    Make enemies of nations who had else,
    Like kindred drops, been mingled into one."

When the Mexican War broke out, our boat was lying at Pittsburg. The Government bought a new boat called the *Corvette*, that had just been built at Brownsville. A cousin of mine was engaged to pilot her on the Rio Grande. His name was Press Devol. He was a good pilot on the Ohio, from Cincinnati to Pittsburg, but had never seen the Rio Grande, except on the map. I thought I would like to go to war, and to Mexico. My cousin got me the position as barkeeper, so I quit our boat, and shipped on the *Corvette*, for the war. Jack McCourtney, of Wheeling, was the owner of the bar.

There was a man aboard, on our way down, who took a great liking to me. He was well posted on cards, and taught me to "stock a deck," so I could give a man a big hand; so I was a second time "fixed for life."

When we got down to New Orleans they took the boat over to Algiers, took her guards off, and part of her cabin, and we started across the Gulf; and you bet my hair stood up at times, when those big swells would go clear over her in a storm. But finally we landed at Bagdad, and commenced to load her with supplies for the army.

I soon got tired of the Rio Grande, and after cheating all the soldiers that I could at cards (as there was no one else to rob), I took a vessel, and came back to New Orleans. When I landed there, I was very comfortably fixed, as I had about $2,700, and was not quite seventeen years old. Here I was in a big city, and knew no one; so I went and got a boarding house, and left all my cash, but what I might need, in the care of an old gentleman that looked something like my father. I thought he must be honest, as he looked like him, and he proved himself so.

I then picked up courage, and said to myself, " I believe that I will go home." But to pay passage was all foolishness, as I was such a good hand on a boat, so I shipped on the steamboat *Montgomery*, Captain Montgomery, and Windy Marshall (as they called him) Mate. I shipped as second steward, at twenty dollars per month.

The boat was full of people, and the card tables were going every night as soon as the supper tables were cleared. We had been out from New Orleans two days and nights before I picked up a game. One afternoon in the texas, I beat my man out of $170; and as there was no "squeal" in those days, I was all right, although they did not allow any of the crew to play with passengers.

We got to Louisville, where the boat laid up and paid off her crew, and I came on to Cincinnati.

HOME AGAIN.

" Be it a weakness, it deserves some praise;
    We love the play-place of our early days."

" Well, now I'll go home to the folks," I said, " and see if they will forgive me." I thought I would take home some presents, so I bought about $400 worth of goods, including coffee, sugar, teas, etc., and took the old steamer *Hibernia*, of Pittsburg, Captain Clinefelter, master. You ought to have seen me when I stepped on the wharfboat at Marietta, my birthplace, dressed to death, with my gold watch and chain, and a fine trunk I had bought at New Orleans for $40. I got my groceries off the wharfboat, and hired a wagon, and I took it afoot, as in those days you could not get a hack except at a livery stable.

My mother knew me at first sight. Father was working at the ship-yard at Port Homer, on the other side of the Muskingum River, and did not come home until night.

I stopped at home a year, and had a fight nearly every week. I then came to Cincinnati again, where I met my brother Paul, who was working at calking steamboats. He coaxed me to stay with him, saying he would teach me the trade. I consented, and soon was able to earn $4 per day. We worked together a few years, and made a good deal of money; but every Monday morning I went to work broke. I became infatuated with the game of faro, and it kept me a slave. So I concluded to either quit work or quit gambling. I studied the matter over for a long time. At last one day while we were finishing a boat that we had calked, and were working on a float aft of the wheel, I gave my tools a push with my foot, and they all went into the river. My brother called out and asked me what I was doing. I looked up, a little sheepish, and said it was the last lick of work I would ever do. He was surprised to hear me talk that way, and asked me what I intended to do. I told him I intended to live off of fools and suckers. I also said, "I will make money rain;" and I did come near doing as I said.

THE GAME OF RONDO.

After shoving my calking tools into the river, I went to keeping a "Rondo" game for Daniel and Joseph Smith, up on Fifth Street, at $18 per week. Hundreds of dollars changed hands every hour, both day and night. At the end of six months I was taken in as a partner, and at that time the receipts of the game were about $600 every day. I had money to sell (or throw away), and, for a boy, I made it fly. In a short time the police began to raid us, and we would be fined fifty dollars each about once a month. Then they raised it to $100, and next to $500. This was too much, so we had heavy oak and iron doors put up; but the police would batter them down, and get us just the same. One night they surrounded the house, broke down the door, and arrested my two partners; but I escaped by the roof. The next day I went up to the jail to take the boys something to eat, when they nabbed and locked me up also. They put me in the same cell with Kissane, of the steamer *Martha Washington* notoriety, who was living in great style at the jail. They fined us $500 each and let us go, and that broke up " Rondo."

After retiring from the " Rondo " business, I took passage with Captain Riddle on the steamer *Ann Linington*, bound for the Wabash River, to visit a sister, who lived near Bloomfield, Edgar County, Ills. There were no railroads in that part of the country in those days. My sister's husband bought 3,000 acres of land near Paris, at $1.25 per acre, and the same land is now worth $300 per acre. During my trip up the river I formed the acquaintance of Sam Burges, who was a great circus man. Captain Riddle and Burges got to playing poker, and the Captain " bested " him for about $200. I told Burges that I could make him win if he could get me into the game. So, after supper, they sat down to play, and I was a looker-on. Burges asked me to take a hand, which I did, and on my deal I would " fill " his hand, so that he soon had the Captain badly rattled, and he lost about $900. The old Captain was getting " full," and I looked for a fight sooner or later. Burges invited all to take a drink, when the Captain refused, and told Burges that he was a " d—d gambler." Burges called him a liar, so at it they went. The Captain was getting the best of it when we parted them, and it was all we could do to keep Burges from shooting. I got one-half of the $900, and no one called me a gambler either.

As the boat was going through the " draw," at Terre Haute, she took a " shear " on the pilot, and knocked down her chimneys. The Captain went up on deck, cursed the pilot, went down on the lower deck, knocked down two deck-hands, and raised cain generally. Burges expected he would tackle him again, but the Captain did not want any of that gun. When we arrived at the landing, I got off, and went to my sister's. I remained there about one month, and had a good time shooting wild turkeys and chickens. On my return trip I got into a game of poker, and took in a few hundred. I stopped off at Louisville a short time, and then shipped for Cincinnati, where I remained until I was very near broke.

NOW A GAMBLER.

> "If yet you love game at so dear a rate,
>   Learn this, that hath old gamesters dearly cost:
> Dost lose? rise up. Dost win? rise in that state.
>   Who strives to sit out losing hands are lost."

I left Cincinnati for St. Louis; and when I landed there, I had just $40 left. I secured a boarding house, and started to take in the town. I made inquiries for a faro bank, and at last found one; and I bolted in as if I was an old sport. I stepped up to the table, and asked the dealer for $40 worth of checks. I then commenced to play, and won; and, pressing my good luck, in two hours had $780 in checks in front of me. I told the dealer to cash my checks, and I walked out.

The next day I was on my way to St. Paul, as at that time there was a great emigration in that direction. I took passage on a steamer that had nearly 300 people on board, going there to buy homes, and, of course, they had plenty of money with them. After the supper tables were cleared, a game of poker was commenced; then another, and another, until there were five tables going. I sat at one of the tables looking on for a long time, until at length one of the gentlemen said to me, "Do you ever indulge?" I said, "Hardly ever, but I do not care if I play a while." The bar was open, and they all appeared to enjoy a good drink, but I never cared for anything stronger than a lemonade. The result was that they all got full, and I thought I might as well have some of their money as to let the barkeeper have it, and I commenced to try some of the tricks I had learned. I found they worked finely, and at daybreak the bar and I had all the money. I got about $1,300, which made me $2,000 strong.

When we arrived at St. Paul I struck another bank, and to my sorrow. I found one conducted by Cole Martin and "King Cole," two old sports, who soon relieved me of my $2,000. I then was without a cent, and too game to let the gamblers know that I was broke. After I had been there about a week, one of them stopped me on the street, and asked me why I did not come around and see them. He said: "I don't ask you to play, but come and dine with us." I accepted his invitation, and went around that evening, and had as fine a bird supper as I ever sat down to.

MY FIRST KENO.

"'Tis not enough to help the feeble up,
But to support him after."

The next day I visited another club-house, where they had keno going at fifty cents a card. I had seen it before, and took a great fancy to the game. I inquired how much an outfit would cost. They said they had two keno sets, and if I wanted one they would sell it to me for $250.

Now came the tug of war—how to get the keno. I at last thought of a plan, and that was to borrow the amount of one of the dealers who had won the $2,000 from me. So I made a bold front and told him what I wanted to do, and he gave me $300 in cash, saying at the same time, "Pay me when you are able, as I like to help a young man who tries to help himself." I bought the keno set, and had $50 left, which paid all my debts and started me in business.

2

Cole Martin, one of the men who loaned me the money, said to me: "Now, after the faro bank closes to-night, at my house, if you bring your keno over I will help you to get up a game." "All right," I said; so I took it over, and opened on the billiard tables, and he brought all of his players into the room, and said, "Let us start this young man's game." They commenced playing at $1 per card at twelve o'clock, and at six in the morning they were playing at $10 per card. I was taking out 10 per cent. They all got stuck. That night my receipts amounted to $1,300.

The result was they put the carpenters at work to fit up a nice room for me, and in eight months my part of the game was $33,000.

Then I began to think I was a blooded boy, and soon began to take the girls out riding and to wine suppers, and to play the bank higher than a cat's back, as the old keno game was a great producer.

About this time the town of Winona was looking up. There were but two or three little frame houses, but a great many people got off there, going back in the country. So I went down there and bought a raft of green lumber, hired carpenters, and put them to work building houses. They soon had five or six done, and in about a week after they were finished, you could stand outside and throw a big dog through the cracks. But they were full every night at $1 a head, bringing their own blankets, and sleeping on the floor.

I sent and got another keno set, and opened a bar room, and was making money like dirt, when one day a man walked in with a bucket of water, and commenced pouring it on one of my billiard tables that I got in Chicago, and which cost me $500. I walked up to him and asked him what he was doing? He told me to go to h—l. I let fly, caught him on the neck, and down he went, and he lay there for some time. Finally they took him to where he and his wife were stopping, and that night he died.

Then I commenced to think about getting out of that hot box. I got together what money I could, and carried a canoe to the river, and started for Dubuque. There were no telegraph lines at that time. I had been there but a few days before the news came to me that the doctors had held a post mortem examination, and decided the man had had delirium tremens, and could only have lived a short time. They sawed open his skull, and found his brain a jelly in the center. So I went back and found his wife, gave her one of the houses which I had built and $700 in money.

I then put a man in charge of my business, and went back to St. Paul, where my keno games were still going on. But the man I left in charge of my business at Winona sold all he could and skipped out, and that was the last seen of him till I went up the Missouri River two years after, when I found him in Kansas City. At that time there were but three or four houses and a hotel down at the river bank. It was a great point for the Santa Fé traders.

I became acquainted with a man named McGee, who owned the largest part of Kansas City. He was a great lover of the game of "seven-up," so we commenced to play at $10 a game, and I beat him out of five lots (as he had no money), which I afterward sold at $10 a piece. Twelve years ago, as I passed through there, I saw those same lots bringing $600 per foot.

I went from there to St. Joe, Omaha, and Council Bluffs, and broke a great many fellows playing poker. I then settled down at dealing faro in St. Joseph, Mo. After staying there one year I went to St. Louis, where I remained two or three months, and then went to New Orleans. I landed there in 1853. The yellow fever was raging, there being 300 deaths per day. Then was the time, if there was any fright in the young gambler, for it to have shown itself; but I made up my mind that if I had to go I might as well go then as at any other time.

I was taken down with the fever, and nurses were scarce;

but I got an old colored woman, and told her to stick to me and I would give her $25 per day as long as I was sick, and if I handed in my checks she might have all I left. In twenty-three days, by the grace of our good Maker, I was up eating chicken soup. They watched me so close I could get nothing else.

During this time I got an answer from a letter written to my partner at St. Paul, telling him to sell out as best he could, and to send me my part, which he did.

INDIANS CAN PLAY POKER.

The year I was in St. Paul they paid off a lot of Indians a short distance from the town. I was told that the Red Man was a good poker player, and was always looking for the best of it. They paid them in silver; so I got some of the hard money, hired a horse and buggy, got some whisky, and started out to give them a game, more for the fun and novelty of the thing than to win their money; for I had the old keno game running, and she was a good producer. When I got among the savages, they were having a war dance. After the dance they smoked the pipe of peace and drank my whisky, and I smoked their pipes. After the friendly smoking was over, they started in to playing poker. They invited and insisted on me changing in, so at last I sat down and took a hand. One of the old bucks soon began to cheat. He had an old hat in front of him, and inside of the hat he had a looking-glass, so that he could see on his deal every card he dealt out. I knew he was after me, so I told him to put the hat away and play fair. He saw I was no "sucker," so he put it away. We played for some time, and it was all I could do to keep even by playing on the square with big "injins," as I found them very good card players. I held out a hand, but had to wait some time for the "wild man of the forest." At last there was a big "blind and straddle," and I kept raising it before the draw. They all "stayed," and drew two or three cards (I do not remember which). I took one, and when we came to "show down," I was the lucky fellow. This was too much for the bucks, so three of them dropped out, and left an old chief and myself single-handed. As I was over $150 ahead of the game, I played liberally, to draw the old chieftain on; and as he had one of his bucks walking around behind, and talking "big injin" all the time, he was getting the best of me. I knew that my hands were being given away, but I did not let them know that I was onto their racket. I waited my chance, and clinched onto four fours and a jack. I kept "going blind," until the chief got a good hand, and then he came back at me strong. We had it hot and heavy. I let the buck see my hand until it came to the draw, and then I shifted the hand, and came up with the four fours and the jack, but the warrior did not get to see *that* hand. I then made a big bet. The old chief called his squaw, and she brought him a sack of silver. He then "called" me. We showed down; the money was mine; and then you should have seen the fun. The buck that had been giving my hand away started to run. The old chief jumped up, grabbed his tomahawk, and lit out after him. I jerked off my coat, dumped all the silver into it, jumped into my buggy, and lost no time in getting out of that neck of the woods. As I was going at a 2 : 40 gait, I looked back and saw the buck and old chief going through the woods. I never knew whether the old man caught the buck or not, but I do know he did not catch me. I took desperate chances to win that pot, and I was very lucky in not losing my scalp. I never inquired when the Indians were to be paid off again, for I had no notion of paying them a visit. Any one who has a desire to play poker with "big injins" has my consent; but I would advise them to play a square game, and keep their eye skinned for the big "buck" that talks to the chief.

A RELIGIOUS CAPTAIN.

I was on board the steamer *War Eagle* going from Dubuque to St. Paul. The Captain was a member of the church, and did not allow any gambling on his boat; and any one caught at that innocent pastime would be put ashore. While walking over the boat I met a gentleman who I thought had money (and I hardly ever made a mistake in my man). I invited him to join me in a drink, and then steered him into the barber shop. I told him I had lost some money betting on cards, but I did not mind it very much, as my father was wealthy. While I was showing him how I had lost the money, my partner came in; and after watching me throw the cards for a little while, he wanted to bet me $100 he could pick the card. I threw them again, and told him to put up. He " turned," and won the money. Then, turning to the man, he showed him one of the corners turned up, and wanted to bet me again. I told him I would not play with a man that beat me. The man then asked me if I would bet with him. I said I would, providing the other fellow would not tell him which card to turn, which was agreed to. The man then got out his big roll, and put up $100. I told him if he won I would only bet him the one time; and if I won, I would only be even; and that I would not bet less than $500. He put up the $500, and turned the wrong card. After putting the money out of sight, I began to throw the cards again; for I saw a diamond stud and ring worth about $1,000. While the cards were on the table I turned around to spit, and my partner marked one of the cards with a pencil, and let the man see the mark. He then bet me $500, and won it; then he walked away. The man began to get nervous and feel for his money; but he had only about seventy-five dollars left, and wanted to bet that. I told him I had just lost $500, and would not bet less than $1,000. He insisted on betting the $75, but I told him to keep it for expenses, and that I would bet him $500 against his stud and ring. Up they went, and I put up $500. Over went the marked card, and he lost again. Out he went, and when I saw him again the Captain was with him. I knew what was in the wind, but I stood my ground. The Captain said to me, " Have you been gambling on my boat?" " I do not know what you mean by that question," says I. " You don't? Well, I will tell you, my boy; you give this gentleman back all the money and jewelry you won from him, or I will have my men take it from you, and then land you on the bank." I laughed at him, and told him to bring up his whole crew, and I would suffer the death of John Rodgers before I would give up one cent. He ordered up the mate and crew. I backed up against the side of the boat, and told them to call for cards, as I " stood pat." They said they did not want any, for they could see by my looks I had the best hand, or at least I would play it for all it was worth. The Captain then said, " You must go ashore." I said, " Land her; both sides of the river are in America, and that big brick house up there is where I live." The old fellow could not help laughing at my cheek, and so concluded to let me alone.

I have often had steamboat captains tell me I must give up the money or go ashore, and I had them to tell the suckers to go and get more money and try it again. I have also had them to say they would put the suckers ashore, and that would break them all up. A sucker thinks when he sees a mark on a card that he is robbing the gambler, and he is just as much of a robber and gambler as the other man.

When two persons bet, one *must* lose; and there is no law in this country to compel a man to bet his money or jewelry on anything. So my advice is, don't you do it.

A COLD DECK.

I was aboard the *Sultana*, bound for Louisville, and got into a five-handed game of poker. When we landed at the mouth of the Cumberland, two of our party got off to take a boat for Nashville; that left our game three-handed. For fear that another would get away, I thought I must get in my work without further delay; so I excused myself for a few moments and went to the bar. I got a deck just like the one we were using, and "run up" three hands, giving one three aces, one three kings, and myself four trays. We played a short time after my return, and on my deal I called their attention to something, and at the same time came up with the "cold deck." The betting was lively. I let them do the raising, and I did the calling until it came to the draw. They each took two cards, and I took one, saying, "If I fill this flush, I will make you squeal." I knew they both had "full hands," and they just slashed their money on the table until there was over $4,000 up. Then I made a "raise" of $1,200, and they both "called." "Gentlemen," I said, "I suppose you have me beat; I have only two pair." "Oh!" says one, "I have a king full;" and the other one said, "I have an ace full." "Well, boys, I can down both hands, for I have two pair of trays." The game came to a close, for there was no more money on the other side.

CAUGHT A SLEEPER.

I was playing poker once on the steamer *General Quitman*. The party were all full of grape juice. Along about morning the game was reduced to single-handed, and the man I was playing with was fast asleep, so I picked up the deck and took four aces and four kings out, with an odd card to each. I gave him the kings and I took the aces. I gave him a hunch, and told him to wake up and look at his hand. He partly raised his hand, but laid it down again, and I knew he had not seen it. I gave him a push and shook him up pretty lively, and he opened his eyes. I said: "Come, look at your hand, or I will quit." He got a glimpse of it, and I never saw such a change in a man's countenance. He made a dive for his money and said: "I will bet you $100, for I want to show you I am not asleep." I told him I thought he was "bluffing." I said in a joking way: "I will raise you $1,000." So he pulled out his money and laid it on the table, and said: "I will only call you, but I know I have you beat." I showed down four big live aces, and he was awake sure enough after that. He never went into any more of those fits, and we played until they wanted the table for breakfast. I used to make it a point to "cold deck" a sucker on his own deal, as they then had great confidence in their hands. My old paw is large enough to hold out a compressed bale of cotton or a whole deck of cards, and it comes in very handy to do the work. I could hold one deck in the palm of my hand and shuffle up another, and then come the change on his deal. It requires a great deal of cheek and gall, and I was always endowed with both—that is, they used to say so down South.

TEN THOUSAND IN COUNTERFEIT MONEY.

We had a great "graft," before the war, on the Upper Mississippi, between St. Louis and St. Charles. We would go up on a boat and back by rail. One night going up we had done a good business in our line, and were just putting up the shutters, when a man stepped up and said "he could turn the right card." My partner, Posey Jeffers, was doing the honors that night, and he said, "I will bet from $1 to $10,000 that no man can pick out the winning ticket." The man pulled out a roll nearly as large as a pillow, and put up $5,000. Posey put up the same amount, and over the card went for $5,000; but it was not the winner. " Mix them up again," said the man, and he put up the same sum as before. He turned, and Posey put the second $5,000 in his pocket. The man then walked away as if to lose $10,000 was an every-day thing with him. We then closed up our "banking house," well pleased with ourselves. The next day we were counting our cash, and we found we had on hand $10,000 in nice new bills on the State Bank of Missouri, but it was all counterfeit. We deposited it in the (fire) bank, as we had no immediate use for it.

BLOWING UP OF THE PRINCESS.

I was on board of the steamer *Princess* on a down trip when she was carrying a large number of passengers, and there were fourteen preachers among them, on their way to New Orleans to attend a conference. The boat was making the fastest time she had ever made. I had a big game of "roulette" in the barber shop, which ran all Saturday night; and on Sunday morning, just after leaving Baton Rouge, I opened up again, and had thirty-five persons in the shop, all putting down their money as fast as they could get up to the table. I was doing a land-office business, when all of a sudden there was a terrific noise, followed by the hissing of escaping steam, mingled with the screams and groans of the wounded and dying. The boat had blown up, and was almost a total wreck. There was but very little left, and that consisted mostly of the barber shop, which was at the time full of gamblers, and not one of them was hurt. The steamers *Peerless* and *McRay* came to our aid; one boat looked after the dead and wounded, and the other took us lucky fellows out of the barber shop. One hundred souls were landed into eternity without a moment's warning, and among them were the fourteen preachers. It was a horrible sight; the bodies were so mangled and scalded that one could not have recognized his own brother or sister. Captain William

Campbell (now of the Vicksburg Packet line) was steward of the *Princess* at the time of the explosion, and there was not a man on the boat that worked harder to save life and relieve the wounded. He richly deserved his promotion, and is now one of the best captains on the river.

A WOMAN WITH A GUN.

I was on a boat coming from Memphis one night, when my partner beat a man out of $600, playing poker. After the game broke up, the man went into the ladies' cabin and told his wife. She ran into his room and got his pistol, and said, " I will have that money back, or kill the man." I saw her coming, pistol in hand, and stepped up to the bar and told the barkeeper to hand me that old gun he had in the drawer, which I knew had no loads in it. She came on, frothing at the mouth, with blood in her eyes. I saw she was very much excited, and I said to her: "Madame, you are perfectly right. You would do right in shooting that fellow, for he is nothing but a gambler. I don't believe your pistol will go off; you had better take my pistol, for I am a government detective, and have to keep the best of arms." So I handed her the pistol, and took hers. Just a moment later out stepped the man who had won the money, and she bolted up to him and said: " You won my husband's money, and I will just give you one minute to hand it to me, or I will blow your brains out in this cabin." Well, you ought to have seen the passengers getting out of the cabin when she pulled down on him ; but he knew the joke and stood pat, and showed what a game fellow he was. He told the woman her husband lost the money gambling, and he could not get a cent back. Then she let go ; but the pistol failed to go off, and he got her to go back into the cabin, and pacified her by giving her $100. After taking the charges out of her pistol, I returned it to her. So, reader, you can see what a gay life there is in gambling.

THE FRENCHMAN AND THE HORSE HAIR.

I knew a Frenchman who used to travel the river play-ing the wheel, who made a great deal of money and sent it to France. One night he opened a $1,000 snap at faro, and I was to loan him my tools. He shuffled his own cards, as he was too smart to use any other; and I went down on deck and pulled some hairs out of a horse's tail, and came back and got one of the coppers and fastened a hair to it. A copper is used to make a bet lose and take the banker's side. When the copper is off, the bet is open. So I got my partner to buy a big lot of white checks, so that I could get my small bet behind them. My checks were $12.50 apiece; he was playing white checks at 25 cents. We took one corner of the table, side by side. He placed his checks between the dealer and me; then I would put my little stack behind his checks, and when the dealer made a turn he would have to rise from his seat to see if my bet was coppered or not. If the card lost that we were on, I would let the copper remain; if it won, I gave the horse hair a little jerk and pulled the copper off, and we both won. I used to take it off when he was going to pay the bet, for fear he would get his fingers tangled in the hair; and in this way we won the bank roll, which made the Frenchman very sick.

SAVED MY PARTNER'S LIFE.

We were once coming down on the steamer *Belle Key*, of Louisville, and my partner was doing the playing that day. We had won some big money, and were about to quit, when up stepped a very tall man, who looked pale and sickly. He watched the game for some time, and then pulled out a $1,000 note and laid it on the card he wanted, and of course he lost. He did not say a word, but started back to his room. I thought he acted strangely, and I concluded to keep an eye on him. Pretty soon out he came with an overcoat on his arm, and he walked up as near the table as he could get, and commenced to push some of the crowd away so as to get closer. Finally he got at my partner's back, with me close at his heels, when he commenced to pull from under his coat a large Colt's pistol. As he leveled it to shoot him in the back of the head, I knocked him stiff, and the gun dropped on the floor. It was cocked, but it did not go off. They carried him to his room, put cold water on him, and finally brought him to. He sent for me, and when I went back he reached out his hand, and said: "Friend, you did me a kindly act, for I had made up my mind to kill that man. I am glad it happened so, for it was all the money I had, and it was raised by my friends, who, knowing that I never would reach home again, were sending me to Florida, as all the doctors have given me up; and I thought I would kill him, as I do not expect to get off this boat alive. I have got consumption in its last stages." So I pulled out $1,000, counted it out to him, and he cried like a child. His pistol I gave to the mate, as I thought he had no need of such a weapon.

LEAP FOR LIFE.

Another time I was coming up on the steamer *Fairchild* with Captain Fawcett, of Louisville. When we landed at Napoleon there were about twenty-five of the "Arkansas Killers" came on board, and I just opened out and cleaned the party of money, watches, and all their valuables. Things went along smoothly for a while, until they commenced to drink pretty freely. Finally one of them said: "Jake, Sam, Ike, get Bill, and let us kill that d—d gambler who got our money." "All right," said the party, and they broke for their rooms to get their guns. I stepped out of the side door, and got under the pilot-house, as it was my favorite hiding place. I could hear every word down stairs, and could whisper to the pilot. Well, they hunted the boat from stem to stern—even took lights and went down into the hold—and finally gave up the chase, as one man said I had jumped overboard. I slipped the pilot $100 in gold, as I had both pockets filled with gold and watches, and told him at the first point that stood out a good ways to run her as close as he could and I would jump. He whispered, "Get ready," and I slipped out and walked back, and stood on the top of the wheel-house until she came, as I thought, near enough to make the jump, and away I went; but it was farther than I expected, so I went down about thirty feet into the river, and struck into the soft mud clear up to my waist. Some parties who were standing on the stern of the boat saw me, and gave the alarm, when the "killers" all rushed back and commenced firing at me, and the bullets went splattering all around me. The pilot threw her into the bend as quick as he could, and then let on she took a sheer on him, and nearly went to the other side. The shooting brought the niggers from the fields to the bank of the river. I hal looed to them to get a long pole and pull me out, for I was stuck in the mud. They did so, and I got up on the bank and waited for another boat.

I was always very stubborn about giving up money if any one wanted to compel me to do it, but I wish I had one-quarter of what I have given back to people that did need it. I have seen many a man lose all he had, and then go back into the ladies' cabin and get his wife's diamonds, and lose them, thinking he might get even. But that was always a good cap for me, for I would walk back into the cabin, find the lady, and hand her jewels back; and I never beat a man out of his money that I did not find out from the clerk if his passage was paid. If not, I would pay it, and give the man some of his money to assist him to his destination. By so doing I was looked upon as being a pretty good robber—that is, if you call it robbing; but I tell you that a man that will bet on such a game as monte is a bigger robber than the man who does the playing, for he thinks he is robbing you, and you know you are robbing him.

THE CHICKEN MEN AND THEIR SILVER.

At one time, before the war, silver was such a drug in New Orleans that you could get $105 in silver for $100 in State bank notes; but the commission men would pay it out to the hucksters dollar for dollar. They would put it in bags and label it with the man's name and the amount. At this time I was coming out on the steamer *John Raine*, and, in looking around for customers, I found fifteen chicken men on board, who had sold their "coops," and had their sacks of silver setting in the office, as there was no room for it in the safe. After supper I got my men in the barber shop, pulled out my three cards, and began to throw them, at the same time telling the men I had lost $1,000 at the game, and that I was going to practice until I could throw equal to the man that had beat me out of my money. They all took a great interest in the game, and could turn the right card every time for fun. About this time the "capper" came up, and said he was positive he could guess the card, and kept insisting on betting me $100; so at last I concluded to bet him, and he lost the $100. Then the fun commenced. One of the chicken men saw the corner of the "right" card turned up; so he jumped up, and wanted to bet me $500 that he could pick out the "right" card. I told him I did not want to bet, but if he made it $2,000 I would bet him, and if I lost I would quit. At the same time I pulled out a large roll of small bills, with a hundred dollar bill on the outside, and laid it on the table. The chicken men held a council of war, and of course they all saw the corner of the "right" card turned up. They went for their sacks of silver, and planked down four of them, with $500 in each. I put up and said: "Gentlemen, you must all agree on one card, and select one man to turn it, as I must have the two

chances. They picked out their man; he turned the card
with the corner turned up; but, of course, it was not the
"right" card. The boat was just landing to take in sugar,
so I said, "Gentlemen, I will have to bid you good-by, as
this is my sugar plantation." I called two of the porters
and told them to take my sacks ashore. They said, "All
right, Massa George." You should have seen the chicken
men look at me when I landed with my sacks; and all the
niggers came to shake hands and say, "Glad youse back,
Massa George," (for I knew all the niggers on the coast).
After the boat pulled out, I opened one of the sacks and
gave each black, one of the "chicken" half-dollars. They
guarded the money until another boat came down. which
they hailed, and I was soon on my way back to New
Orleans to catch some more suckers.

THE HUNGRY MAN.

I was on board the *John Simonds* coming out of New
Orleans one night. I had a very lively game of "red and
black," and did not close up until two o'clock in the morning. We were sitting around the stove in the bar, drinking,
smoking, and telling stories, when there was a man came
in whom I had not seen since the boat left New Orleans.
When he came aboard he was pretty full of "bug-juice,"
and had been asleep. When he woke up, of course he was
dry, and had come into the bar to get a drink. I said to
him, "You look dry, and you are just in time to join us."
After thanking me, he took a drink, and then told me he had
missed his supper. I told him I would send the porter to
the texas, and get him a lunch, which I did. I then
thought if I can get some more of that "go-your-money"
whisky into him, I can size him up. So after taking another
round, I said to him, "You should have been up when the
big betting was going on." He said, "What was it?" I
said, "There was a great tall fellow sat down to the table
just after supper, and called all the men in the cabin to

" The ' Killers ' all rushed back and commenced firing at me," etc.   [Page 30.]

come and see how he had lost $2,000 of his father's money. He pulled out a lot of cards and began to throw them on the table, and he said to us, 'If you see the same fellow who got my money, don't you bet with him, for he has two chances to your one.' I can't explain just how he did it, for I haven't got any of the cards." The barkeeper then said, "I have some of the fellow's cards that he left when he got off the boat." I said, "Let me have them and I will try and show the game." I took the cards and bent them, and then said, "You ought to have seen him throw them through those long fingers; it would have made you laugh."

I was throwing and explaining when my partner came in. After looking on for a little while he asked me if I would bet on the game. I pretended not to hear him, but invited them both to take a drink. Then my partner offered to bet the drinks. I took him up, and he lost. While we were talking he picked up the cards and turned up one of the corners of the winner, and then let the other man see what he had done. I commenced to throw them again, when my partner wanted to know if I would bet just as they lay. I said I would after the shuffle. He said, "You beat me out of the drinks; now I will bet you $100 I can pick up the card the first pick." "Enough," says I, and up went the money in the "hungry" man's hands. Over went the card, and my partner caught me for $100. I said, "Give him the money, as he won it fairly." The stakeholder threw down his bread and meat, jumped up, pulled out his money, and said, "I will bet you $500 I can turn the right card the first time." I saw he had about $1,500 or $2,000, so I said, "I will make but one bet, and then quit; I will bet you $1,500." "Enough said, I'll go you." The money was put up, and over went the card; but, as luck would have it, he turned the wrong one; and, to tell the truth, I was glad of it. He then pulled out $400 in gold and wanted to bet that; but I told him to keep it, for I did not want to win it from him, but wanted to keep what I had.   We sat down and had a drink, and in a short time the man went out on the guards.   My partner and I were talking and laughing about how we won the money, when all of a sudden in rushed the man with his clothes all torn, and very much excited.   We asked him what had happened, when he told us that two fellows had grabbed and robbed him of the $400 in gold.

We got the mate and watchman, and searched the boat until we found one of the robbers in a fireman's bunk, down on the lower deck.   We got all the money from him and returned it to the man.   The other robber could not be found.   We turned the one we had captured over to the police of Baton Rouge, and that was the last we ever heard of him.   I took the next boat back to New Orleans.

COLLARED THE WRONG MAN.

I had been attending to business pretty faithfully, and had accumulated some wealth, when it struck me I must take a rest; so when I arrived in New Orleans I laid off. I was playing the "bank" one night, and was a big loser. There was a big fighter came in and sat down at the same table, and in a short time he began to pick up checks. I thought he would take some of mine next, and I was not in the humor to let any one take my checks. Sure enough, he clinched onto a stack I had on the nine. I said to him, "Those are my fifty." He raised up, took me by the collar, and said, "You're a d—d liar." I thought I would get the old head ready for business once more, so I argued the question with him until I saw an opening, and then I let him have it just between the eyes. He dropped all in a heap, and it was some time before they could get him to sit up. He was pretty badly hurt; his nose was broken down flat with his face; the blood was running out of his ears, and I thought it was about time for me to get out. I cashed in my checks and quit the game over $6,000 loser. So you see a man must fight at times, even when he has quit his regular business, and is laying off for a rest.

MY JEW PARTNER.

I was on board the steamer *Sultana* one evening, coming up from New Orleans, when a "Jew" came up to me, tapped me on the shoulder, and said: "Mr. Devol, I have heard of you for years, and have sat at the same table with you in New Orleans playing the bank. I caught her this trip for over $4,000; but I have often wished I could make as much money as you do; you bet I would take better care of it than you. Come, let us go and have a nice drink." I told him I did not drink anything but wine; and I was very glad he had beat the bank, for they nearly always beat me; but I could hold my own with any man at poker. He said: "Oh, Mr. Devol, I know that no one can beat you at poker, and I would like to put my money in with you and have an interest." Something struck me immediately that I might as well have the $4,000 as not, so I said to him: "I will see Mr. Bush (my partner), and let you know after supper." The first thing to be done was to manufacture a sucker to play me a big game of poker. I knew several good boys on board; some were gamblers and some were horsemen. I selected one of the horsemen, and took him to my room to teach him the ropes. I said to him: "I will cold deck you, and give you three kings, a seven and an eight, and you must put your thumb over one of the spots on the eight, so that the Jew will think you have a king full on sevens when he sees your hand. I will have an ace full, and will bet you $200 or $300 before the draw; then you raise me $5,000." After giving him full instructions, so there would be no mistake, I gave him a big roll and let him out, with instructions not to know me until the time of the game. I told Bush the plan, so after supper we opened up with our three cards and took in a few hundred dollars. After we had closed for the evening, I picked up my manufactured sucker and commenced a divvy game of poker. I told my Jew partner to see every hand that the other fellow held, and to attract his attention so I could cold deck him. I came up with the ice and bet $250 before the draw. The sucker came back and raised me $5,000. The Jew was behind him and saw his king full on sevens; he then came around and saw my ace full on trays. I pretended to be a little short, and called for Bush to bring me some money. Then my would-be partner commenced to get out his money, and was in such a hurry (for fear he would not be in time) that he tore the buttons off his vest. He put up his $4,000; Bush got $1,000 from John C. Heenan (the prize fighter, who was on the boat), and I called the bet. The game had attracted the attention of all the passengers; they were all around us, some on the tables and chairs, and every one was holding his breath waiting for the result, except my Jew partner, who was so delighted with the sure thing of having won one-half of the money that he could not keep still a moment, but kept dancing around, rubbing his hands and smiling as if he had sold a suit of clothes without coming down a cent. When, to everybody's great surprise, the sucker said, "Gentlemen, I have made a mistake in my hand; can't I take my money down?" The Jew said: "Oh, we don't rectify no mistakes in poker." The sucker looked up at him and said: "What in the h—l have you got to do with this game?" The Jew said: "I thought you was bluffin'." The sucker then said: "Hold on, gentlemen, we have not drawn yet. I thought I had a king full on sevens." He then threw down the seven and eight and called for two cards. The Jew said: "We don't care for your mistake," and then walked around behind the sucker to see what he would get in the draw. I dealt him off two cards, but the Jew did not get to see what he got. They had sent me some money from the office, and I bet him $500. The sucker hesitated a moment, and then bet $5,000. I put up all the money I had, my big single stone, pin and ring, but that was not enough. Then the Jew put

The Jew said, " Oh, we don't rectify no mistakes in poker." [Page 36.]

up his Juergersen watch, a large cluster pin and ring, and I called the bet. The sucker said, "I have two pair." The Jew was so glad (thinking I had won) that he could not keep still, but went up and down like a jumping-jack. I showed down my ace full, and then the sucker showed down two pair of kings. You should have seen my " new partner." He threw up both his hands, groaned, and then fell over on the floor dead. We had to throw water in his face to bring him around, and when we got him up he started for the guards, saying· "I go drown myself; I don't want to live." Some one ran and got him a life preserver, and told him to put it on before he jumped overboard. He finally quieted down and went to his room. I took the horseman into my room, gave him $200 in money and my "partner's" diamonds. He was the lion of the boat and did not have to pay for drinks from there to Louisville. I got off at Baton Rouge at daybreak, and was soon on my way back to New Orleans; and when I arrived there, every one I met would ask me about my bad luck. My friends were sorry for me. I could have borrowed almost any amount of money. The papers came out all over the country that Devol had at last found his match.

I saw the Jew in St. Louis some years later. He knew me, and said: "Mr. Devol, come and let us get a good drink. See that clothing store? That's mine. I never play poker since that time on the boat; don't you remember?"

SOLD OUT BY A PARTNER.

One night I was coming up the river on the steamer *Morrison*. I had a partner with me named Charles Bush. He was a good, big-hearted fellow, but did not know much about beating a sucker out of his money. I had to teach him how to handle the blokes. Well, Bush and myself had made some money, and were sitting around looking at the gamblers. There were twenty-five of them on board, going to the Memphis races. Finally one of the sports, named Dennis McCarthy, said to me, "Devol, I will play you seven-up for $100 a game." So I turned to Bush and asked him if he wanted any interest in it. He said "No," so he sat down alongside of me, where he could see my hand. We commenced to play. I could see Bush working a toothpick in his mouth, from the corner to the middle and then over to the other side. I thought I noticed that when the toothpick was in the left side of his mouth I always had one trump; when he had it in the middle of his mouth I had two trumps; when in the right side I had three trumps, and when he took it out of his mouth I had no trumps. McCarthy beat me six straight games. The last game we played we were six and six. I saw Bush take the toothpick out of his mouth. I looked at my hand and saw no trumps. McCarthy stood his hand, and led. He had no trumps either, but as he had some large cards in his hand he made the game, which put him out. Bush was sitting on my right; so I let go with my left, caught him between the eyes, and straightened him out on the floor. They got a piece of beefsteak and put it on his eyes, and he went to bed. There was a big six-foot fellow named Anderson, who said that any man that would hit another for nothing was a scoundrel, and he could whip him. He was not posted, and did not know why I hit him, so he made this bluff. I said to him, "Take off your coat and come and see me." He took off his coat, and after he got it off he weakened, and picked up a big iron poker that lay by the stove. I pulled out old "Betsy Jane," one of the best tarantula pistols in the Southern country, and told him to drop the poker, which he did. "Now," said I, "if you want it on the square, I am your man." So at it we went, and I hit him and knocked him clear through the office door. I then reached down and caught him by the collar, raised him up and struck him with that good old faithful head of mine, and the fight was all over; for I had broken every bone in his nose. The clerks came rushing out of the office, the Captain and passengers also came, and the Captain asked me what was the matter. I told him, and the mate spoke up and said Devol was perfectly right, for he had seen it all. I offered to pay for the door and chairs we broke, but the Captain would not accept one cent.

I went back to the room to see Bush, for I was sorry I had hit him, although I thought he was guilty. I told him to get up and look out for me, and I would open faro bank for the gamblers, which he did. They all changed in except the big fellow with the broken nose; he went to bed. The result was, we broke every one of them, and then got off at Baton Rouge; they went to Memphis, where the races commenced in a few days. Bush was with me for three years after that; and many a night I have sat and dealt for a big game, and in the morning would divide several hundred dollars with Bush, who was in bed and asleep.

THE BIG CATFISH.

My old partner (Bush) and I had been up all night in New Orleans playing faro, and were several hundred dollars winners, and thought we would walk down to the French market and get a cup of coffee before we went to bed. We saw a catfish that would weigh about 125 pounds; its mouth was so large that I could put my head into it. We got stuck on the big cat, and while we were looking at it an old man came up to me and said: "That is the largest catfish I ever saw." Bush was a little way off from me just at the time, and knowing I would have some fun (if not a bet) with the old man, he kept out of the way. I said to the old gent: "You are the worst judge of a fish I ever saw; that is not a cat, it is a pike, and the largest one ever brought to this market." He looked at me and then at the fish, and then said: "Look here, my boy, where in the d—l were you raised?" I told him I was born and raised in Indiana. "Well, I thought you were from some hoop-pole State." We got to arguing about it; and I appeared to be mad, and offered to bet him $100 that the fish was a pike. Says he, "Do you mean it?" I pulled out a roll, threw down $100 and told him to cover it. He lammed her up, and I said: "Who will we leave it to?" We looked around and saw Bush, with a memorandum book in his hand and a pen behind his ear, talking to a woman who sold vegetables, and he was acting as if he was collector of the market. I said: "May be that man with the book in his hand might know." The old fellow called Bush, and said to him, "Do you belong about here?" "Oh, yes; I have belonged about here for a good many years," says Bush. "Well, sir, you are just the man we want to decide our bet," says the old gent. "Well, gentlemen, I am in somewhat of a hurry; but if you do not detain me too long, I will be glad to serve you to the best of my ability," said Bush. "We want you to tell us what kind of a fish this is." "Well, gentlemen, that can be done easily." "Out with it," said the old gent. Bush braced himself up, and said: "I have been market-master here for twenty years, and that is the largest *pike* I ever saw in this market." "Well! Well! Well!" says the old man; "I have lived on the Tombigbee River for forty-five years, and I never saw two bigger fools than you two." I invited the old man and the "market-master" to join me in a cup of coffee. Bush accepted, but the old one from the Tombigbee declined, saying "he did not drink with men that did not know a catfish from a pike." We bid him good morning and went home, and we were both sound asleep in a short time; for we felt we had done an honest night's and morning's work.

THE SERMON ON THE (MOUNT) BOAT.

"The hypocrite had left his mask, and stood
  In naked ugliness. He was a man
  Who stole the livery of the court of heaven
  To serve the devil in."

I was coming from New Orleans on board the steamer *E. H. Fairchilds*, bound for Louisville. She was literally packed with people. After supper, on Saturday evening, we started a game in the barber shop, which was kept up until Sunday morning. Over $8,000 changed hands, and I was a big winner. After eating my breakfast I went out on the guards to take a smoke before going to bed. While I was enjoying my cigar, a fine looking old gentleman about sixty years of age came up to me and entered into conversation. Presently the Captain joined us. The old gentleman told us he was a minister from Louisville, and would like to preach in the cabin. The Captain gave his consent. The minister placed his arm in mine, and, before I was aware of what we were doing, he had me half way down the ladies' cabin, and then it was too late to back out or get away. He sat me down near where he was standing. I was impressed with his discourse, for it was full of practical sayings. He spoke of gambling in very plain terms, and of the game that had been kept up all night in the barber shop. He said: "It was a pity that such a fine looking gentleman as the one who sat near him should play cards for money." To tell the truth, his remarks on the subject of my business did make me feel a little mean. He did not look directly at me, but I thought he was getting close to home. The collection amounted to considerable, and I chipped in my share liberally. After the morning services were over I retired to my room to take a sleep, and it was not long until I had forgotten that we had an old preacher on board.

I spent that Sunday evening reading until near midnight; most of the passengers had retired. There was but one passenger in the cabin, and he was sitting with his back to me, reading. I approached him, and found it was the minister. I had changed my dress so that he did not recognize me. I sat down near him, and he began talking about the gambling game of the night before, and he handled the gamblers without gloves. I sided with him in his views, and then trumped up a story of how I had been roped into the game, and had lost $1,000; but that my father was rich, and gave me all the money I could spend, and that I did not mind the loss very much. He became very much interested, and asked a great many questions. I told him I had picked up some of the tickets that they played the game with, and had them in my room, and if he would like to see them I would go and get them. "Oh, I would like very much to see the way it was played, and I will go to your room if you will show me.' We went to my room, and I showed him the old three-card monte racket. I let him play with the cards until he thought he knew all about them, and he said to me : "My dear sir, I can't see how you could lose money on such a simple thing ; I would not fail to pick out the right ticket every time." I said to him, " I'll make you a proposition ; I will throw the tickets, and put up $100 with you. If you gain the money you are to donate it to your church ; and if I gain it I will do the same, for I want to show you how I lost playing them.' The old fellow accepted my proposition, for he wanted to give the money to his church (and so did I). Of course I displayed a big roll, and told him I would just as soon make it $200 as $100. He agreed, and we put up. He turned the ticket, but he failed to pick the right one. It was such a simple thing that he got excited, and put down $200 more, and again he failed to pick out the right one. We kept on until the old sucker lost an even $1,000, then I said to him, " I am really sorry, for I had rather lost the amount myself. This money will do me no good, and it would hardly benefit your church ; we have had lots of fun, and I want you to gain the money back

I will put up the $1,000 against your watch and chain, and when you gain it back we can have a big laugh over it." He put up his handsome watch and chain (that had been presented to him by his congregation), and, as he was playing in hard luck, I soon had the "ticker." He bade me good night, and went to his room.

I went to see the Captain, and when I showed him the reverend gentleman's watch, with the inscriptions on it, he could hardly believe his own eyes. After having a good laugh with the Captain, I went to the minister's room, and found him on his knees. When he saw me he said, " I have just been praying for you." I replied, " Brother, hadn't you better do a little of that for yourself ? " " Oh," says he, " I have prayed mostly for myself this night." " Well," I said, " since you have prayed for yourself, and me too, here is your watch, chain, and $100. ' Go and sin no more.' " He said (with tears in his eyes), " God bless you.' I left the boat at Natchez, and did not get to see the old gentleman again.

I caught a preacher once for all his money, his gold spectacles, and his sermons. Then I had some of those queer feelings come over me (and when they came upon me I could not resist their influence), so I gave him his sermons and specks back. At one time there were fifteen preachers on the Jackson Road, going to a conference at Hazelhurst. I got in among them, and, just for fun, I opened up monte, and I caught five out of the fifteen for every cent they had. I tell you, my dear readers, preachers are but human, and some of them will steal the livery of the court of heaven to serve the devil (Devol) in.

FIFTY TO THE BARKEEPER.

I was in the St. Charles bar-room one morning —having been up all night playing the bank—when a good looking old fellow walked in and called for a champagne cocktail. I turned to him and said, " Have one with me ; I drew

$6,000 out of the Havana Lottery last evening, and I would like you to join me." He accepted the invitation; and while the barkeeper was mixing the drinks, I slipped out some monte cards, and began playing them on the counter. I told the old gentleman it was a kind of a lottery I saw a man play, and I wanted to learn it. He looked at the game, and turned the card for fun, then for the drinks and cigars. Finally he said, " I will bet you twenty-five dollars I can turn the card." I said, "If I bet, it will not be for less than $100." He got out his wallet, and there was plenty of money in sight. I then pretended that I wanted to back out, and I offered to treat to a bottle of wine. He said, " No sir; I hold you to the bet." I then acted a little huffy (as he thought), and offered to bet him $1,000. He put up $1,000; and as I saw some left, I said, " Here is $500 more, and I will bet but once." He put up the extra $500. I said to him, " You know you must turn over the baby card the first time, or you lose." " All right," he said, and at the same time he grabbed a card as though he thought it would get away, and turned it over; but it was not the baby, and I was $1,500 winner, and did not have to divide with a capper, as I played the old sucker single-handed. I invited him to take another drink, and then bid him good morning. As I was going out, I rolled up a fifty-dollar bill into a little ball, and shot it at the barkeeper. He caught it on the fly, and put it in his pocket. I went to my room and slept until evening, when I was up and ready for the bank again.

LOST HIS WIFE'S DIAMONDS.

I was playing poker with a gentleman on board the steamer *John Simonds*, bound for Louisville, late one night, and had won a few hundred dollars from him, when he got up without saying a word, and went to the ladies' cabin. In a short time he came back with a small velvet-covered box in his hand, and said to me, " Come, let us finish our game." He opened the box, and I saw it was full of ladies' diamond jewelry. I said: "What are you going to do with those?" Said he, "I will put them up as money." "Oh, no; I have no use for ladies' jewelry." "Well," says he, "if I lose I will redeem them when we get to Louisville." I told him I was not going above Vicksburg. "Well," says he, "if you win, leave them with the clerk and I will pay him." I then loaned him $1,500 on the jewelry, and we sat down to play. It was about 3 A. M. when we commenced, and before they wanted the tables for breakfast I had won the $1,500 back. We drank a champagne cocktail, and he went to his room. The barber was at work on me, so that I was a little late for breakfast, and the steward had to take me into the ladies' cabin to get me a seat. There was a gentleman, a very beautiful lady, and a sweet little child at the same table; the lady's eyes were red, as if she had been crying. I looked at the gentleman, and saw it was the same person who had lost the diamonds. Somehow, my breakfast did not suit me; and the more I looked at that young wife and mother, the less I felt like eating. So at last I got up and left the table. I went to my room, got the little velvet box, wrapped it up, and carried it back. They were just leaving the table when I returned. I called the chambermaid, and told her the lady had left a package, and for her to take it to her room. After it was gone I felt better, and I eat a square meal. The gentleman came and thanked me, and wanted my address; but as I never had any one to send me money lost at gambling, I told him not to mind the address; for I knew if I did not give it, I would not expect anything, and therefore would not be disappointed.

THE MONTE KING.

After getting well of the fever in New Orleans, I took a trip up the river on one of the Vicksburg packets. On this trip I met a man by the name of Rollins, who was the

first man I ever saw playing three-card monte. Seeing I
was pretty smart, he proposed a partnership. We first
commenced depradations on the packets. He did the
playing, and I was the capper. I represented a planter's
son traveling for my health. The first party that we fell on
to was a nigger trader, who had forty-five big black coons
on board, taking them to New Orleans to sell. We found
him an easy victim, and downed him for $4,100 and four
of his niggers. We were afraid to win any more from him
on account of a squeal, but he acted very honorably and
made out a bill of sale.

Well, here I was a slave-holder with plenty of money.
My partner was one of the best that I ever worked with,
except Canada Bill, whom I shall speak of later.

We sold our slaves at one of the yards for $4,400; they
averaged $1,100 apiece, and in twenty minutes after I saw
one of them put on the block and bring $1,700. We knocked
about the city, spending our money freely; riding to the
lake, eating big suppers with the girls; and all were our
friends, for we would not allow any person to spend a cent,
and the flowing champagne was a great luxury in those
days.

The next trip we took was on a Red River packet. We
went as far as Shreveport and back on the same boat; and
on the trip, clear of expenses, we were $6,000 winners, as
it was no more trouble to win $1,000 then than $1 now.

Well, the gamblers began to get a little jealous of us,
and at the same time we lost heavily at their games when
we played, as we were both good suckers at any game except our own. One night one of them struck my partner,
and I jumped in between and told them I did all the fighting for both; and at it we went, and the result was I did
him up; for I always kept myself in good condition by
using dumb-bells and taking other exercise. When I was
twenty-five years old, I did not think there was a man in
the world that could whip me in a bar-room or on the
street.

After I got away with this gambler, they made up their minds that they would get a man who would make me squeal. We continued working the boats and making plenty of money, and every time we got out in the city both of us would lose a big sum of money; and then per- haps I would have to fight, for they were looking for a man to start a fuss with me. One night we had been down to the lake and had a big supper, and we drove up oppo- site the St. Charles Hotel and went in. There were about twenty-five gamblers standing in a saloon called the Jewel. I saw at a glance they were drinking and full; I also saw two of my men that I had whipped previously. Well, I could not show the white feather, so I called for a basket of wine and invited all to join me, when one of the party stepped out into the middle of the room, took off his coat, and said: "I can whip any man in the room." I looked around, and saw it was a job to either kill or whip me. I saw at a glance I had only one friend in the house; that was Captain Smoker, of the Vicksburg Packet Company. I knew he could be of no service to me. The door was locked. I turned to the challenger and said: "I know who you mean this for," and I untied my cravat. I had a single stone on my shirt that cost me $2,600. I took off my coat and vest, and handed them all to the barkeeper. The enemy was a powerfully built man, six feet and one inch high, and weighed thirty-five pounds more than my- self; at that time I weighed 195 pounds. Well, to tell you the truth, it was a pretty hard fight; but I got one good lick at him with my head, and that won the battle for me. It took all the fight out of him. He said, "That will do." The doors were thrown open, and in less than a minute there were 1,000 people in there.

We were both arrested and taken to the station-house, or calaboose, where we gave bail, Captain Smoker going on my bond. While they were signing our bonds, my op- ponent made some remark that I did not like, and I hit him a good crack in the neck and brought him down on his knees, but they parted us; and the next day, when we appeared in court, the Judge said he had a notion to fine us $100 apiece for not sending for him, as he wanted to see it himself; "but I will let you go this time " The man's name was John Mortice, of Natchez, Miss.

Well, to tell you the truth, I was pretty well used up; but I staid in my room till I got all right again. We made several successful trips after that together. At last we parted, and he went to California, and soon after died. I was then king of the monte men, and did all of the playing myself. I got a man named Charlie Clark to do the capping for me, and we made a world of money.

"Eph " Holland, Alexander, and I were coming out of the Red River one night. The boat was full of people, and a great many were playing poker. It was 2:30 A. M., when a large and powerful man rushed out of the ladies' cabin with nothing on but his night-shirt, and with a large butcher-knife in his hand. He rushed to one of the tables, where there were seven seated, and before they could rise he plunged the knife up to the hilt in two of the men. I jumped up and ran out into the hall, determined to kill him if he made a break for me; but the Captain hallooed at me, "Don't shoot; he is a crazy man." He had been brought on board at Alexandria by his wife, who was taking him to an asylum. He came rushing through the cabin towards the hall, and I snatched up a big iron poker; for I made up my mind I would lay him out if he came within reach. He picked out another man and started for him, and they had it all around the guards. The poor fellow that he was after was almost scared to death. I jumped inside of the door, and as he came brandishing his knife I dealt him a heavy blow on the side of the head, which brought him down. We then got ropes and tied him, and kept him in that position till the engineer made hand-cuffs for him.

THE DAGUERROTYPE BOAT.

" Good heaven! that sots and knaves should be so **vain,**
To wish their vile remembrance may remain
And stand recorded at their own request,
To future days a libel or a jest."

Before the war, " Eph " Holland, my partner Alexander, and myself were waiting for a boat at the mouth of the Red River. There was a little boat lying at the landing, nicely fitted up for a daguerrotype gallery, and I proposed to the boys that we have our pictures taken all together, and I would pay for it, as I thought it would make a pretty group. They agreed, so we went on board the boat and let the artist take us all in a bunch. Holland was in the middle, and the picture flattered him ; so he insisted on having a dozen copies. I saw that the picture did not do me justice, so I wanted " Eph " to sit alone, telling him it would cost less. He said he would pay the bill, for he could see it was the contrast that showed him off to so great an advantage. Well, to please him we let the artist draw a bead on us eleven times more ; for at that time they could only take one picture at a shot. Holland paid the entire bill, which was so large that I asked the daguerrotype man if he would sell out. "Oh, no ; I am making too much money," says he. Then I thought, I will try and get some of it ; at least the amount that poor " Eph " had paid for his vanity. I told the old story of how I had lost my money, and began to throw the cards. I soon had them guessing ; Alexander turned up the corner of the winner, and then bet me $100 that the artist could turn it. I took him up, and lost the money. The artist got excited and wanted to bet his money. The result was, I won all he had, and told him I would give him a chance to get even, and would bet all he had lost against his boat and contents. He accepted the proposition. Holland made out a bill of sale, the artist signed it, and in a short time he had lost his home and business. Then I said to him :

4

"You have played in bad luck, so I will pay you a salary to manage the business for me." He accepted the employment. We bid him good bye, and took a boat for New Orleans. Two weeks later I saw my picture boat at Bayou Sara. I went on board, and my employe was glad to see me (or at least he said he was). I asked him about the business, and he told me he was losing money; so I told him I would like to sell out. He wanted to know my price; I told him $150. He offered me $40 cash and his note for the balance; so I thought, as he had been losing money for two weeks, I had better sell. I have his note yet, and the first time I see Holland I am going to try and sell it to him. There was no money in the business for me, as it was outside of my line; and I have come to the conclusion that a man should stick to his legitimate business. "Eph" Holland was sorry afterward that he ever had his picture taken in a group, for the next time he went to New Orleans he was arrested on the street and taken to the Chief's office, and there he saw his "group" picture in the rogues' gallery. He tried to explain how it was that his picture came to be grouped with two well known horse-thieves, but the Chief couldn't see it. Then Eph sent for his friends, who went on his bond, and he was let off until the next morning. As he and his friends were leaving the Chief's office he caught sight of me, and then he "dropped," and said to me, "George, *you* gave that picture to the Chief." I said, "What picture?" Then Eph said, "Boys, come on; it's all on me." The Chief joined us; and when Eph had settled the bill, he said to me, "George, the next time I have my picture taken I will go it alone." I said to him, "Eph, all is vanity and vexation of spirit."

PITTSBURG'S BEST MAN.

Before the war there were a great many coal boatmen traveling on the river. I was coming up at that time with Captain Forsyth, on the steamer *Cambria*. Some of the coal boat crew traveled in the cabin, and others on deck. I got into a game with one of their bullies. They said he was the best man in Pittsburg. In the play I bested him out of a few hundred dollars, and he did not like it a bit. He went down on deck and told his party there was a BOY up stairs who had won all his money. "If he comes on deck I will let you know, and we will throw him down and take the money away from him." The news came to me, and I prepared for the boys by putting my money and jewelry in the office, took my pistol and went down on deck. The bully was there; he pointed me out to the gang. They commenced to gather around me. I backed up against a hogshead of sugar, telling them not to come any nearer to me or I would hurt some of them. They took the hint, but began to abuse me. The mate and some of the boat's crew came back into the deck-room, and then I commenced to open out on them. "Now," said I to the bully, "perhaps you can whip me, but I can tell you in a few words you never saw a boy more willing to fight than myself; and if you will give me a boy's show, we will see who is the best of the two." He said, "I can whip you in a minute;" and so saying, he took off his coat. I threw mine off in quick time, ready for a fight. It was a good one. He hit me as hard as ever Sullivan hit a man; but I kept dodging my head, so he would hit that, and he soon had his right hand as big as any man's head. I at last commenced to give it to him about the head pretty lively. And talk about a head! His looked like the hind-quarter of a beef. Finally one of the crew called enough for him, for he was not able to do so. They carried the big bully up stairs and laid him in his bed. To tell the truth, he was the toughest man I ever had anything to do with; for he was a powerful man, weighed two hundred pounds, and could hit like a jack a-kicking. The Pittsburgers did hate to see their man get whipped, as he was their leader. The news went to Pittsburg, and they could hardly believe that he could get the worst of a rough-and-tumble fight.

At one time I was crossing the levee at New Orleans about 6 o'clock in the evening, when a big fellow jumped from behind a cotton bail and struck me on the head with an iron dray-pin, which he held in both hands. The blow staggered me, and I fell on my knees. I caught hold of the dray-pin until I recovered myself, when I got hold of him and took the pin out of his hand. I downed him, and was just getting ready to go to work, when the police rushed in and pulled me off. I would have given $100 if they had let me alone just half a minute. They took us both to the lock-up. I put up money for both of us to appear, as I wanted to get at him again; but he called on the police to accompany him to his place of business. He was a boss drayman, and a particular friend of a stevedore I had whipped a year previously, and he had it in for me.

DIDN'T WIN THE BAGS.

There was a man in New Orleans before the war that supplied the steamboat men with silver to pay their deck-hands. He could buy it at a discount, as it was a drug on the money market at that time. I have often seen him, with his two heavy leather bags, on his way from the bank to the boats. One day my partner (Charlie Bush) and I were in a saloon on Camp Street, when in walked the "silver man," carrying his heavy leather bags. I gave Bush the wink, and began throwing the cards on the counter. The man got stuck looking at the game; and when Bush bet me $100 and won it, he got more interested and bet me the drinks, which I lost; then he bet me the cigars, and I lost again. I then said to him: "You can't guess the winner for $500." He said, "I will bet you $100 I can." I told him I would not bet less than $500; then Bush said, "I will bet you," and we put up the money, and Bush won it. Old "silver" got excited when he saw Bush pocket the $500, and I said to him, "I will bet you $1,000 against the silver in the two bags."

He knew there was not near $1,000 in the bags, so he jumped them up on the counter, and said, "It's a go;" and then he stood close and watched me throw them, until I said "Ready;" then he made a grab, and turned over the wrong card. If he had been struck by lightning, he could not have acted more dazed. He dropped into a chair and lost all control of himself, and I felt a little sorry for him; but "business is business." So I picked up the bags and started to go, when the fellow came to his senses and said: "Hold on; you did not win the bags." I saw he had me on the bags; and as I knew he had them made for the business, I said to him: "If you get me something to put the money in, you can have the bags." He jumped up and ran out; and when he returned with a meal-sack, he found the barkeeper and his two bags, but not Bush and me. We had bought some towels of the barkeeper, dumped the silver into them and lit out, for fear that the little old silver man would bring back a "cop" to hold us, in place of something to hold the silver. The little fellow was game, and did not say anything about his loss. The next time I met him he requested me to say nothing about the play; and every time we met we would take a drink, and laugh over the joke. The last time I met my silver friend he was crippled up with the rheumatism so he could hardly walk, and he was "dead broke." I gave him $10 (for past favors), and I have not seen him since; and I expect he is now in his grave, for it has been many years ago since I won the silver, but not the bags.

THE BLACK DECK-HAND.

Charlie Clark and I left New Orleans one night on the steamer *Duke of Orleans*. There were ten or twelve rough looking fellows on board, who did their drinking out of private bottles. Charlie opened up shop in the cabin, and soon had a great crowd around him. I saw that the devils had been drinking too much, so I gave Charlie the wink,

and he soon closed up, claiming to be broke. Then we
arranged that I should do the playing, and he would be
on the lookout. I soon got about all the money and some
watches out of the roughs, besides I beat seven or eight of
the other passengers. They all appeared to take it good-
naturedly at the time; but it was not long before their loss,
and the bad whisky, began to work on them. I saw there
was going to be trouble, so I made a sneak for my room,
changed my clothes, and then slipped down the back stairs
into the kitchen. I sent word for Clark to come down. I
then blackened my face and hands, and made myself look
like a deck-hand. I had hardly finished my disguise,
when a terrible rumpus up stairs warned me that the ball
was open. The whisky was beginning to do its work.
They searched everywhere; kicked in the state-room doors,
turned everything upside down, and raised h—l generally. If they could have caught me then, it would have
been good bye George. They came down on deck,
walked past, and inquired of a roustabout who stood
by me if he had seen a well-dressed man on deck. He
told them "he had not seen any gemman down on deck
afore they came down." They had their guns out, and
were swearing vengeance. The boat was plowing her
way along up the river; the stevedores were hurrying the
darkies to get up some freight, as a landing was soon to be
made. The whistle blew, and the boat was headed for
shore. Those devils knew I would attempt to leave the
boat, so as soon as the plank was put out they ran over on
the bank, and closely scanned the face of every one who
got off. There was a lot of plows to be discharged, so I
watched my chance, shouldered a plow, followed a long
line of coons, and I fairly flew past the mob. I kept on
up the high bank and threw my plow on to the pile, and
then I made for the cotton fields. I lay down on my back
until the boat was out of sight, and then I came out,
washed myself white, and took a boat for Vicksburg,
where I met Clark the next day, and we divided the

boodle that he had brought with him. He told me that after I had left the boat they got lights and went down into the hold, looking for me, as they were sure I was still on the boat. It was a pretty close call, but they were looking for a well-dressed man, and not a black deck-hand.

HARD BOILED EGGS.

I was going from Baton Rouge to New Orleans on the steamer *Grand Duke*, one New Year's eve, and had spent a great deal of money at the bar for wine. The barkeeper was an Italian with a great name, which was Napoleon. I said to him, " Nap, I hear you have sixty dozen eggs on board; suppose you treat me to an eggnog." " Oh, no; me no treat; if you pay, me make some." " If you don't treat me to an eggnog, I will quit buying wine," I said, and walked out. I went to Daniel Findley, the steward, and told him how stingy old " Nap " was to me. Dan said, " Never mind, George; I'll fix him and his eggs." He told the cook to fire up, and then get those sixty dozen eggs and boil them as hard as h—l. After they were all hard-boiled, they put them into cold water, and then put them back into the box. I went back to the bar, and waited until Dan sent me word that all was ready; then I said to old Nappy, " I was only in fun; I wanted to see if you could make a good eggnog." " I make good eggnoggy as anybody," said Nap. " Well, I tell you what I will do; if you will make enough to treat all the passengers, I will give you $10," I said. "All right," says he, and started to the storeroom to get his sugar, milk, eggs, etc. He soon returned, loaded down with stock. He got out his large bowl, and then cracked one of the eggs. It didn't crack to suit him; he looked at it, and then said to me, " Lookey dat! a chick in the first egg!" He threw that one out of the window, and then cracked another, which was just like the first; then he said, " Me boughty the egg for fresh; no good; all rot." Then he

broke another, and another, and finally he broke one open
and found it hard boiled; then he said, "Who biley the
egg? Me give five dollie to know who biley the egg!"
His Italian blood was up to fever heat, and it was some
time before we could get a drink of any kind. He sold
the eggs in market when we got to New Orleans. We did
not have our eggnog that New Year's eve, but we had
the best laugh at the expense of old Napoleon that I ever
had in my life.

"SNAP GAMES."

I was coming down from the Memphis races on the *R.
W. Hill*. There were about twenty-five gamblers on the
boat, and they were all crazy for a game of faro. I told
them I had a set of tools on board that I would loan them
if they wanted to open. They accepted the offer, and
took turns in opening "snaps." Some opened as high
as $1,000 at a time. I was playing poker, and did not
pay much attention to their game. After supper I told
them that I would open a $1,000 "snap," and they could
tap it when they pleased. When I sat down to deal, I had
a matched set of boxes; you could not tell one from the
other. One box was fixed for all the cases to lose, and
this I kept secreted. They knocked me out of $400 in
one deal; on the next deal I shuffled up the same cards
and put them in the box, so they could see that everything
was on the square. As I did so, my partner tipped over a
big lot of silver on the layout, which he had stacked up on
purpose to draw their attention, and I came the change on
the boxes and threw my handkerchief over the box I held
in my lap. Everything went on all right. The first case
that showed on the case-keeper they all jumped on to play
it open, as they wanted to break the snap, as then I would
open another; but the case lost, and I was a good big
winner over the last deal. When it came to another case,
they played it to win, and it lost; but they did not think

anything was wrong, so they kept firing away till they were all pretty well crippled in money matters. They played the deal out, and nearly all were broke. At the end of the deal I said, "Boys, I will have to quit you, as it is too much of a seesaw game;" and then they commenced to smell a rat, and you would have given $100 to have heard them cursing for not watching me shuffle that deal. The game closed with nearly all the money won; some of them I had to loan money, to pay their expenses.

THE JUERGUNSEN WATCH.

I won a Juergunsen watch one time from a Jew. I put $1,000 against it. After I got the watch the Jew came to me and said: "Look here, I want to tell you something. I bought that watch for $5. It is not worth that much, so help me gracious; but I bought it for a brother on a farm, and he don't know the difference. I'll tell you what I do; I will give you $10 for it, for I don't want to fool him, as I am going out there now." I told him it was good enough to give to a boy, and I would keep it for a black boy I had. "I tell you what I do; rather than let a nigger boy get it, I'll give you $15." I said "No." He kept raising till he got to $400. As I knew I could get no more, I let him have it. After he got the watch he commenced to laugh and said he cheated me, for the watch cost him $600. I knew what they cost, for I had priced the same watches, and they were worth $600 at that time. It was one of the finest make, split seconds, and had an alarm. The cases were very heavy, with a diamond in the stem that would weigh a karat. The Jew thought he had beat me, but he seemed to forget that I had beat him first.

IT MADE A MAN OF HIM.

" Yet fondly we ourselves deceive,
    And empty hopes pursue ;
Though false to others, we believe
    She will to us prove true."

On my way up the river on board the old steamer
Natchez (the boat that was burned up during the war),
I won some money and a check for $4,000 on the Louis-
iana State Bank of New Orleans. The check was signed
by one of the largest planters on the coast, and I knew it
was good if presented before payment was stopped ; so I
took passage on the *Mary Kean* (one of the fastest boats
on the river), bound for New Orleans. We landed in the
city about 4 o'clock Monday morning. I got a cab to take
me down to the French market to get a cup of coffee before going to my room. As I was passing the St. Louis
Hotel on my way from the market, I saw a man that I recognized as hailing from Cincinnati (I will not give his
name). He appeared to be glad to see me ; but I could
see he was not at his ease, so after a little while I thought
I would sound him, so I said, "What was that trouble you
got into in Cincinnati ?" He looked at me in surprise
and said : " How did you hear about it ?" (there was no
telegraph line from Cincinnati to New Orleans in those
days). I told him it was all right, and he could trust me.
I invited him to take breakfast with me ; he accepted the
invitation, and told me he would tell me about himself
when we were in a more private place. After breakfast
we walked over to the bank, and I drew the $4,000 on the
planter's check ; then we went to my room, and he told me
his story. He was a bookkeeper for a large pork house ;
became infatuated with a gay married woman, made false
entries, and finally ran away with the enticing married
woman. I advised him to put on a disguise, for I knew
the police would soon be looking for him. He invited me
to go with him and see his lady love, for said he, " She is

one of the truest and best women in the world." I went with him, and met a very fine looking lady. I did not blame him very much for being infatuated; but I wondered how much money did he get away with, and how am I going to get my share; for I always felt that it was my duty (as an honest man) to win stolen money. I soon found out he had about $8,000 of other people's money and I wanted it. I first taught him to play poker, so he could be in with me the first time we caught a sucker. I got Clark to play the part, and he beat us out of $6,000, most of which was "pork money." "The best and truest woman in the world" ran off with another fellow, which little thing nearly broke my young friend's heart; but in a short time he went to Galveston, Texas, got into a large cotton house, and the last time I saw him he said, "George, we live and learn. That little game made a man of me."

THE COTTON MAN.

My partner and I were waiting at the mouth of Red River for a boat to take us to New Orleans. There was a man who had twelve bales of cotton on the wharf, and he was also waiting for a boat. I told my partner to get acquainted with him, and to keep away from me. The result was they were good friends when a boat arrived. We all took passage, the cotton was loaded, and we were on our way. I opened up the three-card racket; my partner won $100, and then the cotton man was crazy, for he did not have any money to bet. My partner told him he would loan him some on his cotton. They went to the clerk, who made out a bill of sale for the twelve bales. He got the money, and then he was happy, for he was sure of doubling it with me. He was happy but for a short time. I had all his money, and my partner had all of his cotton, so he (being a good friend) let him have some money to pay his expenses. He did not remain long, so the cost was not very heavy. The cotton was worth about 12½ cents per pound at that time, but during the war it was many times that price. I was never very much stuck on cotton, as it was too bulky to get away with in case you had to leave a boat in a hurry.

TAUGHT A LESSON.

I was playing poker with a man, who, after I had broke him, went to a gentleman friend of his and promised him twenty-five dollars for the loan of $500 until he got home. As he was worth a great deal of money, his friend loaned him the $500. After he got a new stake, he came to me and wanted to renew the play. I had played a square game, and, believing him to be a gentleman, I sat down to play the same way; but I soon saw he thought himself a better player than myself, so I lit into the new stake, and it was not long until I had him broke again. Then he went to the Captain and set up a great kick. The Captain said to him, "If you had won the money, would you have given it back?" He said, "Captain, I give you my word of honor that I would." "Then," says the Captain, 'Why did you pay twenty-five dollars for the loan of the money?" "Oh," says he, "I only wanted to teach him a lesson." "Well," says the Captain, "If you pay twenty-five dollars every time you want to teach such men as he is a lesson, you will soon get broke. I can't do anything for you, my fine fellow."

The passengers laughed at him, and some called him "a good teacher" (and that broke him all up). He soon sneaked off to his room, and that was the last I saw of my teacher.

SINKING OF THE BELLE ZANE.

I was a passenger on the steamer *Belle Zane* during the winter season, and navigation was expected to be closed soon, as the river was full of floating ice. We had a large number of passengers on board, and were getting along very well until we left the Ohio. We had left Cairo, and were steaming down the Mississippi, when the boat struck a snag, and in a very short time had sunk down to the cabin. It was about four o'clock in the morning, but I was up (as usual). We had the passengers out of their rooms in quick time, and got them up on the roof in their night clothes, as there was no time for them to dress. In a few moments the cabin separated from the deck, floated off, and then sank down until we were standing in the ice and water nearly knee deep. It was a terrible sight; such a one as I hope and pray I may never see again. Men, women, and children standing amid the floating ice nearly frozen to death, and expecting every moment to sink into a watery grave. Some were screaming for help, others were praying, while others stood as if they were lost. I caught up one poor woman, who was nearly frozen to death, and held her in my arms above the water. Others did the same, while the crew and some of the passengers tore the boards off of the pilot-house, and tried to paddle the wreck to shore. We floated down until we struck a point. The men that were doing the paddling jumped off onto the shore, and then held on to the wreck until they swung it around into an eddy. We got all the passengers off, but it was about a mile to the nearest house. We were all nearly freezing, and there was not one of us that did not have our feet frozen. We had no fire, nor any way to make one. Some of us who were lucky enough to have coats took them off, and wrapped up the women and children. We then took them to a house that was about a mile distant, and the good people did all in their power to make us comfortable. The news reached Cairo, and they sent a boat, with blankets, provisions, and medical aid to our relief. Three or four men jumped overboard, and tried to swim ashore, but got chilled, and were drowned. Some of the women were frozen so badly that they did not survive. I feel the effect in my feet to this day, and the accident happened over thirty years ago.

JEW VS. JEW.

"When Greek meets Greek, then comes the tug of war."
When Jew meets Jew, they want each other's gore.

We were going down the river from Baton Rouge at one time, and I had an old fellow with me they called "Jew Mose." There was a young Jew from Vidalia on board, and Mose got him into a game of euchre. We had not played long until the young Jew said, "I have got a good poker hand." Mose spoke up and said, "My hand is worth ten dollars." Then the young one put up his money; and as Mose had nothing, he backed out. I saw Vidalia had some nerve and money, so on my deal I ran up two hands, giving the young one four kings and the old one four aces. Mose said, "I have a poker hand." Vidalia says, "My hand is worth twenty-five dollars," and he put up. I tipped my hand to him, and raised it $100, at the same time giving Mose the office not to raise, as I thought it was all the fellow would stand. They both called; we showed down, and Mose had won the money. He made a reach for it, when Vidalia made a grab, but Mose was too quick for him. Then the young one jumped up and said to Mose, "You are a Jew and I'm a Jew, and you shan't have my money." Mose would not give up, so at it they went. They hit, bit, scratched, gouged, and pulled hair, until they were rolling around in each other's gore. Everybody came running to see what had broke loose, and it was ducks to see those two fellows fight. Neither would give up, and it is no telling how long the circus tumbling would have kept up, if the officers of the boat had not separated them. After the fight the cabin looked as if we had been fighting a half-dozen Newfoundland dogs from the amount of blood and black hair that was on the floor. The young one told Mose if he ever came to Vidalia he would lick him, so we supposed from that remark that he did not feel satisfied with the result. Poor old Mose did not live long enough to visit Vidalia so the young one could make his word good for he went up to Chicago, and soon after died.

BEAT A GOOD HAND.

I beat a man at poker out of $1,200 on the steamer *Wild Wagoner*. After he quit playing he asked me where I would get off. I told him at the mouth of Red River. When I left the boat I saw my friend had concluded to stop at the same place. It was not long before an officer called on me to take a walk with him, and he said, " We will go up and see the Judge." When we arrived at his Honor's place of business, I found that my twelve-hundred-dollar friend was there before me. The Judge spoke to him before he did to me, and said, " How did this man swindle you out of your money ? " " We were playing poker, your Honor." " Do you call playing poker swindling ? " said the Judge. " Well, your Honor, he must have swindled me ; for every time I had a good hand he would beat it," said he. " If that is all the evidence you have, the case is closed, the defendant is dismissed, and you will be held for the costs," said his Honor. I told the Judge I would pay the costs if he would let the fellow go. He accepted the proposition, and that night I had the honor of playing in the same game with the Judge, and I played a square game for once in my life, for fear I would have another friend who would want to see me at his Honor's office.

THEY PAID THE COSTS.

I had beat a man out of $600 on the railroad from New Orleans to Jackson. I saw that if I got off he would put me to some trouble, so I kept on until I got to Canton, twenty-five miles above. He followed me there, and had me arrested. The trial was to come off in an hour, as it was meal time with the Judge. We were all assembled in he court-room, and the Judge wanted him to tell how I

got his money. He said, "I could show you, Judge, if I
had some cards." I pulled out some of the same cards I
beat him with, and gave them to the Judge, and he wanted
to know how they could bet money on the three cards. I
said, "Judge, I will show you so you can understand."
I took the cards and mixed them over a few times, telling
the Judge to watch the jack. He did watch it, and he
could turn it over every time, as one of the corners of the
jack was turned up, and he said it was as fair a game as he
ever saw. I told him I had two chances to his one; so he
dismissed the case. I came near giving it to the Judge for
a few dollars, and then give them back; but I thought best
not to do so.

When the fellow went out of the court-room, the Canton
boys laughed at him and called him a fool. After he left,
the Judge and I went over to a saloon and had some cigars.
He said he dearly loved to play poker; but I did not want
any of his game, as I thought I might need him again
some time; and it proved I was right, for it was not long
after that I was coming down on the train from Vicksburg,
and beat five or six of the passengers out of a few hundred
dollars. When we got to Canton we were behind time and
missed connection, and had to lay over until night. They
had me arrested for the same trick, and taken before the
same Judge; and you ought to have heard him after he
found out how they had lost their money, for he just gave
them a good old-fashioned turning over. He called them
a lot of babies, and put the costs of the court on them. I
got the Judge a box of fine cigars, and went down on the
same train; but I was in the sleeper, and they did not see
me until I got to New Orleans. I played poker in the
sleeper all the way to the city, and did not lose very much,
as the game was small, and we played on the square. I met
some of them at the opera the same night, and they had
their opera glasses pointed at me for some time. I guess
they wondered how I got there so soon.

MY FIRST LOVE.

"Love gives esteem, and then he gives desert;
   He either finds equality, or makes it.
   Like death, he knows no difference in degrees,
   But frames and levels all."

There was a dance in the cabin of the steamer *Magnolia* one night, which was a fine affair, as there were a great many wealthy people on board. I had not done any playing on the boat, so I put on my good harness, and went back into the ladies' cabin to join in the dance. I was introduced to a number of fine ladies, among whom was a beautiful young widow. She joined me in a waltz, another dance, and a promenade on the guards. I thought her the most agreeable and sweetest woman I had ever met in my life. I was in her society most of the time, until the dancing ceased, and then I bade her "good night, good night; parting is such sweet sorrow, that I shall say good night till it be morrow."

I met the fascinating widow the next day, and before I bade her good-by I had received a pressing invitation to visit her at her plantation; and, "boys," you can bet your life it was not long before I availed myself of the opportunity. During my visit I received every attention. The negroes could not have done more for their master. There was a nice lake on the plantation. The servants would drive the lady and I over to it, and we would enjoy ourselves at fishing for a few hours. On our return she would play and sing for me, and as I sat and looked at her I thought, What would I give if I was a square man, and how happy I could be with such a woman as my wife. I did not tell her my business, for fear she would think less of me. I could not endure the deception, so after three days of happiness I tore myself away, feeling as if I was "unfixed for life." In a short time she visited relatives in New Orleans, and sent me an invitation to call; but as I was acquainted with her friends, the same old dread came upon

5

me, so I declined, with the excuse that I was compelled to leave the city that same evening on the steamer *Judge McLean*. We met again on board a steamer. She had been told my business, but she treated me more kindly than ever before. She begged me to quit gambling, and settle down. I partly agreed to do as she wished. We spent a very pleasant time together (for I would not attend to business while she was on the same boat).

Before she left the steamer she took off a large single-stone diamond ring, and said to me, " Wear this until we meet again." I tried to refuse it, but she insisted; so I at last accepted the token. I bade her good-by at the stage-plank, and went up on deck. She remained on the levee, waiving her handkerchief (and I returned the compliment) until we were out of sight. I talked to the clerk until I felt that I was myself again, and then I started out to find a sucker; for I had enjoyed the pleasure before business.

It was about three months before I saw my lady love again. I was glad to see her, and she appeared to be pleased at meeting me. Before we parted I put the ring back on her finger, but she said she did not want it; and I believe she meant what she said. I received another invitation to visit her at her plantation, which I have neglected to this day, and that has been over thirty years ago. I have often thought what a different man I might have been if I had accepted that last invitation. There is one thing that I am sure of, and that is, if I had married my "first love," I would not now be writing "Forty Years a Gambler on the Mississippi."

THE BOYS FROM TEXAS.

I got on the steamer *B. L. Hodge* at Baton Rouge, bound for New Orleans. It was on a New Year's eve; everybody was feeling jolly, and I felt somewhat that way myself. There were five tables of poker going at one time, so I opened up the good old game of monte for the

benefit of a lot of Texas boys that didn't play poker.
They all got around the table and watched me throw. In
a short time my capper came up and wanted me to show
him how to play the game. I showed him, and he wanted
to bet a dollar. I told him if that was all the money he
had, he had better keep it. He got as mad as a wet hen,
and told me he had just as much money as I had. He
pulled out a big roll and slashed down $1,000, saying,
"I will bet you I can turn the winner." I said, "You can't
bluff me," and I put up. He turned one of the cards and
lost. While I was putting the money away, he picked up
the cards and turned up a corner on the winner, letting the
boys see what he had done; then he said to me, "Mix
them up again," which I did, and he put down a roll,
claiming it to be $500. He turned and won. Then the
boys began to nudge each other and get nervous. The
capper then said, "I will let it all lay, and bet you again."
He turned and caught me for $1,000; and then you should
have seen the boys from Texas. There never was such a
cutting of cloths. One fellow pulled off his new coat and
cut the lining nearly all to pieces; another took off his
coat, vest, and shirt, for his money was sewed up in his
undershirt; others had their money down their boot legs
tied to a string, so that they could pull it up when they
wanted it. They all wanted it just then, and they were in
the biggest hurry of any suckers I ever saw. They all put
up their pile, except two or three who had more than the
rest. I told them to pick out one boy to turn the card, so
they selected Jim, who was their leader. Jim made a grab
for the sure thing; but when he turned it over, all the boys
were *sure* they had lost their money. They took it good-
naturedly, and said it was fair. One said I was the great-
est man in the world, and if he could *do* it as slick as I did
he could get all the money out in their country. I promised that I would come out and see them, and that they
would all be in with me. I did not say just when I would
keep my promise; and as I do not like too many partners,

I have put it off over thirty years, in hopes that some of the boys would give it up and move out of the country, so if a slick man did get all of their money he would not have to divide up so often.

MARKED CARDS.

While waiting for a boat at Donelsville to take me to New Orleans, I fell in with a fellow who proposed a game of cards to pass the time until the boat arrived. We went into a saloon and sat down to play a game of poker. He brought out an old deck of marked cards (which I recognized the minute I saw them). We began to play. I knew the fellow took me for a sucker, so I let him play me with "his cards" until I got a chance to down him, which I did for all he had, amounting to about $80. About this time some one announced that a boat was coming, so I proposed to quit; but Mr. "Gambler" did not want any quit in his, so long as he was loser and he had a sucker. I knew he had but little (if any) money left, so I quit and started for the landing. The boat had arrived, and was just about ready to leave, when an officer stepped up to me and said, "I have a warrant for your arrest." "The h—l you have! What have I done?" "You have swindled a gentleman out of his money, sir," says he. "All right, sir; I will go with you." He took me before a magistrate, and there was the fellow who had played the marked cards on me. The Justice wanted to know how I had swindled him. He said: "He put up the cards on me in a game of poker, and he is a gambler." You ought to have heard that old fellow give it to me. He said: "How dare you, sir, come in this place and rob our respectable citizens out of their money? I will teach you a lesson that you will not soon forget." He was going on in this strain, when I stopped him by saying, "Hold on, your Honor; I would like to say a word." "Go on, sir." "Well," says I, "this man invited me to play a game of poker with him, and when we sat down to play he brought out this old deck of marked cards on me, and I happened to know them as well, if not better than he did. He took me for a sucker, and I beat him at his own game. He calls me a gambler, but he is much worse ; for he attempted to rob me with those marked cards." "Show me the marks on those cards," said the Justice; so I walked up and began reading the cards by their backs to him. He watched me as I read the cards, until I called a ten spot and turned it over; then he grabbed it up and examined the back, and said: "Hold on; that will do; this is the same deck those d——d rascals have been playing on me ; for the other night this ten of hearts fell in the spit, and here is the mark on it now. They have been swindling me for the last six months." Then turning to me, he said: "You are dismissed; but I will fine this rascal $50 and costs, and send him to jail if he does not pay it immediately." I thanked the Justice for his just decision, and took the next boat for New Orleans.

MY CROOKED PARTNER.

My partner, Hugh Foster, and I were on board the *Elonzo Childs*, bound for New Orleans. Foster had the reputation of being a wolf, and I did not have much use for him. He was acquainted with a man on board that claimed to have a man who had five thousand dollars, and he could make him lose against monte, but he wanted half or there would be no play. Foster told him to get his man into a state-room, and they would win the money, and not let Devol know anything about it. So Foster came to me and said, "George, we will not try to do anything until after we leave Cairo, will we?" "No," I said; "I want all the sleep I can get." Foster said he felt tired, and would go to bed. I knew that the sneak had some scheme on hand, so I went to my room, but I did not go to bed; I went out the back door and up on the roof, where I could see what was going on down in the cabin. I had not been on watch very long until I saw Foster come out of his room, and in a short time go into another with two gentlemen. I slipped down off the roof, went out on the guards and called all the men into the barber shop. I told them I had a new game that I wanted to show them. It was a new game to them, and they were very much interested in it, as I let them win several small bets. After I got them well worked up, I said: "Now, gentlemen, I will not take any more small bets, but will bet $1,000 that no one can turn the jack the first time. Just then the barkeeper came in, and I said: "I will bet you $500 that you can't turn the jack." He counted out the money and put it up. I mixed them, and he turned up the winner. He then walked out, and I knew if there was any big money I would get it. I began to mix them again, when up stepped a big fellow and asked me what was the least I would bet. I sized him up, and then I said $1,000. He pulled out and put up. I counted out the same amount and put it up on my side of the table, so if there would be any snatching I could get there in time. I then saw he had some left, so I said I would back out and treat. That made him very anxious, and he said, "No, I will not let you back out." Then I said, "If you will not let me out, I will bet you $2,000, as I might as well be hung for an old sheep as a lamb." He put up the $2,000 and turned the card; but as I had two chances to his one, he made the same mistake that thousands had made before, and turned the wrong one. He walked off without a word, and sat down on the guards. I kept an eye on him; but he was game, and took his medicine just as I had taken it many a time at the bank. I kept on playing until I had taken in all the pan-fish and a large white diamond stud that was worth about $1,000. Then I closed up shop and invited all to join me in a drink. They all accepted except my $2,000 friend. He was too busy thinking how it was that he had turned the wrong card, when he could see so plainly that the right card had one corner bent. While we were drinking, in came Foster, and he looked as if he had just been pulled out of the river; for it was a very hot day, and the fellow had been in a close state-room for an hour, and had not won a cent. I said, "You look warm; come and join us in a drink." He took a drink, saying: "It was so hot I could not sleep." I took the diamond stud out of my pocket and showed it to the barkeeper. Foster saw it, and said: "George, I did not know that you had that stone." "What will you give for it?" said I. He looked at it, then offered me $500. I told him he could have it, so he paid me the money and put the stud in his shirt. In a few moments after he got the stone, a gentleman said to him: "That is a very fine stone; I am acquainted with the gentleman who lost it; he is a large jeweler in St. Louis." "You must be mistaken," said Foster. "Oh, no, I am not; for I saw him lose it in the barber shop about half an hour ago." Foster came to me and said: "George, you did not make a play, did you?" "Oh, yes; did you not make one yourself?" That made him look sick; but when a friend of mine came up and said, "Devol, you must have won $4,000 in that play," then he looked sicker. I said, "Yes, I guess I got about $4,000 out of it, and I will treat." While we were drinking, the barkeeper handed me the $500 he had won. I gave him $200 for his cap; and then Foster began to give me taffy. I told him I did not want anything more to do with him; that I had heard he was a sneak, etc. He got off at Cairo, and I was glad to get rid of him. I had a good wheel game down to Memphis, where I got off and lost $2,500 against faro. I took a boat for New Orleans, and made more than I lost in Memphis before I reached the city.

JUDGE DEVOL.

I was on board the *City of Louisiana*, bound for New Orleans. There was a large number of passengers, and a heavy load of freight. The roof was literally covered with coops full of chickens and turkeys. I had old monte running in full blast, but the chicken men could not bet, as they were going to market instead of coming away. They were so very much interested in the game that they forgot to watch their coops. After a while one of them went up, and found that some one had stolen some of his chickens. The pilot told him he saw the man taking them, so he went down and told the Captain, and he sent for the pilot to pick out the thief. They found him and brought him into the cabin, when some one proposed to try him by judge and jury; so they elected me judge, and I impaneled a jury. We heard the evidence, and the attorneys made their arguments. Then I charged the jury, and they retired to the bar-room (as we did not have any regular jury room). They were out about as long as as it would take a first-class barkeeper to make up twelve drinks, and then they filed back into the court-room, each one putting his handkerchief away, as if they had all been crying over the awful verdict they were about to render. I asked the foreman if they had agreed upon a verdict, and he said, "We have, your Honor." Just at this time there was some commotion in the court-room (occasioned, no doubt, at the sight of the twelve handkerchiefs). I told the sheriff to rap for order, but it was some little time before it could be restored. I then told the jury to stand up and hear their verdict. The foreman read the verdict, which was: "We, the jury, find the defendant guilty." I then told the defendant to stand up and hear his sentence. "You are to return the chickens to their owner, pay a fine of six bottles of wine and the costs of this suit, and be imprisoned in the bar-room until the fine and costs are paid."

As there were no other cases on the docket, I ordered the sheriff to adjourn court (to the bar). The sheriff went up with the man who had lost the chickens, and they picked out three dozen. When they came down and reported to me that they had returned three dozen chickens, the criminal yelled out that he had only taken one dozen. The poor fellow did not have the money to pay for the wine, so he had to give a bill of sale for his chickens.

After all of my judicial duties were performed, and while the bar (of justice) was full of people, and the people were full (of what they got at the bar), I opened up the dear little three-card racket, and in a short time I owned every chicken and turkey on the roof of that boat.

What to do with my live stock I did not know. I had a bill of sale from the chicken men, but what I wanted just then was a chicken buyer. I at last had an offer from the second clerk which was much less than the market value; but as I never had much use for anything I could not put in my pocket, I accepted his offer and sold out. The chicken men had no business in New Orleans, as they had sold in transit, and not one of them had any money; so I called them up to the office, and gave each one money enough to take him back to Cairo.

MY PARTNER ALEXANDER.

I went on board the steamer *Imperial* at Memphis, bound for New Orleans. It was ten o'clock at night, and I did not think of doing any business until the next day. While standing talking to the barkeeper, a man walked in and proposed to shake him for the drinks. They shook, and the stranger lost. He then proposed to shake for five dollars, and asked me if I would come in and make it three-handed. I said I would for a time or two. We shook, and he was a little loser, when he wanted to make it ten dollars. I consented, but the barkeeper dropped out.

We sat down, and soon were shaking for $100 a game. We were drinking during the time, and it was not very long until I had won $1,300. The fellow was pretty full, so I thought I would complete the "filling," and then he would go to bed. As I expected, it was not long before he turned in, and I was at liberty to look around. I went into the cabin, and found three games of poker in full blast. I was looking on at one of the games, when I noticed a man looking at me. He gave me a sign, and I walked out on the guards. He followed me and said, "You do not remember me ; my name is Alexander ; I met you in St. Louis over a year ago. I heard that you and Clark had split up, and I am now on my way to New Orleans to meet you, for I want to go to work." I told him that I was alone, and that we would begin our work on the morrow. We were in the barber shop the next day, when a man came to me and told me that he was a brother of Mike Carroll, and he wanted to cap for me. As I knew Carroll well, I told him to go ahead. We were playing monte, and I had beat a man out of twenty-six twenty-dollar gold pieces. When we came to settle up there was one gold piece missing, so I said, "Boys, there is one gold piece short." Alexander proposed a search, and Carroll said, "I have not got a cent, and that is why I wanted to cap, in order to pay my passage." We commenced the search, and when we took off Carroll's hat the gold piece dropped out ; so I paid his passage and let him go.

At the expiration of four years, Alexander showed me receipts for money he had sent to his home in Dover, Ky., amounting to $44,000, and he was not a stingy man, either ; for he was a good liver and dresser, and I have known him often to spend as much as $200 in one night for wine, etc. He has often talked to me about playing the bank, and wanted me to quit it ; and I can now see if I had taken his advice I might have been worth forty times $44,000.

THE QUADROON GIRL.

I got on the *Belle Key* one afternoon at Vicksburg; and as I claimed to be a planter from White River, I soon became acquainted with some planters that lived on the coast. There was a game of poker started, and I was invited to sit in. We played until supper was ready. I had played on the square, and had won a few hundred dollars. After supper they got up a dance, and that spoiled the game. I was sitting in the hall, when one of the planters came to me and said, "Don't you dance?" "No, I don't care to dance where I am not acquainted." "You are like me in that respect; I had rather play poker; but as those gentlemen who were playing in the game to-day have all got their families on board, they will not play, so what do you say to us having a game?" I said I did not care to play a while, but I would rather be a little more private, and that we might go up into the texas and play. We got the checks at the bar (and the barkeeper did not forget a deck of my cards). We went up and had just got seated, when up came my partner and said, "Gentlemen, are you going to sport a little?" "We are; will you join us?" said the planter. "What are you going to play?" "Poker, of course." He sat in, and then it was a very nice, gentlemanly game. We played on the square for a while (that is, if the cards had been square). Finally I could put it off no longer, so I ran up two hands, giving the planter three eights, and then downed him for over $400. We played a little while longer, and then I ran up two more hands, and guarded them so that nothing could fall in that time. I gave my partner the best hand, and he took in about $600. The planter was then over $1,000 loser, so he excused himself for a few minutes, and I knew that he had gone after more money. He soon returned with $1,500, and that lasted him about one hour. He got up and said, "Boys, I must have some more money." My partner and I went down with him, as I did not think he could get any more. We were at the bar taking a drink, when he turned to me and said, " I would like to play some more, but I can't get any more money, unless you will loan me some on my negro, as I have one on board that I paid $1,500 for, and she is one of the most likely girls you ever saw." I winked at my partner to loan him some money on his wench. He went back and brought out one of the prettiest quadroon girls, about seventeen years old, that I ever saw. My partner loaned him $1,000, and got the clerk to draw up a bill of sale; then we resumed the game; but that did not last him but about half an hour, for I beat him out of nearly the whole amount on one hand, and that broke up the game. He had but seventy-five dollars left. We went down and took a drink, and then went to bed.

The next day he got the money and redeemed his girl; then he said to me, " I have got about $700, so let us go up and play single-handed. We went up, and I soon got that money. He said, " In all my poker playing, I never played so unlucky in my life. He went to my partner and borrowed $1,000 more on the girl, and I took that in. He then went to Captain Keys, and tried to borrow the money to redeem his girl again, but the Captain would not loan it to him. He found a man that loaned him the money, and he redeemed her again. He was considerable loser, but he got some more wine in him, then he wanted more poker; but I told my partner not to have anything more to do with his negro, for it was making too much talk on the boat already. When he got to his landing, he and his negro left the boat, and I tell you she was a dandy.

THE CAPTAIN SPOILED THE GAME.

I was coming out of New Orleans one night on the *Ohio Belle*, a Cincinnati boat, and she was full of good looking suckers. I went out on the guards and called them all into the cabin, and opened up monte. They all gathered around the table, and among them was the Captain of the boat, who insisted on betting. I said to him, "You are the Captain of the boat, and I do not want to bet with you." He kept insisting that his money was just as good as anybody's, and he put up $300. I gave my capper the office to take him away, but he would not have it. I then told him I would not bet less than $500. He called to the clerk to bring him $200, and then he put up $500. I told him not to bet if the loss would distress him, when he told me it was his money. I told him to turn the card, for I saw it was the only way to get rid of him. He turned, and lost; then he got mad, and made me close up. I had no intention of keeping his money, so I walked out on the guards, and then up on the roof, where I found him. I said, "Here is your money; I did not want you to bet, and you have knocked me out of many a good dollar." He was surprised to get his money back, and he said he bet in good faith. I talked to him until he told me I could open up again, and then I told him to give me the $500, and so soon as I got opened up, for him to come up and make a play, and I would let him win it back.

I went down and called all the boys into the cabin again, and had just begun to throw them, when up stepped the Captain and said, "I lost once, but I will try it again." So he put up and won the money. Then he walked away. Then a sucker pulled out his wallet, and offered to bet me $500. I saw he had plenty left, so I said, "I will not bet less than $1,500." While he was hesitating, my partner came forward and said he did not have that much money, but he would bet $1,000 that he could turn the winner. I took him up and he lost. Then the sucker was all excitement, for he saw that he didn't turn the card with the corner turned up, so he wanted to bet $1,000. I would not bet less than $1,500, so he at last put up. I gave them one more shuffle, and then he was so nervous that he turned the wrong card. It made him so sick that he went out on the guards and threw up his supper. The balance of the suckers did not want to get sick, so I closed up; but if it had not been for the Captain's first play, I would have done a much better business on that boat. Such is luck.

TOO SICK TO FIGHT.

I was playing poker on the steamer *Capitol* with a negro trader, and had won some money from him, when he got up and went down on the boiler deck. In a little while he came back followed by an old black woman, and wanted me to loan him $1,500 on her. She was too old for me, so I told him I was not keeping a pawn-shop; but my partner told him he would loan him $1,000 on her, if he would make out a bill of sale. The bill was made out, and he got the money. We began another game, and in about half an hour I had his $1,000; for we were playing with my cards, and they never went back on me or told me a lie. He went off, borrowed some more money, and wanted to renew the game; but as he was getting very drunk, I declined to play with him any longer. Then he set up a kick, and said he had been cheated. I told him all suckers talked that way when they lost their money. That made him hotter than ever, and he wanted to fight. I told him I was sickly and could not fight; so he left me to find my partner, to buy his old woman back again. I never refused to sell a nigger I had won, if any one would give me anything near the value; and I never had any use for old nigger women.

THE GAMBLER DISGUISED.

I started out one night on the *Crystal Palace*. The boat left New Orleans about 6 o'clock in the evening. After supper I opened monte. There were some rough customers from Greenville, and I knew if they lost their money there would be the devil to pay; but I took the chances, and caught some of them for a few hundred dollars, and there were some two or three of the passengers who also lost. After the Greenville killers had lost their money they commenced to fill up, and I knew there would be war soon. I closed up, slipped around and got on another suit of clothes, put on my plug hat and gold glasses. Then I gave my valise to the porter and told him to have it ready to go off at Donaldsonville. I walked out in the cabin; they were all standing by the bar holding a consultation how they could get the money back. One said: "The first time the boat stops he will get off." "Well, if he does he is a good one, for I will fill his hide full of lead if he tries that," says another. The boat blew her whistle to land, and you ought to have seen them break for the lower deck, gun in hand. I walked out through the cabin with my plug hat, white necktie, and gold glasses. You would have bet $500 that I was a preacher. You ought to have seen those fellows make room for me to pass by. My partner remained on board, as they were not on to him. I got a boat soon after and went to Baton Rouge, where my partner was waiting for me. He said they raised the d—l after I got off.

MARRIED HIS MONEY.

I was on board the steamer *H. R. W. Hill* going up the river and had got my work in, and what money I had accumulated was at poker. We landed at Natchez, and most all that were playing in the game got off. After supper I was sitting on the guards smoking, when a man came up and commenced conversation about gambling. He said: "I love to gamble, but my wife is bitterly opposed to it. I did want to play in that game to-day, but I dare not, as I have my family on board; so if you play to-night, I want to sit in." "Well, I guess that we may make up a game after it gets later," I said. About two hours after supper he came out and proposed a game. I asked the barkeeper to pull out a table and put the checks and a deck of cards on it, which he did. I could see that this man was crazy for a game, so I told him to sit down at the table and to ask every man that came by the bar to play, and he did so. Presently my partner came up to the bar and he got the invitation, so he sat in. They counted the checks and got all ready, when I dropped in. Then we had a nice three-handed game, and as we were all first-class gentlemen there could not be anything wrong. I wanted to play along until the passengers got thinned out a little, as they were too thick about the table to suit me; and then my friend wanted his wife to get to bed before he started in. Everything was going on beautifully, and I had not given my man a hand to see if he had any blood in him; but presently he got a hand on the square, and I knew I could beat him before the draw, so I slashed it at him pretty lively, but no big bets, and he staid like a man. When it came to the draw, he filled his hand, and I did not. It was my partner's age and the man's first bet. He bet $100, and I told him to take the pot. I had got in before the draw about $150. Then I knew he was a darling sucker, and I nursed him like a baby. We played a hand or two, then I ran him up three aces and took four nines pat. I did not want my partner to raise it too much before the draw, for fear he would drop out. We had up about $150. It was my deal, and I asked him how many cards he wanted. He took two. I said, "I will only take one." My partner took three, as he had nothing, but had to stay in to cross lift. He tipped his hand to the man, and the gentleman bet $250. I just called the bet, so my partner bet $1,000 better; and the gentleman tore his pockets getting at his money, and he called the bet. So I said, "Boys, I expect you have got me beat, but I will have to raise you back $1,000." That made my partner throw down his hand. Then it was between him and myself. He said to me, "I know I ought to raise it, but will just call the bet." When I showed down four nines, it made him lie quiet. We were just getting ready to give the boy another hand, when his wife came out into the hall, and made him quit and go to bed. I was sorry to see such an angel leave the game; but such is luck. I found out that he was very rich, but had married the money.

THE BEST LOOKING SUCKER.

I was on board the steamer *Eclipse* from Louisville to New Orleans, and she was crowded with passengers. I knew all the officers, and they were glad to see me, as they knew I would make it lively while I was with them. I opened a few bottles of wine, and finally I called them all in off the guards and opened up monte. I explained the game to them. My partner stepped up and looked at it for some time, and at last he bet me $1,000 and lost it. He then took up one of my cards and bent up the corner, then showed it to the best looking sucker that was standing by. Then he turned to me as he threw it down, and said: "Please mix them up once more." So I threw them over again, and then I was ready for a bet. He pulled out his money and put it up in the gentleman's hand that he had picked out for the solid one. I said, "How much have you got there?" He said $1,000. I put up the money, and at the same time I said: "I will make it $5,000 if you wish." "I have not got the money, or I would." He turned the card over and won. Then he wanted to bet $2,000; but I told him, "Whenever I get beat I never want to bet with the same man again." Then the gentleman spoke up and said, "I will try you once for $1,000." I said I would not bet less than $2,000, so by a little persuasion he laid it up and lost. He walked off, and I never saw him again about the table. I played a short time longer and took in a few hundred dollars, and then closed up for the evening.

MY CARDS.

The first trip the steamer *Eclipse* made I was on board. There were five games of poker running at one time in the cabin. I was invited into one, and I represented myself as a horseman. I played on the square, as I wanted to gain their confidence; so when the game closed for the night, they all thought me a square man. After all my new friends had retired to their little beds, I got out six decks of my marked cards and went to the bar. I told the barkeeper what I wanted, but he objected, as he did not own the bar, and was afraid it would be found out, and then he would be discharged. I told him that no one but old gamblers could detect the marks, and not one in fifty of them, as it was my own private mark. I had been a good customer at the new bar, so the new barkeeper finally consented to take my cards and send them to the table where I would be playing. The next morning after breakfast the games were started, and my new friends wanted me to sit in. I accepted the invitation, and when the barkeeper put the checks and cards on the table, I saw my old friends (I mean the cards). The game was five-handed, and it was pretty hard to keep the run of all the hands; but I quit the game a few hundred dollars winner. After the game one of the gentlemen came to me and said: "I don't like a five-handed game; suppose we split up and make two games." That was just what I wanted, provided I could get in the game that had the most suckers, so I said to him: "I do not care to play, if you gentlemen can make up your game without me; but as we are all going through to New Orleans, I will play a little to pass the time. You can arrange the games to suit yourselves, and can count me in if you are short a man." The gentleman arranged two nice games, with me in one of them. I had no partner, so I had to depend entirely on myself and my old friends, the marks on the back. We played until the engines were stopped at the landing in New Orleans, and I was $4,300 ahead. I might have won a great deal more with the assistance of a good partner, but then, you know, I would have had to divide with him; so I was very well pleased with my last day on the new steamer. I did not forget the new barkeeper, but gave him $50 for using my cards at one of the tables in place of his own.

FIGHT WITH A LONG-SHOREMAN.

A big fellow tackled me by the name of Barlow. He was a long-shoreman, and a tough one, but I did him up in seventeen minutes. He came into a saloon where I was in company with Bill Leonard and Bob Johnson. Leonard is well known, having kept stables in New Orleans and Cincinnati for many years. I had given races that day, and it appears that this man Barlow had lost some money. Five or six toughs entered the saloon with Barlow. He approached Johnson and said to him, "You throwed that race, you s— of a b—, and I am going to lick you for it." He cut loose and hit Johnson, and he must have hit him pretty hard, for he knocked him clear into the street. As Johnson was getting up, an officer ran up to him, when Johnson cut loose and knocked him down, thinking it was Barlow. They arrested Johnson and took him off. Then Barlow turned to me and said, "You keep the race track, and you are as big a thief as that other fellow. You whipped a good man when you whipped Fitzgerald, but you can't whip Barlow." I looked around to see how many friends he had with him, and I saw there were six or seven, and only Leonard on my side, who turned the key in the door, jumped on the counter, pulled his pistol, and said : "Gentlemen, if these men fight, they shall have it on the square, and the first one that interferes I will fill him full of lead." So at it we went. He was a good, scienced man, and had his hands up very quick. He made a feint to strike me with his left, and let go with his right. I gave him my head for a mark, which he hit clearly, and his fist looked like a boxing glove two minutes afterward. I ran under his guard, caught him under the arms, and downed him. In the squabble I got one solid crack at him between the eyes with my head, which ended the fight. He just was able to cry "Enough." I did not see him for several weeks after that. The next time I saw him was on St. Charles Street. He was drunk, and looking for me with a big knife up in his sleeve. I saw him coming, then I grabbed my gun and stood pat. I said, "Don't come one step more towards me, or I will cook your goose." He came to the conclusion that I meant business, and walked off. About that time there was a man done for every day in the Crescent City, but now New Orleans is a moral place, and some of the best people in the world live there.

DON'T DYE YOUR WHISKERS.

We were on board the steamer *York Town* one day, when I thought there were no suckers aboard. I had looked around, and had about come to the conclusion that we would not make our expenses, when I saw a large, well-dressed fellow who had his whiskers dyed black as ink. I got into conversation with him, and we walked around over the boat, and finally up on the roof. Bob Whitney was at the wheel, and his partner, Bill Horricks, was with him in the pilot-house. I knew the boys were all right, so I invited my new acquaintance to go up, as we could see better than on the roof. He accepted the invitation, and we were soon enjoying the scenery. I threw some of my cards on the floor, under the seat. The gentleman noticed them in a little while, picked them up, and turning to me he said, "If we had a full deck we could have a game." I told him I hardly ever played, but I saw a fellow playing a game with three cards that beat anything I ever saw, but it took a smart one to play it. I began throwing them, when

Bob Whitney got so interested that he came near letting the boat run away with him. He wanted to bet me fifty dollars, and he told Bill Horricks to hold the boat until he could make a bet. I told him I did not understand the game well enough to bet on it. About this time the capper put in an appearance, and he wanted to know all about the game. I explained it, and he made the usual bets. The pilot wanted to bet very bad, but I kept refusing. Finally my friend with the black whiskers got worked up to $1,000, and lost it. Then my partner put a mark on the winner, and beat me out of $1,000. The sucker saw the mark on the card, and wanted to bet $100. He was sure of winning, but he did not want to win but $100. So I took his bet, and just as he was about to turn the card I said, " I will make it $1,000;" but he only wanted the hundred dollars, and he got it. After winning the $100, and seeing the mark still on the card, he thought it was all his way, so he put up $1,000. I saw it was about all he had, so I put up, and he turned the marked card ; but it was not the winner for $1,000 so much as it had been for $100. He walked out of the pilot-house and went down on deck. My partner followed him.

After they were gone, Bob Whitney said he would have turned the same card. Then Bill Horricks laughed, and told him he could hold a steamboat, but he could not beat Devol at his own game. I went down to the bar, and there was my black-whiskered friend talking to my partner. I invited them to join me, which they did, and then the gentleman said he would like to speak with me a moment. We walked out on the guards, when he said to me, " I know I am a fool, but I want to ask you one question, and I want you to be candid with me. Why did you pick me out from among all the passengers for a sucker?" " Well, I said, " I will be honest with you ; don't you dye your whiskers?" "Yes," said he." " Well, that is the reason I picked you out." He said, " I thank you, sir," and walked off.

I went into the cabin and opened up again. I caught a

few suckers, and then closed up monte.   I then got out my wheel, and took in all the pan-fish.   After closing up for the evening, I walked into the bar, and there I met a fine looking smooth-faced gentleman, who asked me to take a drink, at the same time saying: "Do you think shaving off my whiskers has improved my looks?" I told him there was not as much deception in him as there had been in the card with the pencil mark on it. We took another drink and separated, I with about $2,000 of his money, and he with the experience.

CALLED A GAMBLER.

I was coming from New Orleans on the *Duke of Orleans* at one time, and had won a few hundred dollars from some of the passengers, but had quit playing, and was standing in the hall talking to some gentlemen that had played in the game, when a big fellow stepped up and said he believed we were a set of gamblers, and had divided the money he lost in the game.   I gave him the laugh, and that made him hot. He then pulled off his coat and said he could whip any man in the crowd, and he kept his eye on me all the time.   I told him I could lick him for fifty or one hundred dollars in a fair rough-and-tumble fight down on deck. He said if any one would see he had a fair show he would fight me.   The mate asked me if I was going to fight him? I said, "Yes."   So he told the big fellow he was an officer on the boat, and that no one would interfere if he wanted to fight.   So he put up his fifty dollars in the mate's hand, and I covered it; for those days I would rather fight than eat, and I could fight for a man's life. We went on deck, and they cleared a place for us.   While this was going on I offered to bet him fifty or a hundrd dollars more that I would make him squeal.   He said he had no more money to put up.   We stripped off and got in the place prepared for us.   He struck at me with one of those old-fashioned Dutch winders.   I ducked my head, and he hit that.   I knew it hurt him, for he did not use that duke any more. I got in under him, let fly with my head, and caught him square in the face. It made him grunt, but the next time I got one in on him I made him look silly, for the blood came out of his ears and nose. He said, "That will do."

The mate took him up stairs, and had the barber wash and patch him up. I changed my clothes, as they were covered with the fellow's blood. I asked all hands to take a drink, and my man came up and joined us. I then paid the bar bill, and gave him back the balance of the fifty dollars I won from him on the fight. He claimed that it was his first whipping, but he could not stand the old head; it was too hard for him.

I have had a great many fights in my day. There was a fellow tackled me on the levee in New Orleans at one time when I was all alone, and he had a lot of his friends with him. I got him down, and was getting the best of him, when some of his friends began kicking me pretty lively. I guess I would have been licked that time, if it had not been for some men on a ship, who saw too many on one; so they came to my assistance, and then I made the fellow squeal in a short time, They had it in for me for a long time, but finally gave it up as a bad job; and I was glad of it, as I never wanted to kill a man, which I expect I would have done if they had not let me alone.

THE ALLIGATORS.

I went up on the *Princess*. My old friend Truman Holmes was the Captain of her. I was standing on the hurricane deck when we landed at the mouth of the Red River to take in some passengers. I saw the negroes carrying some long boxes built like chicken-coops. I asked Captain Holmes what was in the boxes. He said, "Alligators;" so I went down stairs and found the man that owned them. I took him up to the bar and had a drink; then I asked him what he was going to do with the alligators. He said he had a side-show, and he was going to play the fairs all over the entire Northern country, and he wanted them to draw custom. I told him I thought it an excellent idea, and said, "I have a ten-legged wolf in a cage that I will get on board at Vicksburg, and I will sell him cheap." This pleased him, and we took another drink. I insisted on paying for the drinks, but he would not consent, so we got to be good friends. After supper we got to playing whisky poker, as I told him I never gambled much, only once in a while, as planters would play a quarter antee. He insisted on changing it into a little draw; and as I had some very good cards in the bar, I was not hard to coax. We commenced at a quarter antee, and after we had been playing about an hour he insisted on raising it to $1. He flattered me more than I ever was flattered before, in telling me I was the luckiest man to draw he ever saw. The result was, before we reached Natchez I had won all his money and his alligators. But he took it so much to heart about losing his pets, that I sold them back to him and took his note. It is now older than the daguerrotype man's; and when I hand in my checks, I will leave the notes with my dear old mother-in-law for collection.

CONTROL OVER SUCKERS.

I was playing euchre one night on the old *Vicksburg*, and had a good sucker down in the game, and the clerk was watching us very close; so after I gave the sucker a good hand, and he wanted to bet on poker, I whispered and said, "If we make a bet we must put the money in a hat, and we must not speak about betting louder than in a whisper." We had up $900, when I saw the clerk coming; I grabbed the hat and threw down my hand. When the clerk got there the bird had flown. He told the Captain it was all foolishness in trying to keep those gamblers from winning a sucker's money, for they could make a sucker whisper or do anything they wanted him to do; so that made two good men out of the Captain and the clerk, for they never interfered with our innocent games after that, and we made many a dollar on that boat. She was a nice steamboat to travel on in those days; but they got to building them so much finer that a sucker was afraid to go on board one of them, thinking that they would charge him more money.

NIPPED IN THE BUD.

I went on board the *General Quitman* late one night, and as I had been up all the night before, I got a room and went to bed. I saw some gamblers playing in the cabin as I went through, but I was too tired to notice them much. I had not been in my bed long until I heard a racket out in the cabin. I peeped out and soon understood what was up. Some one had lost his money, and was doing the grand kicking act. I got up and was into my clothes in double quick time, and out among them, with old " Betsy Jane" in my pocket. I soon learned that a contractor on the levee, who had a lot of men down on deck, had lost his money playing poker with one of the gamblers, and he was going to have it back or he would bring up his men and take it by force. I told the gambler to stand his ground and not give up a red. The barkeeper told me the kicker had sent down for some of his men to come up; so I started for the stairs and met the contractor in the hall, waiting for them. I asked him what was the difficulty; he said " that was his business." Then I said to him, " You are one of those d——d scoundrels who try to beat others out of their money, and kick like h——l when they get the worst of anything." He did not want to say anything until his gang was at his back, and they were then coming up. I ran out to the head of the stairs with old " Betsy Jane " in my hand, and ordered them to stop. They did stop, for I had her pulled down on them, and the other gamblers were standing by me. I said, " The first man that takes another step to come up these stairs will get hurt." They didn't come. Then I turned to the kicker and told him if he made a move I would cook his goose. He saw we meant business, and weakened. The gang went back to their bunks, the kicking contractor went to his room, and we held the fort. I was told that the same man had lost his money about a year previous while playing poker with John Deming, and he brought his men up, threw Deming down, and did not only take the money he lost, but a large amount besides. I had the same thing tried on me once ; so when I saw a fellow-gambler imposed upon, I went to the front. Besides, if we let such a thing go too far it would ruin our business, so I thought it was best to nip it in the bud.

THE BIG SUCKER.

We were out from New Orleans with Captain Bill Harrison one day on board the steamer *Doubeloon*, and was having a good game of roulette, when we noticed that most of the fish were suckers, and did not bite so well at roulette ; so we changed our tackle, and used monte for bait. We were fishing along, and had caught some pretty good fish, but none of the large ones we saw about the hooks. Every time we would get one of them to come up and begin nibbling around, something would scare him away. We put on fresh bait, spit on it, and threw it out with all the care that we were capable of; but somehow or another they would not suck in the hook. I knew the bait was good, for I had caught thousands of suckers with it, and I could see that there was plenty of that kind of fish around us. I began looking, and soon discovered the trouble. It was a great big old sucker who wanted to be a kind of teacher over the school ; for every time one of the young suckers would get up too close, he would pull his tail, and that would scare the young one so he would not take hold in earnest. I watched the big sucker for some time, and I saw it was no use trying to catch anything until I caught the old school teacher. So I put up my tackle, and began looking for a bait that would land the old one.

I was walking on the guards, when I saw the man that had back-capped and spoiled my game. I went up to him and entered into conversation. I did not let him know I was mad; but I was, all the same, and would have given $100 to give him one between the eyes; but I soon thought of a plan to make him contribute a part of what he had kept me from winning, so I said to him, " I was surprised to see you back-capping my game, for I could see you were a sporting man. I tried to give you the wink, and have you come up and win out something, so the suckers would take hold, but I could not get your eye." He said, " I did not understand it, or I would have been glad to help you." I told him that after dinner I would open up again, and for him to walk up and make a good big bet, and I would let him win; then for him to walk away, and I would catch all the suckers on the boat. After all had been arranged, I went to my room and got old " Betsy Jane;" for my new capper had one on him so long that it stuck down below his coat-tail. I told my partner to look out for the big gun and our new capper. I called the passengers around a table, and began to throw the hooks. Up came the big fish, and wanted to know what was the least bet I would take. I told him $200. He planked her up, when I saw about $50 left, so I told him I would make it $250. He put up the extra $50, for of course the more he put up the more he would win, as he was to suck in the hook with the extra kink in it. I gave them a little mixing and said " Ready !" He darted in and nabbed the bait more like a goggle-eye than a sucker, but he was caught all the same. He did not swim away (as he had been told to do), for he was held by a line that cost him $250, and he could not break it without a great struggle. I thought I had let him play about long enough, so I said : " Gentlemen, there are no more suckers to be caught on this boat," and that landed the biggest sucker I ever caught in all my life.

I put up my fishing tackle and invited all hands to the bar, for I was feeling like all fishermen (a little dry). My big sucker joined us, as he had been out of water just long enough to want to get back. After we had quenched our thirst he said he would like to see me a minute. I told him he could see me for an hour, as I had no other business to look after. We walked out on the guards, and my partner was not far away. The big fellow said to me, "Why didn't you let me win the money?" I looked up at him, but kept my hand on old Betsy Jane, and said, "My business is to catch suckers, and you are the biggest one I ever caught in my life if you think I will give you back your money." He went back for his gun, but I had old Betsy out and up to his head before he could say Jack Robinson. I told him to put up his hands, and be d—d quick about it, too. He put them up, and said he did not want any gun to whip such a fellow as I was. I told him that he might be a good man down in Texas, where he came from, but he was a sucker up in this country, and I could eat him up. I said: "We will put our guns in the bar, and have it out just as you like it." We went in the bar, and he handed over his young cannon, and then I put up Betsy Jane. I told my partner to get the Captain and tell him to land the boat, and he would see some fun, for I knew he would rather see a fight than eat when he was hungry. So just as we got our guns behind the bar the Captain walked in, and some one said, "Here comes the Captain." The Texas fellow said, "To h—l with him; I don't care a d—n for any captain." That made old Bill hot, and he wanted to know what was all this racket about. I told him the big fellow wanted to lick me. He said, "I'll soon settle this; you will go ashore." The big fellow said there was not men enough on the boat to put him ashore. The Captain then sent word to the pilot to land, and also sent for the mate and some of the deck-hands. The pilot ran the boat up on a point, and she got aground. I jumped off as soon as she struck; and the mate, assisted by two big deckhands, soon had Mr. Texas off. The passengers were all out on the guards, for they had heard the racket, and wanted to see the fun. I pulled off my coat, and told Texas to clean himself and come a-fighting. He was just as sure of licking me as I was of catching him for a sucker, but he had forgotten " Nothing is sure that grows on earthly ground." He was onto me in an instant, and if he had hit me just where he aimed, he would have hurt me, for he was a hard hitter; but I gave him my dear old head, and he hurt himself very bad; but I did not care if he did. I then ran in under him, and had him down on his back before he recovered from the blow he struck against a rock (as he afterward called my head). After I got him down I gave him one just between the eyes, and he saw stars (although there were none in the sky just then). I gave him one more punch, and he said, " That will do." I let him up, and he was so dazed that he staggered and fell into the river. They pulled him out, and I heard some one remark, " That's the biggest sucker ever caught in this river."

While the fight was going on, they were trying to get the boat off the point; but I guess they did not try very hard, for as soon as they fished out the sucker, the Captain called for me to come aboard. I said, " Captain, it is only three miles to Donaldsonville, and as I want a little exercise, I will walk; but take good care of my " big sucker."

THE CRAZY MAN.

I was going up the Illinois River once with Dad Ryan. We did not try to do anything the first night out from St. Louis. The next day I picked up a man who had been to St. Louis with wild game and butter, and had a great deal of money for a man of his calibre. I told him I lived in Galena, Ill., and had some of the finest lead mines in that part of the country. We got pretty well acquainted with each other, and had some drinks together. He got to feeling lively, for whenever he took a drink he would take a tumbler half full of whisky. After getting him warmed up pretty well, I walked him in the barber shop to see a white squirrel. During the while the barber was after it, Dad opened out the three cards, and my friend and I had become very interested in the game. I looked on a while, then I said to Ryan: "I think I can turn the winning card for $100." He accepted the proposition, and I laid up the money and turned the wrong one. I then picked up the jack, as that was the winner, and bent the corner, showed it to my friend, "whispered" and told him not to say a word, as he would not detect its being bent. He said, "All right." I told the dealer to throw them over again, which he did. I then said, "I know you have two chances to our one, but I will try you for $200." We put up our money into the butter man's hands, and I turned the card. The dealer told the butter man that he lost fair, and to give the money to me. Then I wanted to try it for the $400, but he would not bet with me, saying: "When a man beats me once, I will not bet with him again." So I handed the money to my friend, and told him to bet it for me. "That will do," said Ryan. He mixed them up again, and my friend turned the card and won for me.

Ryan took it very pleasantly, laughing all the time, so my friend thought he would try it with his own money; but Ryan said: "You beat me once, and you know what I said." "Well," said my friend, "I did not bet for myself." I coaxed Ryan to let him bet, as he was entitled to one bet at least. He consented, and my friend got out $100; but Ryan said: "No; I will not bet less than $500." I said to my friend, "If you have not got the money, I will loan it to you; and if you only win one small bet, he will not bet with you again." He pulled out a big roll with a string around it, and counted out $400 more and laid it on the table. I told him I would hold the stakes, so he handed me the money. Ryan saw that big roll, and hated to have him get away, as he might quit after losing. When he saw that I was holding stakes, he said : "I guess I will back out." I spoke up and told him he could not, and my friend said that it was not fair to back out. Then said Ryan, "I will raise you $2,000," and he laid it up in my hand. Then my friend wanted to back out and take his money down, but Ryan would not stand that. I insisted on putting up the rest, but Ryan would not allow it, as he said, "I will bet but one at a time." I told him to lay up the money. He put it up at last, trembling like a man with the palsy ; but finally he grabbed the card and lost.

Just about that time there was a little boat landed alongside of us, as we were lying at a landing putting off freight. I gave Ryan the office to get on her. He slipped over on the boat, and the sucker just then came to his senses. When he saw that Ryan had gone out, he said to me, "Where did he go?" I told him he had gone back in the cabin ; so he started back to look for him, and while he was gone the little boat backed out. I walked out in the hall to see what had become of my friend, and found him searching all the rooms in the ladies' cabin. He then rushed into a gentleman's room where his wife was, and then there was h—l to pay. The man came near shooting him, but I ran back and told the gentleman that the fellow was crazy and did not know what he was doing. He ran all around the boat, frothing at the mouth, and never said a word to any one. Finally some of the officers grabbed him, got a rope and tied him, for they all thought he was crazy ; and I commenced to think so myself, as all he would say was, "Where is he? Where did he go?" No one had seen the game but the barber, and I slipped him a twenty-dollar bill and told him to keep mum. They kept the man tied for about one hour, until he promised he would behave if they let him loose, which they did. He sat perfectly still and did not have a word to say. I knew he was not broke, for I saw he had about $200 left; and that amount, together with his late experience, was capital enough for any man.

DIDN'T WIN THE KEY.

We were playing monte on board the steamer *Magnolia*, out of New Orleans, one night, and had a very lively game. We had won a few hundred dollars. There was a Jew on board who had no money, but he had a fine watch. During the play he was very anxious to bet it, but I told him I did not want to play for his watch, as I knew I could win it whenever I saw fit. So, just as the game was about to close, I said to him, "What is your watch worth?" "Three hundred dollars, and I can get that for it." I told him I would put up $300 against it, and bet him he could not turn the picture card. He pulled out, put her up, and then turned over the wrong card. The passengers all laughed. He never said a word, but appeared to take it all right. After a while he came to me and said: "I have the key, and would like you to keep the watch wound up, as I think a great deal of it; and as soon as we get to Natchez I can borrow the money on the wharf-boat, from Charley Frazier, to redeem it." When he spoke in that way I handed him his ticker, and he ran away with it. I laughed, and began thinking how to get it back again. So I took my partner, Alexander, to one side and told him to get in with the Jew, then tell him he heard me say I was going to give the watch back. "Tell him you have been watching me play, and that you believed you could play it as well as the man he played against." He got in with him, and finally got some cards to show the Jew how I played. The Jew got very much taken with the game again, so he said to my partner, "I know that I could beat you, if you will play for something." So he won the drinks and cigars from my partner, and at last he wanted to put up his watch against $500 that he could turn the card. My partner put up the money, and the Jew the watch; but he missed it that time; and you never did hear such laughter as there was on that boat, for the passengers all turned loose and plagued the poor Jew all the way up to Natchez, asking him what time it was. He did not redeem it at Natchez, so I had to buy a "key," and that nearly broke my heart.

WAS IN WITH THE JUDGE.

I was on the train from Jackson to New Orleans. I opened in the smoking car, and won a good deal of money. We were just coming to a station called Amite, about sixty miles above New Orleans. I waited until the car got in motion, after learning the station, as I did not want to go into New Orleans; for they were kicking like the d—l, and I knew there would be a big crowd at the depot. I slipped off, and told my partner to bring my valise, and come up the next day. They went into the city kicking like steers, and they had the officers looking for me, but they did not find me. Two of them took the train and came back to Amite that night, and in the morning when I came to breakfast there they were. I could not help laughing at them. After breakfast they went to the magistrate, and swore out a warrant for my arrest, and the constable came over to the hotel looking for me, but I had skipped out. I walked down the railroad and kept hid until they were satisfied I had gone. They left orders if I showed up to have me arrested, and telegraph them. I took the first train and went to the city. They came in on the evening train. The next day they found out I was in the city, and then I was arrested and brought before the Recorder's Court, when the Judge asked me if I had an attorney. I told him I could plead my own case. I soon convinced him that the gambling was done in another parish, and I was discharged. They then took a train and went back, got the

7

warrant they had out for me, and brought an officer with them. The officer stepped up to me and said: "I have a warrant for you." "All right; but we can't leave here until night. Let us pass away the time until the train leaves." There was a big crowd followed us to get a look at the notorious Devol, and the officer kept pulling out the warrant and showing it to the throng. He was getting pretty full of whisky, when I saw a thief in the crowd. I gave him the wink, and in less than five minutes he had the warrant. I got one of my friends to ask the officer to show him the warrant. He dove down in his pocket, but could not find it; so I told him he must have the paper, or I would not go with him. It sobered him up, and the last time I saw him he was with the two fellows going to the train to get fresh papers. I went up myself to see what they could do with me. I took a train and passed them coming down. They went into the city, and found that I had left for Amite that morning, and that they had missed me. When I got there I took the Judge and Prosecutor out, and we had several drinks; then we went to a shoe shop, and ordered two pairs of boots for them, and took the size of their heads, and sent to New Orleans for hats. When they came back, and the case was called, the Judge heard their story, and then mine, and decided it was nothing but a case of gambling, and that he would have to fine us each five dollars and costs. We paid our fines, and they all took the train that day but myself. I stayed a day or two, and had a fishing game, as it was a great place to catch the little flappers. They said, when they came back to the city, that no law down here would do anything with that fellow, and his name ought to be "Devil" instead of Devol. They thought I must be some relation to Claude Duval, the highwayman. They were Vermonters. They said if they had me down East they would fix me for the balance of my life; but I was not down East, and I had often been, before I met those suckers, "Fixed for Life."

THE BRILLIANT STONE.

We were on board the steamer *Southern Belle*, bound for New Orleans. There were several planters aboard, that I was acquainted with, and we were drinking wine, telling stories, and enjoying ourselves, when a large, fine-looking gentleman stepped up to the bar and took a drink. He had a diamond stud in his shirt that was so large and brilliant that it attracted the attention of us all; so after he went out we began commenting on it.

I finally said to one of the planters, "What would you give for that stone?" He said, "I would give $1,000 for it, but I bet it could not be bought for the money." "What will you give me for it?" I asked him. They all laughed, for they understood by my question that I thought the man was a sucker, and I could win it from him. One of them said: "Devol, you are a good one, but that fellow is too smart to be caught by any of your tricks." I said, "Gentlemen, I will bet two bottles of wine that I will have that stone inside of an hour. Who will take me?" They all wanted to take the bet, and raise it to a basket; but I told them the odds were too much in their favor, and I would bet but two bottles; so it was settled that I was to win the stone, or pay for the wine. Then we all went out in the cabin, and I called everybody to join me in some wine. My partner went up to the man with the brilliant stone, and asked him if he knew the man that was treating. He said he did not. Then my partner told him that I was a planter; that I owned six plantations, and so many niggers that I did not know the number myself. The gentleman was introduced to me and the other planters, when he said: "I am very glad to form the acquaintance of you Southerners; I'm a New Yorker." The compliment cost me the wine for the entire party. While the barkeeper was serving the wine, I told him to bring me some of those tickets that they played

the whisky game with. He brought the tickets, and I began to mix them. One of the planters bet me the wine
that he could turn the ticket with the baby. I took him
up, and he stuck me. Then another bet me the cigars, and
I stuck him. While we were lighting our cigars, my partner put a pencil mark on the baby ticket, and told the New
Yorker that he wanted to have some fun with me; that I
was so good-natured, I would take it as a joke when I
found it out. I commenced mixing them again, and
wanted to know who would be the next man to try his
luck. My partner came to the front, and wanted to know
if I would bet money on the game. I told him so long as
I had two chances to his one, I would bet a plantation,
and a hundred niggers besides. He put up $1,000, and
said: "I will try you once for $1,000." I pulled out a
roll so large that it made everybody look wild, saying:
"That just suits me." I mixed, and my partner turned
the ticket with his pencil mark on it, and caught me for
$1,000. I laughed and said, "You're a lucky fellow; I
don't want to bet with you any more." He then slipped
away, as though he was afraid I would detect the mark
and raise a fuss. He gave the $2,000 to one of the plant-
ers, and told him to go and play it. The planter came up
and said: "I'll try you for $2,000." I said, "All right;
plank her up." He turned a card, but not knowing anything about the mark, he lost. I laughed and said, "Try
it again; you're not as lucky as the other fellow." "No,"
said he; "I've got enough." Then my partner came up
again and wanted to bet; but I told him he was the lucky
fellow, and I was afraid of him.

The New Yorker could see the mark on the card, and
he could not stand it any longer; so he pushed up to the
table and laid down a roll, and said: "I will bet you
$400." I told him I would only make one more bet and
then quit, and I would bet $2,000 or nothing. He picked
up the money and turned away. My partner said, so I
could hear him, "Bet him." The man said, "I have not

got the money." Then my partner offered to loan it to him, when I told them I would not bet if the lucky fellow was in with it; but if the gentleman had anything worth the money, he could put it up. The lucky fellow told him to put up his diamond stud, saying in a whisper: "It is only for a minute; don't you see the mark on the card?" The gentleman put up the stone and the $400. I told him I would only take the stone for $1,000. Then my partner told him to put up his watch. He did so, and I put up $2,000 in money. I mixed, and he turned the marked card. He was very much excited; and when the card turned over, it had the mark on the back, but the baby had crawled off the other side. He drew a long breath and walked back to his state-room, and that was the last we saw of him. As he was walking away, some one called to him to join us in some wine; but he could not hear so well as when the capper told him in a whisper to put up, as it was only for a minute. We looked at our watches (I had two), and it wanted just five minutes of the hour. The planter that made the bet of two bottles spent over $200 for wine that night, and before he left the boat he gave me $1,000 for the " brilliant stone."

LUCKY AT POKER.

One night I went out on the steamer *Belle Lee*. She was running from Memphis to New Orleans. Captain Hicks was her commander, and a jolly fellow was he. He said to me: "Devol, I never saw a gambler in the world that I was afraid to play with. I am just as smart as any of them." I said, "Captain, you will get no game out of me, as I do not want any of your money." After supper I noticed the Captain had a man, and they went to his room in the texas. I opened up and had a fine play at roulette, but it fell off at 12 o'clock, and I closed up. I was sitting in the hall when the Captain and his man came down. The man said: "Captain, I am winner; let's have a bottle of wine." They invited me to join them. The Captain said: "George, I will turn this gentleman over to you, as I can't beat him." "Well," I said, "Cap, if you can't beat him, I can't; for you are a better poker player than I am."

Then I winked at the barkeeper, who had a few decks of my cards that I had put in when I came on board. He knew what I wanted. I said to the man, "I'll tell you what I will do: I will play one game of seven-up for a bottle of wine;" as I thought that was the best way to get him started. He agreed. I said, "Barkeeper, give us a deck of cards, and we will see who is the lucky man." We began, cut for deal, and I beat him. I dealt, and I knew every card in his hand. He had no trumps, and I had the jack alone. He begged; I gave him one and made four. He dealt, and I made three on his deal, which put me out. He was as hot as a pepper pod, but he called for the wine. After we drank it, he said: "I wonder if you are that lucky at poker; if so, I will try you a little while." I said, "All right; I think, myself, I am in luck to-night." We went at it, but he said the limit must be $50. We played till daylight began to peep through the skylight of the cabin, and I had to loan him money to defray his expenses. He told the Captain it was the hardest game he ever struck. He sent me the money I loaned him by express, and wrote that if he ever met me on the river again he wanted to be in with my play. It was not long after that when I met him on the steamer *Natchez*, and we made some big money together, as he got up some fine games with the planters. He was known all along the river, and Captain Leathers thought it strange to see him playing with me; but the gentleman understood it, for I was always "lucky at poker."

THE HIDDEN HAND.

While in St. Louis just before the war, I got acquainted with a man from Detroit by the name of James Scott. He was dealing faro bank, and was such a square fellow that all the boys would play against him. He had a big game one evening, and had downed quite a number of the boys, but he did it on the square. He quit dealing to go and get his supper, and while he was out the boys tried to think of some scheme to stick him for enough money to get a square meal for themselves. Finally one of them thought of the same racket that I played on my Jew partner, and they manufactured a sucker. When Jim came back, they were playing a single-handed game of poker. Jim loved poker, and as he had not finished picking his teeth, he stopped at the table to look on. That was just what the boys expected and wanted, so the two hands were run up. Jim was behind the fellow that had the three kings and a pair of sevens; but just after he saw them, some one spoke to him on the other side, so he went around the table. The man with the kings made a big raise, and the other fellow said it was more money than he had. Jim saw his three aces and a pair, so he said: "I am with you, old boy, for $1,000." The money was put up, and then the sucker said he had made a mistake in his hand, and wanted to take down his money; but everybody said he could not take down. Then the fellow threw down two cards and called for two more. The old boy (Jim's partner) gave them to him, and the sucker made another raise just large enough to use up the balance of Jim's thousand. The old boy called the bet just in time to save Jim from putting up another thousand, for they did not want to strike him too heavy the first time. They showed down, and the sucker had caught another king in the draw, and he won the pot. Jim did not say a word, but began to deal the bank. The next night some of the boys that had eaten a good supper at Jim's expense invited him to the theatre. Jim wanted to know the play; they told him " The Hidden Hand." Jim said, " No, boys; I saw that play last night, and I would not see it again for $1,000." Jim is now living in Detroit, and is one of the wealthiest men in the city. His father left him a fortune, and he has not laid down a dollar on a gambling table since; yet he likes the boys, and can tell some of the best stories of any man in this country. He is very fond of the theatres, but he says he never goes when they play "The Hidden Hand."

CAUGHT AGAIN.

While sitting in the hall of the steamer *Petonia*, I noticed a fellow who kept looking at me so closely that I at last said to him, " Do you live on the river, sir?" He replied, "Are you speaking to me?" " Well, yes; I asked you if you lived on the river." He answered me very gruffly, "No sir." I let him alone, for I thought I had seen him before, and it might be I had beat him out of some money; so I got up and walked down the cabin. After I left, he asked the barkeeper who I was, and he told him I was a planter, and the son of one of the wealthiest planters on the coast. The fellow said " Darn me if he don't look just like a fellow that beat me out of $5,000 some years ago." " I guess you are mistaken; although all planters gamble more or less," said the barkeeper. " Well, let's take a drink; but I was sure he was the same man."

Just as they finished their drink, I walked up and called for some wine. The fellow spoke up and said, " Have a drink with me." I said, " No, you join me, as I see you have finished yours." He accepted, and I ordered a bottle of wine. We sat down to drink the wine, when he said: " You must excuse me for the manner in which I spoke to you a while ago, as I took you for a man that beat me out of $5,000 on one of these boats, some years ago, at a game

they called monte." " Well, now," I said; "it must have
been the same fellow that beat me, for that's what they
called it, monte; but I did not care very much, as I was
spending the old gent's money at that time." He replied:
" But I did mind it, for I had just sold my place, and was
going to put the money into business; but on account of
that d——d rascal, I have had to work hard ever since;
and I have sworn to kill him the first time I meet him."
" I do not blame you for feeling as you do, for you could
not afford to lose the money; but I did not care, as the old
gent had plenty more that I could get whenever I asked
for it; and as he sometimes lost pretty heavy himself, he
would say to me, ' Son, if you bet you will win or lose;
but if you lose, take it cool; for if you could not afford to
lose, you had no business to bet.'" " You're right! I did
not have any business to bet; but I thought I had a sure
thing of winning. I would have killed that fellow the
next morning; but when I began looking for him, I found
he had got off the boat, and I have never seen him since."
I laughed and said, " If you had won the money, you
would not have felt like shooting the fellow, would you?"
" Oh, no."

I found out the fellow had about $60; but he was just
as much a sucker as he was when he lost the $5,000, and
I made up my mind to win his money, and then tell him
that I was the same man that beat him before. I excused
myself, and told my partner all about the fellow, and that
I wanted to win his money.

After supper I opened up monte, and caught a good
many suckers. My old producer was watching the game
and me too. We had about finished up, when my partner
said to my old friend, " I would like to make a bet, but I
am unlucky; will you bet this $50 for me?" He took the
$50, put it up, and won. Then he put up $50 for himself,
and lost. My partner wanted to know how he had made
such a mistake, when he swelled up like a porpoise, and
said: " I believe that is the same fellow that beat me out

of my money before." He walked away, and my partner followed him. They were standing at the bar when I came up, and I invited all hands to join me in a drink. Everybody accepted the invitation, except my Arkansas killer. I made up my mind that we would have a fight, so I thought I would not put it off any longer. I turned to him and said, "Come and take a cigar with me, for I see you are not drinking." He replied, " I pick my company." Then I said, " You are in better company just now than you ever were in your life, except the time, some years ago, when you were in my company and lost $5,000." He said, "You are a d——d rascal." I then called him a liar and a coward. He attempted to draw, when my partner caught his arm and gave him one in the face, which was not a very heavy one, for he did not appear to mind it. I had old " Betsy Jane" out and had him covered; then I said, "Lay away your old pop, and we will go down on deck and have it out. You are a much larger man than I am, but I will take a licking from you, if you are man enough to give it to me." We gave our guns to the barkeeper and started down. I heard some bets $50 to $25 on the big Arkansas man, so I gave a friend of mine a roll and told him to take all the odds.

When we got down on deck, the mate made a ring with some barrels, and said: "No man but the fighters shall get inside the ring." The big fellow stripped down to his undershirt, and looked like a young Samson; then the bets ran up $100 to $25. I pulled off my coat and vest, and stepped inside the ring. We shook hands, and time was called, the mate acting as referee. He made a lunge; I dropped my head, and he hit it a terrible blow. Then he got one in below the belt, and I thought for an instant I would lose my supper and the fight; but I rallied, and got a good one in on the side of his neck, which doubled him up like a jackknife; then I ran in, caught him, and let drive with my head. I struck him between the eyes, and he fell over as if he had been shot. I took a seat on one of the barrels, folded my arms, and waited for time to be called. The mate said: "That will do; this man can't fight any more." They took him up stairs, and had the barber fix him up. I was not much the worse for having been in a fight. My friend handed me all my money, and over $400 besides, that he had taken in on the result. I treated all hands, and sent some wine, also the $50 I had won, back to my Arkansas friend. He told the mate and some of the passengers that he had been in a great many fights, but that was the first time he was ever whipped. He said he "whipped himself when he hit my head; but when I gave him that butt, he thought he had been struck with a bar of iron." He told them they did not fight that way out where he lived, and he did not think it was fair. The mate told him everything was fair in a rough-and-tumble fight. I felt sorry for the big fellow when I saw his face, for his nose was broken all up. He forgot all about that he was going to shoot the man that beat him out of his $5,000, for you see I returned the money that I won from him when I had him caught again.

MY LITTLE PARTNER.

A man by the name of Dock Chambers was working with me at one time, and he was like my partner Foster— he would stoop to little things. I was playing poker one night with a man, and broke him. He got up from the table and went back into the ladies' cabin, and in a short time returned with some diamonds and a lady's watch and chain. He wanted to put them up, but I told him I never played for women's finery. A man offered him about one-half what the stuff was worth, and he was so crazy to play that he was about to let them go, when I advanced him much more on them than the stranger had offered; for I knew he would lose them. We began our play, and in about an hour I had won all the money that I had advanced him on the jewelry. I asked him if he was broke,

and he told me that their passage was paid and his wife
had some money. I bid him good night and went to bed.
The next morning I put the jewelry in a cigar box, gave it
to my partner, and told him to find the lady and return it
to her. He found her and returned the box. She opened
it, and found everything her husband had lost; then she
gave him $300, and told him to thank me for her. He
came back and gave me' the thanks, but did not say one
word about the $300. I was well paid with the thanks,
until I found out that she had sent $300 with them, and
that my partner had hogged onto it. I did not say a word
at the time, but waited until I could get big even.

We were coming out of New Orleans a short time after
the Chambers trick, and had a good monte business, which
we closed up as soon as we had caught all the suckers. I
went to a friend of mine who kept a drug store in Vicksburg, and told him I wanted to get even with my partner.
I gave him some money, and told him I would open up
red and black, and that the jack paid eight for one. I said
to him, "You come up and bet $10 on the jack three times,
and the fourth time you put a one hundred-dollar bill inside
of the ten and put it on the same card, and I will make it
win." He did just as I told him, and the jack lost the
first three times, but the fourth time it won. I paid the
$80, and started to make another turn, when the drug man
said: "You will have to come again." I said, "There is
your $80 and your $10, sir." "Please look at the $10,"
he replied. I did look at it, and there was a great, big,
live $100 inside of it. It was over the limit; but I had
turned, and there was no getting out of it. To tell the
truth, I did not want to get out, for I was just getting in on
my partner. I paid the $800 over to the pill-mixer and
shut up shop, as I did not want to lose any more of my
" little partner's " money.

LACKED THE NERVE.

I made a mistake one time that came near getting me licked, and it was only the want of nerve that saved me. I feel the effect of the shock to this day, and I believe it will follow me to my grave. I will tell how it happened.

I was playing the little game of monte, and had caught some pretty good fish, when I noticed a Jew, that I had seen in Natchez, standing near the table and watching me and my cards very closely. I took him for one of the finny tribe, and expected to see him swim up and take hold of the hook; but he walked over to the bar and commenced talking to the barkeeper. I found out afterward that he asked the barkeeper who I was, and told him he could beat me at that game I was playing; for says he, "Do you know, there is a little spot on one of the cards, and I don't believe he can see it." The barkeeper was a friend of mine, and he told the Jew that I couldn't see very well, as I was up so much at night. I was fishing along, when back came the sucker. Then I began to think a little better of myself; for I had spotted the fellow, and when I saw him walk off, I began to think that for once I had made a mistake in my man, and was losing some of my conceit. He got up very close, and then he asked me how much I would bet him that he could not turn the card with the old woman on it. I looked at him for a moment, as I had lost a little of my confidence when I saw him go away; but soon I remembered that the best fish will sometimes play around the bait and then swim off, only to come back, dart in and swallow it, hook and all; so I said to him, "I will bet you $500 you can't pick up the old woman the first pick." I had $500 worth of confidence, thirty years ago, that no man could pick up the old woman; but I am married now, and have quit gambling, but I will bet $5,000 that no man can pick up my old mother-in-law the first pick.

Well, the Jew put up $500 and picked up one of the cards, and as his eyesight was so much better than mine, he got the one with the little spot on it; and while he was looking for the old woman on the other side of the card, I put the $500 in my pocket and rang down the curtain. The Jew stood and held on to the card, until I told him if he was done with it I would like to have it. He handed it to me, and then walked over to the barkeeper and said to him, "That man Devol can see better than we thought he could."

I was standing out on the guards smoking, when up came my food for the brain. He said to me: " Mr. Devol, I am a poor man, with a wife and four little children. That money I lost was all I had in the world, and it was given to me by my friends to start me in a little business. If I don't get that money, I am a ruined man, and my poor wife and little children will starve to death, for I will never see them again. Oh, Mr. Devol, take pity on my poor wife and four little children, and give me back the money. You are a rich man, and can make money so fast; and my poor wife and four little children will pray for you as long as we live; and I will tell my children's children what a good man Mr. D—" "Hold on," I said, as I saw the big tears running down the heart-broken man's face. "Here's your money; take it and give it to your family." I handed him a five hundred-dollar bill and turned away, took out my handkerchief, and was just wiping something off my cheek, when I thought I heard something like a laugh. I turned around, and there, a little way off, stood my poor Jew with seven five hundred-dollar bills in his hand, shaking them at me; and he said, "I haven't got no wife nor no four little children, Mr. D—." He did not finish, for I started for him, and he lit out as if the devil, instead of Devol, was after him. When we got to the city, I went into the first harness store I came to and bought a whip, but I never had the nerve to use it.

THE THREE FIVES.

At one time I was going down the river below Baton Rouge, and there were a lot of raftsmen on board They all loved to gamble, so one of them opened a chuckaluck game. They were putting down their money with both hands, and the game was over $400 winner. I thought I would give him a little play, so I went to my room and got a set of dice the same size as he was using, and then changed in a five without winning a bet. Then I asked him if I could shake them once for luck. "Oh, yes," he said, for he was playing on the square. I came the change on him, then I put $100 inside of a dollar bill, and put it on the five. He shook them up, when, lo and behold, up came three fives. He picked up my money, and when he saw the $100 he looked worse than a sick monkey; but he paid up like a man. I then came the change back, and quit. A man should learn all the tricks in his trade before he takes down the shutters.

SNAKED THE WHEEL.

We were going up with Captain Bill Harrison on board the *Doubeloon*, and just after leaving the wharf I took a look around to find some good-looking suckers. I had not found anything that I thought suited me, and was standing at the bar talking to Captain Bill, when he asked me if the fellows in the barber shop were with me. I said, "What fellows?" For I could see my partners, Brown and Chapple, sitting out on the guards. He said, "Go back and take a peep at them." I did go back, and I saw some fellows with two tables covered all over with jewelry and silverware. They had a wheel with numbers on it, and the corresponding numbers were on the table under the jewelry, etc. They were just getting started, and had some customers who were paying their dollar, and trying their luck

turning the wheel. I looked on until I thought I understood
the game, and then I went to the pantry and came back.
I saw a nice looking watch on one of the numbers, but the
space on the wheel that had the same number on it was so
very narrow that the wheel would not stop on it one time in
a thousand. I asked the boss if the watch was good ; and he
told me that any one that won it could have $100 in gold
if he did not want the watch. I fooled around a little
while, then I put down my dollar, and gave the wheel a
pretty heavy whirl. She went around about twice, and
stopped on the number that called for the watch. The fellow was all broke up, but he gave me $100 in gold, and I
put up another dollar. I started the wheel again, and I
hope I may never see the back of my neck if she did not
stop on the watch again. The boss was dumbfounded. He
looked at the wheel, paid me another $100 in gold, and as
he paid over the money he looked at me as if he did not
like me ; and as I make it a rule not to stay where I am not
wanted, I went out to see the boys. I told them how it was
done, and they went in and got $100 in gold. As they
were coming out they heard the fellow say, "Who in the
h—l put this molasses on the wheel ?"

We opened monte, and caught the wheel man for his
entire stock, and we had more Christmas presents than anybody in the State. Molasses will catch more suckers than
soft soap.

THE KILLER.

At one time I was dealing red and black on the wharf-
boat at the mouth of Red River, and as there were a number of Texas boys on the boat I was doing a good business.
While I was very busy watching the game, a big fellow
who was employed by the proprietor of the boat came up
and asked me to loan him $100 for a few minutes, as he had
made a bet with a man that he could show up that much
money. I saw he had been drinking, but I was too busy
just then to argue the case, for I knew if I refused him he

would want a fuss, as he had the reputation of being a great fighter, and I had been told that he had killed three men ; so I handed him a hundred-dollar bill, and went on with my game.

After getting about all the money that the Texas boys would give up, I closed my game and went out to find my $100. I inquired after the fellow, and was told that he was up on the levee, so I waited for him. It was not long until he showed up, and he was pretty drunk. I asked him to give me back the bill, and he told me he had spent it. I was mad, but I did not want to have a fuss just then, as the Texas boys were standing around, and I did not want them to join in ; so I said, " If you have spent it, all right ; you can hand it to me to-morrow." I was just giving him taffy, for I knew he intended to rob me out of the money, thinking I would not dare to tackle him, but he did not know me. The Texas boys had gone to bed, and there were but few persons in the room. The big killer was standing near the bar, when I saw a chance and let fly ; I caught him under the chin and knocked him as stiff as a poker ; then I took his big gun out of his pocket and threw it out into the river. I told a black boy to go through his pockets and see if he had my hundred-dollar bill. He did so, and finally found it in his fob pocket. After I got my money back I let him up, and told him to get off the boat ; and I said, " If you come back while I am here, I will beat your head off." He lit out. I gave a black man a gun, and told him not to let the fellow on the boat. The next day I was told he was saying he was going to kill me ; so I got a double barrel shot-gun, and sent him word to come down and see me. He did not come, but went down to Hog's Point, took a boat, and left that part of the country, as it had got too hot for him around there. I saw him some years later at Laramie City, Dakota, and put the police onto him. They gave him one hour to get out, and that is the last I have ever heard of him.

8

CAUGHT A WHALE.

An old friend of mine by the name of William Hines (who was one of the best steamboat mates that ever ran on the river) and I were laying off at one time in New Orleans, and we took a notion we would get a yacht and have a big sail. We laid in a supply of provisions, and did not forget a five-gallon jug of whisky. We went out to the lake, hired a yacht, and started. Bill was pretty full, so I told him to go below and lay down for a while, and I would look after the boat. The wind was shifting about, and I was afraid the boom would knock him overboard. I was sailing along at a fine rate, tacking about with the wind, and did not notice that Bill had come up on deck until I heard him yell out to me. I looked around and saw the big fat fellow floundering in the water about 100 feet away. I I gave her all the rudder, downed sail, and then threw out a line. Bill swam up and caught hold of the line, and then I began pulling him in. I had landed many big suckers, but Bill was no sucker; he was a whale. I got him up alongside, but I was not man enough to pull him up, as the boat stood about four feet out of the water. He was so full of whisky (and water) that he could not help himself. He was about played out, when he said to me, "George I'm a goner." I told him to hold on just a minute. I got a small line, took two half-hitches around his arm, and then made fast to the boat. I knew he could not go down unless his arm pulled out, and there was no danger of that. I took a rest, and then let on as if I was going to raise sail, when Bill said, "George, what are you going to do?" I looked back at him and said, "I have caught a whale, and am not able to pull him in, so I'm going to tow him ashore." Bill looked at me just long enough to satisfy himself that I was in earnest, and said, "For God's sake, George, give me one more pull, for I don't want you to sail in with me in tow." So I went to him, as I had got rested, and he had got sober; we pulled together, and I soon had the big fellow on board. We sailed around for some time; but when we had to make a tack, you can bet your life that Bill was on the lookout for the boom. Every time we would consult the jug, Bill would say, "George, don't tell the boys about how much fun we have had on this trip, will you?"

THE DECK-HAND.

The deck-hands of the steamer *Niagara* had been drinking, and some of them were a little drunk. They came up to get more of the fighting stuff, and got into some difficulty with the barkeeper. I was sitting near the bar at the time; and as I was always ready to do my friends a favor, I went out on the guards and tried to stop the fuss, and get the men to go down on deck. One big fellow, who was the fighting man of the crew and a favorite with the mate, thought it was none of my business, and the first thing I knew he cut loose at me. I saw it in time to get up my guard. I did not want to have any difficulty on a boat with any of the officers or crew, so I tried to quiet the fellow down; but he would not have it, but came at me again. I could not avoid it, as he was too drunk to have any sense; so I let fly, caught him under the chin, and brought him down. He was a game one, for he was up and at me once more. I then let into him and gave him a pretty good licking. They took him down on deck, and it was not long until Tom Hawthorn, the mate, came up and asked who it was that had whipped one of his men. The barkeeper told him all about the fuss; but he was mad, and would not excuse any man for defending himself against one of his men. I was in the barber shop at the time, but the barkeeper sent me word to look out for Tom. I went and got my old friend (Betsy Jane), and waited for the fray. I was in the hall when Tom came up looking for me. He walked up and said, "Can't you find any one else to whip, without jumping on to one of my men ? " I knew he had been told the circumstances, and if he had any sense he would not blame me; but he was mad; and then he intended to teach me a lesson. I knew he would not listen to reason, so I said, " I gave that fellow just what he deserved." He began to pull off his coat, and at the same time said, "Any man that licks one of my men has got to lick me." I saw I had to fight, so I off with my coat and waited for him. He struck out, but I caught it on my arm. I did not want to use my head unless it was necessary; but as he was a tall man with a long reach, he had the advantage. So I watched my chance, then ran in, caught him around the waist, and downed him. It was hard work to keep the old head from taking a hand, but I gave him several good ones on his face and neck. He tried to rise up, when I got in an upper cut which settled him. I let him up, and he went down on deck. He had it in for me, until one night in a saloon, when he hit a man; the fellow got the drop, and would have shot him if I had not taken a hand. After that we were good friends, and he would say to me, " George, you are the only man that can whip my deck-hands."

THE BLACK (LEG) CAVALRY.

" For those that fly may fight again,
    Which he can never do that's slain;
    Hence, timely running's no mean part
    Of conduct in the martial art ;
    By which some glorious feats achieve,
    As citizens by breaking thrive."

When the war broke out, some of the gamblers in New Orleans got up a cavalry company, and named it the Wilson Rangers. I was a member of the company. We armed and equipped ourselves, and the ladies said we were the finest looking set of men in the army. If fine uniforms and good horses had anything to do with it, we were a fine body. When we were ordered out to drill (which was every day), we would mount our fine horses, gallop out back of the city, and the first orders we would receive from our commanding officer would be: " Dismount! Hitch horses! March! Hunt shade! Begin playing!" There was not a company of cavalry in the Southern army that obeyed orders more promptly than we did ; for in less than ten minutes from the time the order was given, there would not be a man in the sun. They were all in the shade, seated on the ground in little groups of four, five, and six; and in each group could be seen a little book of tactics (or at least it looked something like a book at a distance). We would remain in the shade until the cool of the evening, when the orders would be given: " Cease playing! Put up books! Prepare to mount! Mount! March!" When we would get back to the city, the people would come out, cheer, wave handkerchiefs, and present us with bouquets ; for we had been out drilling in the hot sun, preparing ourselves to protect their homes from the Northern invaders.

After we had become proficient in drill, we were ordered to do patrol duty in the city. The citizens called us their defenders ; and we did defend them, so long as there was no hostile foe within five hundred miles of them. We were as brave a body of men as there was in the South, until the news reached us that Commodore Farragut was bombarding Forts Jackson and St. Philip ; then we began to realize that the war was getting pretty close to home, and we were a little fearful that our knowledge of the tactics would be but little protection to us if the forts should capitulate. We threw aside the old books we had been studying for so long a time, and took up a new edition that our commander told us was much better in times of immediate danger. So for about six days we devoted ourselves to studying how to get out of the "jack-pot" we had got into, without losing our stake.

We were not kept very long in suspense, for early one beautiful April morning we learned the terrible news that

Farragut's fleet had passed the forts, and General Butler with a large land force was marching on the city. We heard the old familiar orders: "Prepare to mount! Mount! March!" But we did not swing into our saddles feeling as gay as when we were on our way to the drill-grounds. We were ordered to the front, and as we rode through the streets the ladies presented us with bouquets, and cheered after us; but then there was but little cheer in that fine body of gamblers. We had many times before attacked the enemy (Tiger) without fear or trembling; but now we were marching to meet a foe with which we were but slightly acquainted. As we passed the old drill-grounds on our way to the front, there was a sigh passed the lips of every man, and our horses turned in, for they (poor dumb brutes) did not know that things had changed.

We were about six miles below the city when the Yankees saw us; but we did not see them, as they were about four miles distant. They were up in the rigging with their glasses, looking for just such suckers as we were; and they turned loose a salute of canister, which came buzzing about our ears, and the next instant we heard an order that we had never heard before: "Retreat!" but we understood it, and lost no time in obeying the command; for I believe we would have executed the movement without orders, if they had not been given just after the first salute. We had a great deal just then to make us feel nervous, but we were thankful for one thing, and that was, we had good fast horses. I had taken mine off the race track, and I was glad of it, for in that race I came out several lengths ahead. When we got back to the city we dismounted without orders, and even forgot to tell the darkies to give our horses a good rubbing-down. We cut the buttons off our coats, buried our sabres, and tried to make ourselves look as much like peaceful citizens as possible; for we had enough of military glory, and were tired of war.

After destroying immense quantities of cotton, sugar, steamboats, ships, and other property, to prevent its falling into the hands of the Unionists, General Lovell with his Confederate troops retreated into the interior of the State, and left the city without any other defense except our company of cavalry ; but as we had buried our arms and cut the brass buttons off our beautiful brown corduroy suits, the citizens hadn't as much confidence in our ability to defend as they had when the enemy was five hundred miles away. The merchants expected that the Yankees would sack the city, so they threw open their stores and told everybody to take all they wanted. Bush was boarding with me at the time, and as he was one of the biggest eaters in the world, I wanted more than I could carry ; so I hired a dray (for which I had to pay $10), and loaded it down to the guards. We put on a hogshead of sugar, twenty-five hams, a sack of coffee, box of tea, firkin of butter, barrel of potatoes, some hominy, beans, canned fruits, etc. I would have put on more, but the dray wouldn't hold it ; and as the load started up Canal Street, I thought, when Bush gets away with all that stuff, I'll make him change his boarding-house. After laying in my stock, I went down to the river to see the fleet come in, and there were all of our company, but they did not make the slightest resistance. The Captain said, "It's no use trying to bluff them fellows, for they have got a full hand."

BUTLER IN NEW ORLEANS.

General Butler took possession of the city the 1st day of May, 1862. His troops gutted the bank, but did not molest the merchants ; so those fellows that had given their stuff away were kicking themselves for doing so. He closed up all the gambling-houses, and then issued licenses for public gambling to any one who would pay the fee and take his brother in as a partner. His profits must have been enough to make him independently rich without the spoons. He kept the city very clean, but old yellow-jack got in, and then Ben got a furlough and went up to Washington, and he took the spoons with him. He took the marble statue of Henry Clay out of the state-house at Baton Rouge and shipped it to his home in Massachusetts. He could not hide that as easily as he could the spoons, so after the war the United States Government made him return it, and that nearly killed him.

I had the race-track, and was running games out at the lake. I was making a great deal of money, and would work the boats when I had time. Some one told Butler that I called him names, so he sent for me, and threatened to send me to Tortugas, but I talked him out of that. Some of his officers lost their money against my games and then kicked. The result was, old Ben sent for me again. This time I did not get off so easily. He took me before the Provost Judge, who fined me $1,000 and sent me to jail for one year, and no amount of money could get me out. There were some of the best men in the South in with me, and our friends on the outside did not forget us. We had good beds, and everything to eat that the market afforded. We played poker, and I was making money all the time. I would fee the jailer, and at night he would take me out in the city, so that my prison life was not so very bad. Butler made us a visit one day just at dinner time, and when he saw the birds and wine, you should have heard him roar. "Why," said he, "those d——d rascals are living better than I ever did." The jailer told him that our friends sent in the luxuries. He looked at our big beds, shower bath, and other surroundings and said, "I have a d——d notion to send them to the penitentiary;" but the jailer told him it was pulled down, so he had to give up his d——d notion, and we were glad of it.

I had been in jail for six months, when one day Governor Shipley visited us. He asked the jailer, "Which is Devol?" I was introduced to him, and he asked me where I was raised. I told him in Ohio. He said the crime I was in for was not so very serious, and he told the jailer to turn me out, and I should come to his office. I was let out, and I reported to the Governor. He told me not to beat the officers; I promised I would not, so I was once more a free man.

When Butler heard that I was let out on the Governor's orders, he was as mad as the d—l; so, to get even, he confiscated all my horses, which had cost me over $50,000. I had promised the Governor that I would not beat the officers; but I took my promise back when Ben took my horses, and it was not long after that I caught a sucker paymaster for $19,000, and they did not find out who it was that won the greenbacks. I made a pile of money, bought substitutes for some of my horses, and opened up the race-course again. Ben Butler and I got to be friendly, and he gave me two silver spoons to remember him by, and I have them yet.

THE PAYMASTER'S $3,500.

I remember a game of poker I had once coming down from Cairo to New Orleans, during the war. There was a paymaster in the game who lost about $3,500, and when we got to Memphis I found out before we landed that he was going to squeal; so I went to the mate and asked him to put me away where they could not find me, as I knew when the soldiers came down to the boat I would have to divulge. He put me down in a little locker that was forward of the main hatch, and rolled barrels on it to hide the trap-door. Well, they came down, took lights, and searched the boat and hold, the ladies' and gentlemen's cabin, and at last gave up. After I had staid down there for eight hours, the boat left for New Orleans. I came up into the cabin, and you ought to have seen the passengers look at me. They did not know what to make of my appearance before them; but I told them I was up town and did not know anything of what was going on; and I took in many a dollar after that.

GENERAL BANKS' DETECTIVE.

I had a big game of roulette one night during the war, when the Northern officers were traveling up and down the river. The boat was full of officers, and General Banks was on board. Up stepped a big fellow from Texas, who was a detective for General Banks. He pulled out a $100 Confederate bill, and laid it on the red. I picked it up and said I had no Confederate money to pay him in, in case he won. He got very saucy, and went over to the bar, where I could hear every word he said, and told the barkeeper that as soon as I closed that game he would whip me. So I closed up and sent my wheel down stairs in the locker, and walked up to the bar and asked him to take a drink, so that he would make some remark. He said, "I pick my company." I let drive and knocked the ginger out of him, and kept him spinning around until he yelled out. Then came the rush. General Banks and staff, followed by all the boat's officers. The fellow was bleeding like a stuck pig. The clerk told the General how he talked, and he said he got just what he deserved. I then sent down and got my wheel, opened, and all the officers played except General Banks. I was sorry he did not appreciate the game, and change in a few greenbacks.

THE U. S. DETECTIVE'S BLUFF.

I was coming up once on the steamer *Fairchild*, of Louisville, and had won considerable money. There was on board a United States detective. He was asleep at the time the games were going on, and when he came to his breakfast the next morning, there was a great deal of kicking going on about the money and diamonds that the gamblers had won the night before. Some of the passengers at the table knew the detective, and when they got through breakfast they all got with him, and they told him finally they would give him half they had lost if he would get it back. So he saw a big opening, and concluded to make a big bluff to get the money. He came to me as I was standing by the office, and said, "Are you the man who won all the money and diamonds last night?" I told him I was the man. He said, "You must give it all back—every cent." That made me laugh, and I think it made him mad, for he pulled back his coat and showed me his badge. Well, I thought he was as good a sucker as any of the rest, or he would not make such a break as that; and when he spoke of my swindling them, I said to him, "Now, sir, I will show you just how I beat those fellows; and I pulled out three cards, and said, "If you will walk over to the table, I will show you; then if you think there is any swindle about it, I will refund every dollar." He said, "All right." I commenced to play them over, and had him guessing lively, when up stepped the capper and took a look at the cards, and said, "I will bet you $500 I can turn the king." He put up the $500, and did not turn the card; so he and the detective began to whisper to each other, the capper telling him about a spot that was on the right card. Then he made a proposition to go me $500 more. I put up the money to cover his, and he turned the right card, took his money and walked away from the game. Then the detective said, "I will bet you $50 myself." I put up. He laid up $50 and turned the right card. One of the bystanders spoke up and said, "He is only baiting you along till he gets a big bet." I replied, "You are about right." He said, "I will bet you $50 once more." So I put up the amount, and he turned the winning card again. So up stepped the capper and said, "I will bet you $1,000 I can turn it." "That is just the kind of a bet I like to get." I put up $1,000, and he put up his. Just as he was going to turn, he got the detective by the collar and got his advice. So the detective told him which one it was. "Are you sure?" said the capper. "No, not sure when he gets a big bet like that; but I think so." You see, he had been told I was only baiting for a big bet. Well, the result was, the capper won the bet, and that made the detective swell up like a toad. He would not listen to any of the outsiders' talk any more, but offered to bet $200. I said, "If that is all the money you have, you had better keep it." That made him mad, and he pulled out his long pocket-book and said, "I have got as much money as you." "Perhaps," said I, "you might cripple yourself if you lost much money." "No," said he; "I am no child. When I bet on a fair game like this, I expect to either win or lose." He counted out the money, and I saw he had the $100 he won from me and a little more left. I told him I would bet him $1,100 that he could not turn the king; so he put up. Just as he was about to turn the card, I looked at him and said, "I will let you back out, and give you $100 to take down your money and not turn." "No, no," said he; "not I." "Well," I said, "let her go;" and over she went, but he lost this time.

He drew a long breath and sat down in a chair, and he looked like a sick kitten. Then he got up and went to his room, and finally came out. I thought there would be the d—l to pay. He called me to one side, and said, "Did you think I was betting in earnest?" "Oh, no," said I, "you were only betting in fun; but I was just keeping in earnest." "Well," said he, "you are not going to keep my money?" "Oh, yes." "I don't care what you do with those other fellows' money, but I want mine," said he, "and I must have it." "Well, you can not have a cent of it." I backed against the bar, and told him he must be crazy if he thought I would give him a cent back, as I never gave a sucker back his money. He then made a motion to his hip; but I had old Betsy Jane in my coat pocket with my hand on it, and my partner was there to assist in holding the fort. He saw his bluff was no good, and he began to give me taffy, saying he had just got that money as a reward for catching a man, and that he had worked six months to get it, and that he had a large family. I told him to go out among the passengers and tell them that he had lost his money at a fair game, and then come to my room and "knock at the back door, and they will not see you come in." Well, he got among them all over the boat, and told them it was a fair game, and he had not a word to say. He came to my room and told me what he had done. I counted out $500 and gave it to him, and told him that if he had not worked so hard for it he never would have got a cent back. So he went off contented, and there was no more squealing on the boat.

THE YOUNG MAN FROM NEW YORK.

During the war I took my gambling tools and started for Brownsville, Texas, and Metamoras. I took passage on board a screw steamer, which had sails also. There were about forty-five passengers, all told. The first two days out of New Orleans were pleasant; but there came on a squall, which tore the sails into threads and came near swamping the vessel. It stopped blowing in about half an hour, and all was calm. There was a young man on board whose father was a very rich man in New York, and had sent his son over to attend to some business. While in New Orleans he became acquainted with a rich firm, and through his letters from his father they intrusted him with $12,000 to be delivered in Brownsville.

It happened that the young man was on deck during the storm, and had to lie flat down and hold on to a coil of chain. After the storm he came into the cabin and said, "I have had bad luck." Of course we were all anxious to know what had happened to him. He said he had had twelve one thousand-dollar notes in the side pocket of his coat, and the wind had blown his coat over his head, and the bundle went into the Gulf. He said it was money that had been put into his care to be delivered at Brownsville, and that his father would have to stand the loss. We all felt sorry for the fellow, but it soon died out, and there was no more said about it till we got to Brownsville.

When we got to Bagdad and took the stage, he sat close to me and commenced talking about losing the money. He said he felt ashamed to show up at the firm's office. That made me think he was crooked, and I concluded to keep an eye on him. We had not finished our dinners at the hotel in Brownsville, when in marched a squad of soldiers, and the Captain asked which man was Devol. I raised up and said, "That is my name." He said the General in command wanted me. "All right," I said. I went down to headquarters, and when I got there the General said, "Where is that money you won from that young man, coming over on the ship?" I told him I played no cards with any young man on the vessel. "Have you got proof of that?" said the business man to whom the money belonged. "Yes," said I, and I sent to the hotel and got the Captain and the purser, who testified that the young man did not play a card coming over. So I was acquitted, and that was the last of it, as they were all satisfied that the boy did nothing wrong, and really had lost the money.

But I had him spotted; for it takes a rascal to catch a rascal. The Captain and the purser were the only two who did gamble going over, and they were very fond of poker. So my partner and self sat in, and we played four-handed all the way over. We realized about $1,300, which paid our expenses and a few hundred dollars besides.

About six of us agreed to go over to Metamoras that night and spend the evening. The young man said to me that he would like to go along. I said "All right," so we all started, and we had a fine time drinking wine and pony brandy. We went into a gambling-house, and the roulette wheel was going, and a lively game at that. There was one man who was playing very high, and I asked his name. They said it was the Mexican General Cortenas, who was in command of Metamoras. Well, I took out a twenty-dollar bill and laid it on the red, and it came red ; I let it lay, and it came red again. I took the $80 and put it over on the black, and it won again ; so I picked up the money and walked out into the bar-room, and called up every one in the house. At that time a Spaniard would run a knife through you for a dollar, if he caught you in the dark ; and a man was not safe to step outside, if they knew he had money on his person. He wanted his pistol in his hand.

Well, the young man was delighted with my playing, and said : " I wish you would play again. I want to put in with you and take half of your game." "All right," said I ; " after a while." I wanted to get a few more ponies into him, for I was sure he had the money. So I changed the drinks to wine, and I could see his eyes snap at every glass. At last I said, " I guess I will make another play." He stepped back into another room, and came to me and handed me a brand-new one thousand-dollar bill that had never been crumpled. I handed it back to him, and told him I would put up $500 of my own, and for him to put his money back ; that if I lost, he could get it changed and give me $250. "All right," said he ; and I bet $100 on the black, and won it. I bet the same on the red, and it came black again. Then I bet $200 on the red, and it came red. The result was, I played along see-sawing until I was $400 winner, and I quit. I handed my friend $200, and told him I was too tight to play with good judgment.

We had our fun out, and got over to Brownsville about daylight in the morning. We all slept that day, and went over that night again. We did not gamble any that night, but drank wine and smoked our Havanas, and had a good time in general. That night my friend said to me : " I wish I was as smart as you at cards. I could make plenty of money." I said to him, " I can teach you." " Well," said he, " if you get into any game, I want to be an equal partner." He did not know anything about my partner who came over with me, as I had posted him to keep away from me. My partner was a very quiet fellow, who lived in New Orleans. His name was William McGawley.

Well, I told him perhaps I might get up a game with some one. As I was saving him for myself and partner, I did not want the money split up into too many parts. I had too much sense to play in Brownsville, so I fixed up a plan for him and me to take the stage and go to Bagdad, to see if I could not find some one there to play poker. I told McGawley to pay the bill at the hotel, and come to Bagdad the next day with the baggage, which he did. The next evening my young New York friend and I were sitting on the porch at the hotel, when my young friend espied him, and said to me, "You recollect the man who played in the game coming over in the vessel?" "Yes," said I; "there were three besides myself; which one do you mean?" "I don't mean the Captain or the purser, but the other gentleman." "Yes," said I, "I recollect him." "Well," said he, "I just saw him down stairs. I am positive that it is he." I said, "Let us go down and see him." So we both went down and shook hands with him.

My New York friend was very much pleased to see him, thinking I might get a game of poker out of him. So I said, "It is very dull here; what will we do to pass away the time?" I said, "Perhaps we might get up a little game of poker to help us out." McGawley consented to play a little while, so we went and got a room in the hotel and some checks   McGawley asked, "What limit will we play?" I said, "There will be no limit in the game." "All right," said he. I did not want to dwell too long on that $12,000. McGawley went out on purpose to let the gentleman get out his money. The New Yorker asked me how much I would require. I said, "It is going to be an unlimited game, and you had better give me what money you can spare, for if I beat one good hand for him I will break him." He handed me six one thousand-dollar notes. Well, we went to work; and you bet it was lively. I started in $2,000 winner, and you ought to have seen my partner's eyes snap. I don't mean McGawley, of course, for he was as quiet as a lamb. Finally my luck changed, and he beat one hand for $4,000. Then I did commence to kick at my bad luck, and we soon made up another purse. After playing some two hours more, McGawley had all our money; so I said to him, "As you have broke us both, will you lend me $1,000 for a few days, until I get some from New Orleans?" He said, "Certainly," pulled out the money and handed it to me, and I gave my New York partner half, saying, "Perhaps we will have better luck next time, as I will have all the money I want, soon, from New Orleans; then I will tackle him again, and of course you are in with everything that I do."

I had some $600 in silver that I did not know how to get on board the ship, that laid outside of Bagdad, without paying duty on it. So I went to a man from New Orleans, whom I knew well, by the name of Eugene Dupratt. I told him I had this silver, and asked him if he could get it on board the vessel, as he had lighters running all the time. It was about equal to running the blockade, or smuggling. "Well," said he, "I will take yourself, partner, trunks, and silver, and land you safe on board the ship, for $200." "I will give you the money." That night we slipped the things out of the hotel and got them safely on board the lighter, and were soon on board the vessel, and in two hours were under sail for New Orleans. We got home all right, and in ten days after we landed we were both broke, and ready for another trip.

BROKE A SNAP GAME.

We left New Orleans on a Red River packet, and had been out about an hour, when a man came up to me and said, "Captain, have you any objection to a man opening faro on your boat ?" I said, "No; you can open any time you please." He took me to be Captain Heath, and I knew he did not care. He said, " I will open after supper." It was near that time then, and I thought I must go to work if I wanted to beat this man. I found out what room he occupied, then told my partner to stay and entertain him till I returned. I went to his room, and found an old-fashioned valise that held his tools. I tried the keys I had, and found one to fit: I opened the valise, took out the cards and punched every one of them; then I put them back and carefully locked the valise, went back and invited them to take a drink. Then we went to supper, and after it was over the old fellow brought out his kit and opened a game. He shuffled and put the cards in the box. I asked him what limit he was going to deal. He said, " If any of you put too much on a card, I'll tell you." A good many of the passengers changed in, and he had a lively game. I stood alongside of him, so I could look down into the deck; and when I saw white show, I would copper in the big square, and my partner would play the other end and middle open—for when the white showed, it would be an ace or deuce. In this way we got the old fellow rattled. He changed decks every deal, but had the same bad luck. We finally broke him, and then won his tools. We returned the latter, paid his passage to Shreveport, and gave him $50. After breaking up the faro man, I said, " Gentlemen, I have a game here in which I only need three cards." I opened out, had a fine play, and took in all the money, watches, and pistols that they had. We were then ready to light out, as we had won $2,400 from the old faro dealer, and about $1,200, besides the watches and pistols, at monte. We bid the boys good-bye, and got off at Baton Rouge.

STOLEN MONEY.

I landed at Natchez one evening just after dark, on the steamer *General Quitman*. Some one told me that a lady had been robbed of $3,500 that day by some smart thieves They had watched her go into the bank and draw the money, and then walk over to her carriage, a short distance from the bank. One of the crooks took off his hat, put a pen behind his ear, ran over to the carriage, and said: "Madam, you must excuse me, for I have made a mistake in the money I gave you. You need not get out, but sit still; I will go back and rectify it." She handed him the money, never to see it or him again. After we backed out from Natchez, I opened out my wheel in the barber shop. The passengers came in and played until I A. M., when I closed up. While I was packing up my wheel, a fellow came up to me and said, "I've got a man with me who has got about $1,700, and I want him to lose it. He loves to play poker; do you think you can beat him?" "Oh, yes," I replied, "I can come pretty near doing it." He said, "I want half, as he is a thief, and no good. I had to divide $3,500 with him that I got in Natchez to-day." 'Well, bring him to me, and I will try it;" and he did so. I was not long in doing him up for his part of the stealings. I divided with the other thief, and then opened out my rouge et noir game. The other fellow dropped in, and I won his part of the money, so I had it all. I bid him good night and went to bed; but I could not sleep, because I knew that the one I beat last would rob me if he got a chance. I laid in my bed a long time. Presently I heard some one feel the knob of the outside door. I was in the upper berth, and had my pistol under my pillow. My partner was in the lower berth, for he had not been well that night, and went to bed early. Pretty soon, bang went the lock, and a piece of it fell on the floor. Then everything was still for some time, and at last in he came. Just as he commenced to look about him to see how the land lay, I pulled down on him with my gun, as I could see him plainly by the light through the transom. He saw the gun, and did not stop on the order of his going, but he went at once. I got up, dressed myself, and went out to the bar. There was Mr. Thief. I accused him of being in my room, but he denied it. I knew he was lying, but I thought best not to do anything with him, for fear I might have to give up the " stolen money," and I had not lost any myself.

SIGNAL SERVICE

Before the war they had an old steamer fitted up as a wharf-boat and lodging-house at Baton Rouge, to accommodate people that landed late at night, or would be waiting for a boat. This old boat was headquarters for the gamblers that ran the river. Many a night we have played cards in the old cabin until morning, or until our boat would arrive. When thoroughbred gamblers meet around the table at a game of cards, then comes the tug of war. We would have some very hard games at times, and we found it pretty hard to hold our own. My partner proposed that we fix up some plan to down the gamblers that played with us on the old boat, so we finally hit upon a scheme. We bored a hole under one of the tables, and another under one of the beds in a state-room opposite. Then we fixed a nail into a spring, and fastened the spring on the under side of the floor, so that the nail would come up through the floor under the table. Next we attached a fine wire to the spring, and ran it up into the state-room. Then we bored a hole in the bulkhead of the state-room, just over the top berth, so that a person could lie in the berth and look out into the cabin. Now we were ready for the thoroughbreds. When we would get one of our smart friends, we would seat him at our table in his chair, which was always on the side of our state-room. We called it ours, for we had fitted it up just to suit us; and for fear some one would use it when we were out traveling for our health, we paid for it all the time. We had a good boy that liked to lie down and make money, so we would put him in the upper berth while the game was in progress. He would look through the peep-hole, and if our friend had one pair he would pull the wire once; if two pair, twice; if threes, three times; if fours, four times, etc. We would kick off one boot and put our foot over the nail, and then we would be able to tell what hand our friend held. One day I was playing a friend at our table, and he was seated in his chair. I got the signals all right for some time, and then the under-current seemed to be broken. I waited for the signals until I could not wait any longer, for I was a little behind (time), so I picked up a spittoon and let fly at our room. That restored communications, and I received the signals all right. My friend wanted to know what I threw the spittoon for. I told him the cards were running so bad that I got mad; and that an old nigger had told me once it was a good sign to kick over a spittoon when playing cards; so I thought I would not only kick it over, but would break the d——d thing all to pieces. He replied, "I noticed that your luck changed just after you threw her, and I will try it the next time I play in bad luck."

GOT UP TOO SOON.

We were passengers with Captain J. M. White on board the steamer *Katie*, bound for New Orleans, one night, and I had taken a look over the boat, but there was nothing in sight. I was sitting in the hall near the bar, drinking wine and enjoying myself, when a fine looking gentleman came out of his room near by and asked me if supper was over. I told him it was, and asked him to join me in some wine, as he looked like he wanted something. He accepted the invitation, and told me he was hungry. I called the porter and told him to go to the pantry and get the gentleman a lunch, which he did. He thanked me for my kindness, for he thought I acted from pure motives (which I did), and then invited me to join him in some wine. I accepted, for I thought his intentions were honorable. While we were talking and drinking, I asked the barkeeper if he had any of the tickets that the gentleman played the new game with before supper. He said he had, and gave me some of them. I began throwing. We bet the drinks, cigars, and drinks again. I lost most of the time. My capper lost a bet of $500, when the gentleman said: "Good gracious, man! where are your eyes? Can't you see that the baby card has a spot on it?" My partner told him he had not noticed the spot, so the man pointed it out to him. Then he made me another bet, and won.

The gentleman then began to think he was smarter than the man who had lost $500 and could not win it back until he told him about the little spot. I saw he was worked up, so I asked him if he wanted to win something before I quit, as I had no idea of betting money on the game when I sat down; but I would bet him $100 he could not turn the card with the baby on. He flashed his leather, when I saw several large bills; but I pretended not to notice them, and said, "Perhaps you had better not bet, for if you lose it might distress you; but if I lose I will not mind it much, as my father has five plantations." He did not like for me to think that the loss of a paltry $100 would distress him, so he said, "I can afford to bet you $2,000, win or lose." That made me mad, so I said, "I will make it $5,000, if you like." He knew he would win; but he was no hog, and did not want me to ask my old dad for money so soon. My partner wanted him to make it $5,000, and offered to take half, but I said, "No; one at a time, gentlemen." Then the fellow put up, saying to my partner, "I thank you, but I am able to take it myself." He turned the spotted fawn, and found that, if he was not a hog, he was a sucker. I then told him I thought he was too much excited, and invited him to join me in a drink; for I was

always very liberal about treating a man that had but little
if any money. He accepted the invitation, for now he
knew I was a gentleman, and that my motives were honorable. After taking our drinks, he bid me good-night
and walked away, and I thought I heard him say, " I
would have been better off if I had remained in bed until
morning." I thought myself that he "got up too soon."

THE YELLOW JEANS.

At one time on the Upper Mississippi, while playing
monte, I caught a Jew from Quincy, Ill., who had been
down to St. Louis buying a stock of jewelry. I won all
his money and the most of his best jewelry. I would not
gamble for anything but good stuff in the jewelry line.
After I beat the Jew he set up a big kick, and got some of
the other losers to join him. They finally agreed that they
would make me give up ; so they all got after me, and I
knew there would be some fun. I got my gun, backed up
against the side of the cabin, and said : " Now, gentlemen,
I am ready to pay out ; the bank is open. The first one
that comes shall be the first served, so don't be backward." But, somehow or another, no one wanted to be
first, and I stood pat until the boat landed at a town called
Warsaw ; then I backed out of the cabin, down stairs, and
off the boat. When they saw me on the shore, they set up
a yell of " Police ! Police ! Arrest the fellow with the
yellow jeans suit." The marshal came running down, and
I told him I was the man they wanted arrested ; so he
waltzed me up town, and nearly all the passengers followed
us—some to get their money back, and others to see the
fun. The Captain said he would hold the boat if they
would decide the case at once, so the Mayor convened his
court and we went into the trial. I had sent for the best
lawyer in the town, and he said he would clear me for
$50. The Jew was put on the stand, and he swore I
snatched his jewelry from him, and a great deal more of

the same sort. Some of the passengers that had seen the game swore they did not see any one do any snatching except the Jew. My lawyer handled the case so nicely that I was acquitted. Then you should have heard the passengers laugh at the Jew for all his trouble. They would ask him if he did not want to trade some jewelry for a yellow jeans suit; but he did not have any good jewelry left, and he knew I was not sucker enough to trade for any other kind. There was another boat at the landing, and many of the passengers went up to hear the trial. I went on board the other boat, and in a short time was on my way back to St. Louis. During the trip I ran up a poker hand in a game of euchre, and lifted a man out of $300. which more than paid the expenses of the trial.

HE KNEW MY HAND.

We were on board a Red River packet called the *J. K. Bell*, and we had not made any preparations to gamble. After a while a gentleman came up and asked me if I ever played poker. My partners, Tom Brown and Holly Chappell, and some of the officers of the boat, were sitting there and heard the conversation. They had to put their handkerchiefs in their mouths to keep from laughing, when they heard my answer, "No, I did not." "Well," said he, "I will teach you if you will sit down " He got a deck of cards at the bar, and commenced to show me which were the best hands. I at last agreed to play ten-cent ante. We played along, and I was amused to see him stocking the cards (or at least trying to do so). He gave me three queens, and I lost $10 on them, for he beat them with three aces. Presently he beat a full hand and won $25. That made him think his man was a good sucker. I always laughed at my losing, and kept telling him that after a while I would commence to bet higher. I pulled out a big roll of bills and laid it on the table. Finally I held out four fives, and then I went a big blind on his deal, so that if he did not come in I would throw down my hand, and perhaps there would be no pair in it. About this time he commenced to work with the cards, but I paid very little attention to his work. After playing a while I got three jacks, and then we commenced to bet high. He raised me, and I raised him back, and at last he thought we had enough up. Then I got away with the hand he gave me, and pulled up the four fives. Then the betting became lively. I made him call me; and when he saw my hand, and I had got the money, he grabbed at me and said, "That is not the hand you had." "How the d—l do you know what I had?" "Well," says he, "where are the other five cards?" "I don't know what you are talking about." He counted the cards and found the jacks, for I had palmed them on top of the deck. Then he pulled out his knife and said, "You are a gambler, and I want my money back." "Oh, is that all? I did not understand. I will give it back, as I don't want to keep your money if you think I did not win it fairly." I let on as though I was taking out the money, when I pulled out old Betsy Jane. He saw her looking him in the face, and he wilted like a calf. I made him apologize, and you never saw a man get such a turning over as they all gave him. They told him he must not pick out such apt scholars, for they learn too quickly. What hurt my feelings more than anything else was, that he would not speak to me all the way up to where I got off. As I was leaving the boat I said to him, "Good-bye, sir. We are never too old to learn."

HER EYES WERE OPENED.

High Miller and I were playing monte one night on the first *J. M. White*, and had a good game, and made some money. We were about to close up, when a lady and gentleman passed by and saw High throwing the little tempters. They stopped and watched him. I saw they were interested, so I stepped up and lost $100. Then they came back and asked High what kind of a game he was playing. He told them it was the pawn-shop game. The lady wanted to know why he called it pawn-shop? "Because I have two chances to your one," said High. They laughed, and were starting away, when they noticed me turn up a corner on one of the cards. The lady nudged her husband. I made a bet of $500, and won it. The gentleman dropped the lady's arm, got out his money, and put up $100. High told him that he would not bet less than $500; but the gentleman did not want but $100 worth. Then his help-mate tempted him, saying, "It is good." So the man hearkened unto the voice of his wife, put up the $500, turned a card and lost. While High was putting away the money, I grabbed up the right card and turned up the corner again. Then I offered to bet him $1,000 that I could turn the winner. While this was going on the lady was giving her better half a piece of her mind. She was telling him that he was a fool; that he could not see anything, and that she could turn the right card every time. She got out her purse, took out $80 in gold, and asked him how much money he had left. He told her $70. She said, "Give it to me, and I will show you that a woman can beat a man every time." I was counting out my money to put up, when the lady asked me if I would not let her bet first. I said, "Certainly;" for I knew a man never lost anything by being polite to the ladies, and in this particular case I could see we were going to gain $150. High told her he never bet with ladies, but if she would hand the money to her husband he would bet with him. "Him!" says she, "He can't see as well now as when he picked me out for a wife. No, no; he shan't bet any of my money." "All right," says High. So she put up the money. High put up the same amount, and she watched him as though she was afraid he was not going to put up the full $150. After mixing them up a little, High said, "Ready!" The woman took up the card, turned it over, saw it, and then threw it down, instead of giving it to her husband that he also could see. She then took her husband's arm and said, "Come away; *my eyes are open*; if we stay here that man will win you next, and I don't want to lose you if you are a fool, and can't see as well now as when we were married."

We had a good laugh, took something, and then High said, "George, that woman's a game one; what do you say to giving her back the gold?" "All right," says I. So he offered me the $80, and wanted me to return it. I told him I was not afraid of any man, but, said I, "That woman has got her eyes open, and she may think I am your partner." "No, George," says he, "You closed her eyes when you were putting up that $1,000, and gave way to accommodate a lady; she knows you are a gentleman, and would not have anything to do with gamblers, except to do them the favor of returning money they had won from suckers." His fine words lured me into the trap, so I took the gold and found the lady. I told her that the gambler was sorry he had allowed her to bet, and had requested me to return the money. She looked at me a moment, with her eyes wide open, and said, "I will greatly multiply thy sorrow by refusing to accept the money, and may it be a sorrow to you gamblers all the days of your lives."

THE JACK-FISH.

My old partner Bush and I would play the trains on the Jackson Road out about forty miles above New Orleans, and then get off and wait for a down train. Some times we would be compelled to get off before we had gone that far; but, as a general thing, it would be about that distance before we would get our work in on suckers. We would go up in the morning to a place called Man-shak, and fish until the train would come down in the evening. One day we were fishing and had got some distance apart, when I saw a school of large jack-fish coming down like lightning. I jumped up and grabbed a pike pole that was lying near, slipped the noose over my hand and let fly at them. I struck a big fellow, but he did not stop; he kept right on and pulled me after him. I yelled to Bush, and he came running to assist me; he reached me a long pole, and then pulled me out. The rope was still on my hand, and the fish was on the pike pole, so we pulled him out, and he weighed about sixty pounds. We took him down on the evening train, and had a part of him broiled for our supper. Bush said it was the largest fish he ever caught. I told him I caught it, when he said: "Why, George, I caught you both."

RED AND BLACK.

I have been in some big games in my day, and have always been ready to win a dollar or so whenever I saw a chance. Often in the flush times after the war I have stood up in the bar-room and tossed up a silver dollar or a twenty-dollar gold piece, "heads or tails," for from a hundred to five hundred dollars a throw, and have even indulged in the innocent amusement of spitting at a mark—the money, of course, going to the one that came nearest the spot. But of all the games that I ever ran, I think the biggest was during the war, just after Captain Leathers had purchased the elegant steamer *Magenta*. The soldiers of the Union Army had burned his fine boat, the *Natchez*.

The story illustrates the old saying, that one good turn deserves another. When we left New Orleans the boat was full of passengers, and the trip was worth $3,000 to the boat. Reaching Memphis, the Captain soon saw that his chances for a big trip were the best that he had ever had. The boat was loaded to the guards with cotton, and the passenger list was 250, most of them being cotton brokers, who, of course carried a great deal of ready money with them. After supper the boat laid up, and commenced blowing off steam. I stepped up to the Captain's office and said to Bob Owens, the clerk:

" Bob, what's up—what's the boat laying here for?" "We are in a fix, haven't got money enough in the office to pay the charges on the cotton. It's too late to get anything from the banks, and we shall have to borrow."

I took in the situation in a twinkling, and said: "You needn't look any further; perhaps I can let you have all you want." Bob's face brightened up as he said: "I can get along with $1,000." In ten minutes the money was in his hands and the boat under way.

The supper was over and tables cleared, when I opened out my game of *rouge et noir*, and it started in big at once. There were twenty-five players, and the smallest money on the table was fifty dollars. At the end of every deal I opened four bottles of wine, which cost me twenty dollars, as the sparkling vintage was then worth five dollars a bottle. There was one man at the table who got pretty full, and finally commenced to put down a thousand dollars at a bet. I was somewhat surprised to see him roll out three thousand-dollar snapping new bills, and put them down. At first I supposed he was a paymaster in the army, but soon learned that he was a cotton buyer, operating for a rich New York firm. Everything was moving on swimmingly, when up came a contractor from Memphis, whose name was Harper. He was a knowing sort of a chap; perhaps best described as a "smart aleck." He began to "nip out." I stood it for some time, but finally let go all holds, and started after him, and soon had him broke, though in so doing I lost $12,000 that I had won from the New York party. Then he began to kick, and said the game was not fair; that he was going to have his money back, and threatened to bring up the crew of seventy-five men that he had on board, who had been working on the levee. I sent a message to the mate telling him what to watch out for, so he armed all of the boat's crew, roustabouts and all, with clubs and stone coal, and stationed them at the foot of the stairs; that brought matters to a stand-still. The contractor's men weakened, and the play-

ers who were the heaviest losers wanted to throw the contractor overboard, as they said the game was on the
square and perfectly fair.   There was so much noise made,
however, that the passengers began to come out of their
state-rooms.   The Captain hurried down from the hurricane
roof, and ominously shook his head ; so I cleared the game,
and all was quiet once more.   I settled my bar bill, which
was $375 ; and, counting over my money, found I was
exactly $19,000 winner, and had I not been disturbed
or molested might have won $150,000, as there was more
money on board than I ever saw in my life before, and all
the men were "high rollers."

That night the contractor and his men got off; the players sobered up, and we resumed operations ; but the playing
was not so large, nor the players so venturesome.   Still I
kept the game open till we reached our destination, and
came out a few thousands more ahead.

HE NEVER KNEW.

There are always men who have some scheme on hand—
some trick or device that is a sure winner.   It may be a
system, a combination, marked cards, or something of that
sort.   Such a man was John Brogan, of Alexandria.   His
stronghold was marked cards.   He had played with them
for years, and had been remarkably successful, having accumulated considerable property.   I was once coming down
the Red River, when I made the acquaintance of a shrewd
fellow named Neice.   He used a small concave reflector
about the size of a gold dollar, which he placed in the pile
of chips before him, and which in dealing the cards enabled
him to see every card, and where it went.   He generally
played with gamblers, and so adroit was he in his manipu-
lations that they were unable to catch him.   I made up my
mind that we could both make some money, so I told him
that I had a man for him who was well heeled.   He was
willing to help me, and we started for Alexandria.   I got

the Captain to land about three miles above the city, and put off my partner, whom I had thoroughly posted. When I reached Alexandria I went at once to the Ice House, for that was the odd name given to the hotel, where I soon found Brogan; and having had a good shake of the hand and a few drinks, we sat down for a social chat about old times, beguiling away the time with choice Havanas.

We had been chatting away for about an hour and a half, when a rough-looking fellow walked into the bar-room and asked if he could get a dram. "I've come a good distance," he said, "and am very tired. The fact is, I have been out in the back country looking up a mill site, and tramped 'round a good deal more than I calculated."

"Take something with me, my friend," spoke up Brogan. "I don't mind," and we all three took a drink together. The stranger called shortly for another round, and as he settled, pulled out a roll of bills as big as a pillow, that at once caught Brogan's eyes. He gave me a significant hunch. After supper the miller walked into the barroom, purchased a cigar, and walked out. Then Brogan said to me, "How is the best way to get some of that money?" I told him, "I'll play monte for you; perhaps he'll bite at that." John hunted around, and soon brought the miller into the bar-room again. I was up to snuff, and made my talk and showed my cards, and John won $100 from me. Then the miller said, "I'll take a hand." He lost $200. I kept on playing the cards, but the miller would bet no more, remarking to me, "I think you are a sharper."

John then asked the miller if he ever played poker. "Oh, sometimes; I used to play for a quarter ante." "Let's have a little game, then, to pass away time." The game began, and Brogan trotted out his marked cards. I insisted on playing, but the miller said, "No, that I was too smart." So, somewhat crestfallen, I walked out and took a stroll, and was gone perhaps a couple of hours. When I returned they were playing for ten dollars ante, and Brogan was losing very fast. I remained around the card table only for a short time and then went away. When I came back the miller had won every dollar Brogan had, as well as his diamonds, amounting to something like $4,500. Brogan came to me and wanted to borrow $500. I said, "Certainly, you can have it; but, John, you are drinking too much; take my advice and wait till morning." "All right; then my luck will change." "Of course, and that miller will be on hand."

Late that night a boat came along, and the miller skipped out. Morning came and I bade John Brogan goodbye. Poor fellow; he never knew why his marked cards didn't work, and I never told him. Both John Brogan and Neice have been dead many years, and, I trust, are happy in the spirit land—perhaps playing chuck-a-luck, marked cards, and concave reflectors with St. Peter and the Apostles.

THE BLACK MAN.

We were playing monte in the barber shop on board a steamer on one occasion, when a big black fellow, who had been watching the game through the window, asked me if I would bet with a black man. I had never gambled with the niggers, for in those days they were nearly all slaves, and had but little money, and I was looking for suckers who could afford to lose. So I inquired of this big fellow how much he wanted to bet. He said, " I'll bet five or ten dollars." I replied, " If that is all you have, you had better keep it; for I don't want to win a black man's money anyway." That got his African blood up, and he pulled out a pretty big roll, saying, " I got money, massa, if I is a black man." I saw he was well fixed, and so I asked him how he made his money. He replied, " I's a planter, sir, and I just done and sold my cotton." I took out ten twenty-dollar gold pieces, and said, " I will bet you all this against what you have in your hand." "Oh, no, honey," says he, " I got more'n dat." " Then I'll bet you this," I said, pulling out a thousand-dollar note. He put his money down and turned the card, and it was fun to see him open that big mouth, roll the whites of his eyes up, and then throw up both hands, ejaculating: "Laws golly! if dis old nigger hasn't done gone and lost his eyesight, sho 'nuf."

THE PERSUADER.

Bluff is a good game, and sometimes it will turn a trick when everything else fails. I boarded Morgan's Railroad, as it was called, upon one occasion at Algiers. Trains on that road were generally full of suckers, as the road connected with the Galveston steamers at Burwick's Bay. Tom Brown and Holly Chappell, my partners, were both along; and as game was plenty along the road, we carried our shotguns along, and in the event of no bigger game were accustomed to get off and shoot snipe, catching the return train to the city in the evening. Sure enough, there was a party of traders aboard, and Brown lost no time in making their acquaintance and opening out. One of them commenced to cut his clothes the minute he got a glimpse of the corner after Chappell made one cap. To make matters more binding, I came up and lost $1,200. Then the ball opened, and it was not more than half an hour before we had downed the party. Then the devil was to pay. One of the party said: "Look here; I must have my money back, or h—l will flop around here mighty quick." Then they all joined in and made a big kick; and as I saw fun brewing, I slipped into the baggage-car, changed hats and coats with the baggage-master, got his badge and my double-barrelled shotgun. Then I rushed into the car and drew the bead on the party who had collected around the boys, giving a war-whoop and demanding in stentorian tones, "Who has been playing cards in this car?"

"I have," said Brown.

10

"Get off this train mighty quick;" and I pulled the rope. My partners lost no time in getting off. Pulling the rope again, the train started; and when the conductor came back, I explained that somebody would have been hurt, had I not acted as I did. This was satisfactory, and going back he told the party that gambling on the road was against the rules, and that he could have them all arrested when the bay was reached, if he wished. This had the effect of quieting them down, especially as they knew that the man who had won their money was off the train. I was not long in reaching the baggage-car and returning the borrowed articles, and quietly slipping off at the first station, not forgetting my shotgun. Hunting was good that day, and I bagged ten snipe and thirteen robbins, which the boys helped me eat at our old friend Cassidy's restaurant, on Gravier Street, opposite the St. Charles Hotel. The boys all agreed that my conduct was all that saved the boodle, which consisted of $3,300 and two gold watches. Thus it is that a little management, backed by a double-barrelled shotgun and an official badge, is oftentimes a powerful persuader.

I HAD FRIENDS.

I was coming down from Baton Rouge one night in a stern-wheel boat. The night before I had gone up and had been pretty lucky, so I resolved to try and reach New Orleans in time for the next evening's packet. McGawley, my partner at the time, was along; and as we took a survey of the passengers, we noticed that most of them were raftsmen who had just been paid off. They were a pretty tough lot, but appeared to be well heeled, so I was not long in making up my mind to see the color of their money. I managed to scrape an acquaintance with a couple of them, and invited them to drink; then I proposed a game of euchre, to which both agreed. We made it four-handed, and played for the drinks, then the cigars, until finally I resolved to feel one of them ; so I ran him up a hand. He sat on my left, and ordered me up. I gave him the laugh and said, " I'll euchre you."

" I'll just bet you $20 you don't," he quickly replied.

" Here's $100 I do."

Borrowing $30 of his partner, he said, " I'll take that bet."

Of course I euchred him, as I said I would ; but the game broke up, and as I was winner I paid the bar bill. It was not long before I noticed some of them talking suspiciously together among themselves, and I deemed it the part of prudence to slip into my state-room and get my gun, for then I was not particularly disturbed as to what they proposed to do. They began to patronize the bar pretty extensively, and asked the barkeeper who I was. He replied that he did not know. They said that one of the negroes had said that I was a gambler, and they were going to lick me before I got off the boat. The barkeeper soon found an opportunity to tell me what was up ; and as I did not have much confidence in my partner as a fighter, I concluded I was in for it. I knew, however, that he was no coward, and if he was attacked would fight. The barkeeper handed me a " billy," and I strolled back to the barber shop, where several of them were gathered together. Returning through the cabin to the bar, I was accosted by one of them, but paid no attention. Two of them at last approached me as I stood with my back to the bar, when one of them remarked, " I don't think you won that money fair."

" I don't care a d—n whether I did or not," I quickly retorted. So he cut loose at me, and I caught his blow on my arm, let go my left duke and downed him at once. That was the signal for the circus to open. They all rushed in, and I began to lay them out as fast as I could with the billy. Every whack brought blood and a heavy fall. McGawley and the barkeeper took a hand, the former hurling a spittoon that cracked a fellow's head open and sent the blood spurting, while the latter brought a bottle on a raftsman's skull that raised a welt as big as a cocoanut. Then the Captain rushed in, and the mate followed with a gang of roustabouts, who soon had quiet restored. I was hit pretty hard with a chair, otherwise my injuries were not serious. I did not use my revolver, as none were drawn, for I never wanted to kill any man.

THE LAP-ROBE.

My dear old mother—she lived to be ninety-three years old—God bless her. I can see her now, with her silvered hair and tottering step. She used to pray for her wild son George, and on one occasion (I guess it was the result of her prayers) I did a good act that I have always been proud of, and I received the prayers of all the ladies of the church for it. I was in the South at the time, and on board a packet that was laid up at Natchez for a few hours. Some of the ladies of a prominent church there sent down a magnificently embroidered lap-robe, wishing to raise $100 on it. I took ten chances at $5 a chance, and then circulated among the passengers and easily raised a good sum. We shook the box, and one of my throws won. Of course I had to set up the wine; but I put up the robe again, and got one of the blackest men on the boat to throw for me, and a second time I won. A third time the robe went up, and this time for good; but not until $400 was realized, which was sent to the delighted ladies. I think that money spent did me more good than any that I ever squandered, for I was the recipient of the thanks as well as the prayers of the ladies.

THE PREACHER AWAY FROM HOME.

Ever since the days when Joseph's brothers gambled for his coat of many colors when they put him in the pit, the desire to venture in games of chance has been rampant in the human breast, and even "men of the cloth" have proved no exception to the rule. I recall an instance when I was going down the river on the *Natchez*. As I got aboard the boat I said to myself, "Everything looks blue; I've got no partner, and I don't think there is a dollar in sight." I scanned over the faces of the passengers, and soon found one of the old boys who formerly used to play a little, but who had now foresworn cards and become a prominent railroad magnate in New Orleans. Bob and myself were soon talking over old times and sipping julips, until at last we got a stack of chips and a deck of cards, and began to play for a small limit.

Presently a tall, portly, fine looking gentleman came up to the table, and appeared to be so interested that I invited him to take a hand, as we were playing for a small limit just to pass away time. He readily consented, and the game went on smoothly enough, when I ran him out three queens and helped myself to three kings, and gave Bob the office to remain in, as I wanted him to cross-lift, which he did. The game was a two-dollar limit, and at last we got him in for about fifty dollars before the draw. After the draw things livened up; he bet two dollars, Bob went two better, and I chipped in two better than both of them. We got him in for about $100, when he borrowed $20, and we still kept on raising him until we were confident he could raise no more money. Hands were shown, and the portly man wilted like a leaf before a November blast, but never even murmured a kick, and I soon knew the reason why, for Captain Leathers came up to me and whispered: "Why, George, do you know who that was you were playing with?" "I do not." "He's a preacher; I have heard him in the pulpit many a time, and I know that he stands very high all along the coast. I don't know what to make of his gambling here to-night." I never mentioned his name, and I knew that the Captain would not; and as for Bob, he'd never say a word, for he was afraid I'd give the snap away; and as for me, I had my reasons for keeping quiet, since Bob was always generous with his passes, and John Kilkenny would have the laugh on him; for all are now strict church goers.

A SHREWD TRICK.

Some men are born rascals, some men have rascality thrust upon them, others achieve it. This is a story of a chap that I think must have had a birthmark of knavery somewhere concealed about his body. It was during the war, and I was going up on the steamer *Fashion*, Captain Pratt. I was dealing red and black, and had a big game, as there were a number of cotton buyers on board. One of them was a fine appearing gentleman from New York, who was soon $3,800 loser; then he began to play reckless, and was still followed by his bad luck. I noticed his nervousness, and came to the conclusion that he was not playing with his own money.

Finally looking up, he said, "How much will you turn for?"

Noticing his excited condition, I said, "Put down as much as you think proper, and if you go too high I'll tell you." With that he pulled out a long pocket-book, and drawing forth a roll of hundred-dollar bills threw them on the red. I picked up the money and counted it, and found there were thirty-three one-hundred-dollar bills.

"That's beyond my limit," I said; "but as I know you are a great deal heavier loser than that, I'll give you a chance to get even, so crack her down."

I made a turn, he lost. With a trembling hand and wild eye he counted out the balance of his money and laid it before me, saying: "This is my last bet; if I lose, there is $4,000, and there is $200 more. Will you turn for it?"

"Lay her up," was all I said."

Down it went, just as any high-roller would do if he had some one else's money; he lost, and fell back in his chair in a dead faint; ice water was brought and he was revived.

After the game he came to me and said, "Not a dollar of that money was my own; it belonged to a wealthy New York firm, one of the members of which I was to meet in New Orleans, and render an account." I told him that he would have to say that the money was invested in cotton that would be shipped in a few days. "That will give you time to skip," I said, "for the affair is bound to come out, and then you will be in trouble."

"No," he said, "I won't run away. I have thought of a plan that will let me out of the scrape. There is another man on the boat who is buying for the same firm. I will go to him and get a bundle of money which I will hand to you privately, and then you come before the passengers and hand it to me. You can say, 'I don't want your money, so here it is, take it.' I will thank you kindly, and there will be plenty of witnesses to say that I did not lose the money gambling." I did exactly as the fellow wanted, much to the astonishment of the passengers, who said that I must either be the biggest-hearted man in the country, or the biggest fool that ever ran unhung, to give a man back that much money after fairly winning it.

When New Orleans was reached I was arrested, but easily proved that I had returned the money, or rather refused to take it, and was discharged; but the good old greenbacks were safe in my inside pocket, all the same.

MULES FOR LUCK.

In the flush days of gambling on the Mississippi I used to take everything. If a man did not have the money, I would not refuse diamonds or a stock of goods. On one occasion, when I was going from Memphis to Cairo on the *Belle of Memphis*, a little game was started, and I won ten first-class mules. A bill of sale was drawn up, but when I went to land the mules at Cairo, the former owner began to kick, so I had them transferred to another boat that was lying alongside of us, and bound for St. Louis. The man hated to part with his mules, and went down pawing and clamoring among them until one of them gave him a severe kick which nearly proved fatal. At last they doctored him up so he could talk. We were then *en route* for St. Louis, but I was too smart to take them there, so I disembarked at Cape Girardeau, and sold the mules at a reduced price; for what did a gambler want with a pack of hungry mules trailing around after him anyhow?

THE CATTLE BUYER.

We had been playing monte one night on the steamer *Southern Belle*, out from New Orleans, and had closed up. My partner was sitting out on the guards, and I was in the hall near the bar, when I saw a gentleman coming down the cabin toward me. I stepped up and ordered a drink, and as the man came up I invited him to join me. He accepted, and we entered into conversation. I proposed a game of euchre to pass the time; he assented, and we sat down. He proposed to play for ten dollars a game, as it would be more interesting. I said, "All right." I found him one of the best players I had ever met. He beat me two straight games, and I saw I could not beat him on the square, so I began to complain of my bad luck, and said the deck was unlucky to me. He proposed that we get another, so I told the barkeeper to bring us a new deck of cards, which he did, and when he put them on the table I saw they were my old friends. We played two more games, and I won both of them. At this time my partner came up to the table and remarked: "You gentlemen seem to be enjoying yourselves." "I replied, "We have played four games, and it's a stand-off." He then said, "If you were playing poker, I would like to take a hand." The gentleman said, "That will suit me, if you are satisfied." I said, "All right," and I invited my partner to sit in, which he did. We bought fifty checks each at a dollar apiece, and commenced playing. There were a great many of the passengers around the table, so we played on the square until everybody went to bed and left us alone; then I ran him up three large jacks, and gave my partner three queens, and guarded both hands so that nothing could drop in. Our friend was on my left, and had up a big blind; my partner just saw his blind. I exposed my hand and said, "That is too good a pot to lose, so I will raise you gentlemen $150." Our friend put up, and my partner said, "I believe you are both bluffing; I see that and raise you $100." I did not want to drive our friend out, so I raised $100. He put up, and we came to a draw. They both took two cards, and I stood pat with a nine-spot high. It was my partner's first bet; he hesitated, and finally bet but fifty dollars. I gave them one of those old "go-your-money" laughs, and said, "Boys, I have you both," and I put up $500. Our friend saw it and raised back $500. My partner looked at his hand, and after a while said, "I will call." I then bet $1,000 cold. They both called, and we showed down. The three queens just beat the three jacks, and I said, "I was trying to win that pot on a bluff." Our friend remarked it was not safe to bluff when such hands were out against you. I said, "That is so, but I thought you were both bluffing." We had something to drink, and started in again. I ran up two hands, giving our friend three aces, and taking four tens myself. I did not give my partner anything, as I wanted him to do the tipping. The betting began, and it was pretty lively. When we came to the draw, our friend took two cards and I took one, remarking at the same time, "If I fill this flush, good evening to you fellows." The betting was lively, and finally came to a call. We showed down, and I took in $4,700. Our friend was no kicker, but was as game a man as I ever met. He got up, laughed, and said, "Gentlemen, let's take a drink, and I will go to bed." He bade us goodnight and went to his room. I learned during our play that he was a large cattle buyer from Texas. We got a nice slice of his cattle money; but I must say that he could hold his own with any one in a square game of poker; but with two old sharks, and a deck of marked cards, there is no man that can win much money, as his bluffs don't go.

EVEN THE JUDGES DO IT.

The love of gambling is confined to no class of people. Preachers and lawyers, doctors and men of business, are as susceptible to the smiles of the fickle goddess of fortune as well as the roughest men.

George Hardy and myself were once going from Jackson, Mississippi, to Vicksburg, and, for want of something better to do, fell to talking over old times and tricks with cards. Near by sat a gentleman who appeared interested in our conversation, and I asked George who it was, as I had often seen him at Vicksburg. "Why, that's Judge so-and-so," and he introduced me. Pretty soon George remarked, "Devol, you ought to show the Judge the baby ticket," and as I had just played the trick for a joke, I said, "Yes, Judge, I have one of the best games for the drinks in the world; they play it out West altogether now instead of dice." Of course, he was anxious to see how it was done. Taking out some cards, the Judge was greatly amused, and at last George offered to bet me $50 that he could turn the card I took him up, and he lost. Then the Judge, not at all discouraged by George's ill luck, said he could turn it up for $50; but I told him I did not want to bet with him, since he never had seen the game before. At last I consented to go him once. He turned the card and lost, and then I thought that George would die with laughter. This only riled the Judge, who was now bent on getting even; so he put up his gold watch and chain, and lost them. He was satisfied then, and the next day sent around a friend and redeemed them.

George remarked, "The Judge stands very high in this vicinity, so never say anything about this transaction;" and as I never did, I do not suppose George did. George had no idea that the Judge would bet. Both the parties are still living, and will, when they see this in cold type, heartily enjoy the story.

NO PLAY ON THIS BOAT.

Captain Dan Musselman, who was running the *Belle of Memphis* from Memphis to Cairo, said to me one day as I got aboard his craft at Memphis, "George, I don't want you to play that monte on this boat." "All right," I replied, as smiling as a maid of sixteen. As we were near Hickman, Ky., I downed a fellow in the barber shop for the trifling sum of $900. Up stairs the fellow rushed in hot haste to the Captain to try and get his money back. I remained talking with Captain Bill Thorwegon, of St. Louis. In came the Captain and said, "George, did you win this man's money?"

"Yes, sir, I did;" as frankly as a school boy saying his catechism.

"Did I not tell you not to play that game on this boat?"

"Yes, sir; but, Captain, the man dared me to bet, and I wouldn't take a dare from any man."

"Well, you'll have to go ashore at Hickman."

The boat was then about three miles below, and I had a faint recollection that there was a man living at Hickman that I had beat only a short time before, so I said to the Captain, "You can't land her too quick to suit me. Put her into the bank as soon as you can." Captain Thorwegon tried to dissuade me, but I was obstinate, and insisted on being landed at once. Dunlap, my partner, was ripping mad at my obstinancy, as it was dark, raining, and in the woods. Out went the gang plank, however, and we on it, armed with some matches, cigars, and a bottle of whisky. A big tree was soon found, a fire started, and after patronizing the whisky bottle, and sampling the cigars, we turned in for the night. Towards morning I was awakened by a noise, and found that Dunlap, my partner, was on fire.

I woke him up and rushed him down into the river, only a distance of about fifty feet, and he came out looking like the worst tramp that ever was on the road. His coat was burned off, and also one leg of his pantaloons, so he walked to Hickman and purchased new clothes, and, boarding the first boat down, induced the Captain to stop for me ; and we returned to Memphis $900 ahead, but sadder and wiser men.

THE GREEN COW-BOY.

I always had a great love for horse-flesh, and it is many a dollar I have won and lost on the turf. In flush times, just after the war, I was taking a lot of race-horses over to Mobile, and had got them all nicely quartered on the boat and was taking a smoke on the boiler-deck, when a stranger approached me. "Are you the gentleman who brought those horses over from New Orleans ?"

" Yes, sir."

" There is one that I would like to buy."

" And that one ?"

" The pacing horse."

" Can't sell him ; need him in the races that I'm giving every week."

At supper we sat together, and after supper we chatted for a long time. My partner sat near by, and knew what I was nursing him for. He let me know that he was from Texas, and towards 10 o'clock I asked him if he played euchre. He loved the game very much, and played a great deal. "Suppose we amuse ourselves, if we can find a deck of cards," I suggested ; and we sat down, playing single-handed until most of the passengers had retired. When I took out my watch at 1 o'clock, a rough looking fellow, unshaven and long-haired, with a huge Buffalo Bill hat on his head, came up to the table and said he was from Texas, and had never been in this part of the country before.

" What part of Texas are you from?" asked my friend,

who appeared to be taken with the green country manners of the Texan.

"Wall, I live on a ranch twenty-five odd miles from El Paso."

"What brought you so far away from home?"

"Me and my pap came over with cattle, sir, and they's all over in pens in New Orleans. I reckoned as how we'd lose 'em all coming across the sea, and pap was skeered, so he never went to bed till we got them thar steers in the pens. I didn't want to go with pap when he started with them thar steers; but pap is the oldest, and I had to mind him."

"But what did you come to Mobile for?"

"Well, I'll tell you. I got talking to a fellar, and he told me that if I would go over with him on the ship that he would buy all my critters; so I asked pap if I might go, and he said yes; but I'm kinder sorry I went now, for I got lost from that fellar and never laid eyes on him after we got over thar. He told me to pay his fare, and when he got over thar he would give me back the money; but I reckon he went after the money and got lost. But I haint going to say a word to pap, for I got to pranking with a fellow on the ship, and I'll be gol darned if I didn't lose $1,000; but pap wont find it out, for I had $10,000 what I been saving to buy me a ranch, and I shan't tell pap anything about it."

"How did you come to lose your money, stranger?" I asked.

"Wall, look here; I never seen such a thing. He had some tickets, and he would mix 'em up—sorter jumble 'em together—and then he would bet you that you couldn't lift the one that had the little baby on it. So I just watched it, and I just cut my coat to get the money, for mam she sewed it up before I started. Well, I just laid down my greenbacks, and I didn't lift the boy, and he kept my greenbacks; then he went off and left his tickets lying on the bench, so I'm going to take them home with me, but I wont tell I lost anything."

"Let me see them," I said.

"Will you give 'em back?"

"Oh, certainly." So he pulled them out, and my friend and myself had never seen anything like them before; so I said, "Show us how he did the trick." He showed us the best he could; then I caught up the one with the boy on it, and turned the corner and showed it to my friend, and gave him a quiet hunch under the table as I laid it down, and asked if he would bet on it.

He said, "When I get back home I'm going to larn it, so I can win all the money I want."

"Will you bet a drink that I can't guess it the first time?" I said.

He mixed them up and observed, "I'll go you a dram."

I bet, and my friend was pleased to see what a fool I was; and I told my friend to bet him another dram that he could pick it up. But I said, "Don't touch the one that has the corner turned up;" and he did as I said. That made the cow-boy laugh, who broke out in his peculiar vernacular: "Oh, you old fools with store clothes on can't tell it no how." Then I observed to my friend, "I am going to have some of that money; for that fool will never get back, for some one will win it sure." I began jesting and playing the fellow, till at last I dared him to bet me $100 on it, and he said, "I won't take a dare," and pulled out about $4.000 in greenbacks, all in hundred-dollar bills. I laid my $100 on the table, all in small bills; so when he commenced to put up his, I counted him out of $100, and that made it two to one; but I turned the card, and he told my friend to just hand me the money.

"What is the least you will bet?" said my friend to the cow-boy.

"Wall, boys, you have got me at it, and I had just as leve bet it all; but I know you fellars with the store clothes on haint got that much ; and I knows you darnt bet a dollar—if you did, the old woman would broomstick yer."

My friend could not stand this sort of racket any longer, for I kept telling him to just lay up his money, and take it and put it in his pocket.

At this stage of the game a tall, fine looking fellow with long black whiskers came up and said, "I'll bet $1,000 that I can turn the card."

The cow-boy observed, "If I can win that bet, I'll be even on what I lost going over," so he put the money up and said, "Come on ; I'll go yer ;" and the black-whiskered man put up his money and turned the wrong card. The cow-boy was delighted. My friend trembled, for he saw that the new comer did not take the one with the corner turned up. Of course he began to get his money out ; and he had lots of the long green stuff, for he was a large cotton buyer from Galveston. He offered to bet $1,000, but the cow-boy said, "I wont bet less than $5,000." I offered to take half, but the cow-boy would only bet with one person at a time ; so I told him to lay it up. He did so and turned the card, but missed the winner. I grabbed up the boy ticket and turned the corner so quickly that he supposed he had made a mistake. The black-whiskered man at once pulled out his money and bet him $1,000 again, and this time he won.

My friend wanted to try it again, for I made him believe that he made the mistake himself. He said, "Shuffle them up, and I will make you one more bet." He counted out another $5,000 ; and says I, "That will only make you even if you win." So he took out $3,300 more, which was all he had, except perhaps $100 in small bills.

The cards were shuffled. The cow-boy counted out his money. The black-whiskered man wanted to chip in enough to make it even $10,000, but the cow-boy wouldn't have it. My friend made a snatch at what he supposed was the boy card, and—lost.

I felt very sorry for him.

The fellow with the black whiskers was Holly Chappell, the cow-boy was Tom Brown. Both were my partners. The cow-boy invited us all to the bar. My friend and I retired to our state-rooms for the night.

NO MONEY IN LAW.

A man by the name of Levy (of course he was a Jew) and myself were once traveling on the Jackson Railroad, amusing ourselves playing in the smoking car, when along came a horseman from New Orleans, and dropped in, thinking he could pick up the right card. I was doing the playing, and I asked the horseman if he thought he could pick out the card with the baby on. He said that was just what he could do for $300.

"Put her up," I said, and in a twinkling I covered his $300. He turned the card, and lost. Then he studied for a moment and remarked: "I am going to try that once more." So he planked down his watch, which was a fine Howard movement, worth about $200. He lost, got mad, and kicked by telegraphing ahead to arrest a couple of gamblers on the train who had been robbing a man. We were then a few miles below the Sixty-two Mile Siding, and I knew there were no officers there; so we got off at the Siding, and on the down train we spied an officer who was coming from Winona after us. Then we took to the hills, and kept a sharp lookout, where we could see and not be seen. The officer asked where we had gone, and the railroad people told them down the road. They returned to Winona, and he offered a reward of fifty dollars for the watch, and $100 for the return of the watch and money.

Bad news travels fast, and I soon heard of this, and I decided not to go so high up on the road. At last, however, I went to the town, though before I reached the depot I handed my money to a gentleman who resided there, who was a good friend of mine; and sure enough, as I expected, the constable served his warrant on me immediately. My friend at once stepped up and said that we would not go to jail, and forthwith furnished bail. We gave the officer the laugh, who only got mad and telegraphed to New Orleans that he had the party who had won the watch and money belonging to the horseman. On the first train, up he came. When the case was called for trial, I asked the Judge for a continuance on account of the absence of a material witness. He granted me one of three days. The horseman then offered to compromise if we would return the watch and money. Failing in this he fell to abusing the Judge for granting us a continuance. This reached the ears of the Judge, who was anything but pleased, and when I had an opportunity I told the Judge that if he wanted I would stand trial for gambling, and be fined; although I was aware that he had no jurisdiction in gambling cases, but I presumed that he and the constable wanted to make a piece for themselves.

The trial came off, and the Judge fined us thirty dollars apiece for gambling. My friend paid the fines, and then I turned to the Judge and demanded a warrant for the horseman, for gambling in the State. He too was fined thirty dollars; and when he returned to New Orleans, and told his story, the boys all gave him the laugh, and told him he had better have staid at home, for we all told you that you could never get a cent back from Devol.

When I reached New Orleans I hunted the horseman up, and he redeemed his watch, giving me $200. This transaction made a man of him, for afterwards I met him and he wanted to help me skin suckers, and did make money. Many business men whom I have at first won money from came to me afterwards and stood in with the game, so that I was given an opportunity to get into games that I never could have done without their influence.

THE POLICE SIGNAL.

They have a signal service on board the vessels running from New Orleans to other points on the gulf, by which they can notify those on shore what is wanted some time before the vessel reaches the landing. If they run up the police flag, there will be twenty or more police at the wharf when the vessel arrives. We would play one vessel out to some point of landing, and then wait for another to bring us back. We had played a boat over to Mobile at one time, and was on our way back, when we got a fellow down in a game of euchre. Several times during the progress of the game, remarks had been made about good poker hands, so I ran the gentleman up the old hand of four queens and an ace. He picked it up and said, "I have a poker hand." I turned my head to spit, and in doing so I purposely exposed (or tipped) my hand so he caught a glimpse of it. I then said, "How much will you bet?" He replied, "Fifty dollars." I then raised him $100. My partner said, "Gentlemen, as this is a game of bluff, I will raise you $1,000. I threw down my hand, remarking, "I started in to bluff you out; but you fellows are too much for me." The gentleman then said, "You can't bluff me; I will call the bet." They showed down, but the fellow's four queens and an ace were not enough, for my partner had four large live kings, and he took down the money.

The fellow got up and raised a h—l of a kick, and finally, when he saw he could get nothing back, he went to the Captain and told him we had stolen his money. The Captain was a stranger to me, so I could do nothing with him. He ordered the police flag to be run up, and then I knew we would be arrested when we reached New Orleans. I did not fear the result if we could get rid of our money, but I did not want the fellow to get a chance at that. I commenced looking around, and soon found a friend I could trust, so I gave him all the money my partner and I had, and then I did not care how quick they nabbed us. When we started off the boat, we were met by about twenty police. The kicker was there, and when he saw us he pointed me out and said, "There is one of them." The officers laughed when they saw us, for they knew me. We got into a cab and went up to the court, which was then in session. They searched us, but only found a few dollars. I employed a lawyer, and in about ten minutes we were free ; but if we had not got away with the stuff we would have had more trouble, as he was ready to replevy. After being released we started out to find our friend, and when we got our money we had more wine than was good for our heads. I have often seen the police flag run up, but always managed someway to keep from giving up the boodle. If I could find no friend to trust it with before we landed, I would find one in the officers or the cab boys, and not one of them ever went back on me.

A PAYMASTER'S BLUFF.

The yellow fever was raging in the South in 1867, and nearly every one was trying to reach the seaboard, as it is considered that the disease is not so violent there. On the steamer to Mobile one night a big game was in progress. Ten dollars was the ante ; no limit. I was $1,300 loser, and soon resolved that I must stir myself and do something. There was no time to lose, so hurrying to the bar, upon some excuse, I got a deck such as they were using, and ran up four hands, being careful that I got the best of it. Returning, I played fully half an hour before I came out with my deck. At last it came my deal, and I gave them threes and let them fill. It would have brought a smile to a dead man to have seen them bet, for they put up all the money they had, and one of them went to the office, and bringing out a valise, said, as he laid it on the table, "There is $18,000 in that valise, and I raise all of you that much." What to do I did not know. I was in a quandary, when, quick as thought, a plan flashed upon me. I jumped up, and rushing to the office, got all the small bills they had—mostly ones and twos—and securing a piece of brown paper, wrapped these bills around it, which made an enormous roll. There was a five hundred-dollar bill on the outside, and, putting a strip of paper around it, I marked it $20,000. Then rushing up, I said, "Boys, I have at last raised the money;" and as I was about to put it on the table to call the bet, the owner of the valise snatched it off, saying, "That was only for a bluff." So I deemed it best to show down for what money we had up, as I knew all the rest were up all they had, and I have always made it a rule never to bet a man more than he had, to run him out, but always to give every man a chance for his money.

Turning to the fellow with the valise, I said, "I will bet you $1,000 on a side bet that my hand beats yours." He counted out the money and put it up, and there was nothing to do but show hands; but in the draw I took in another nine, which made four, and a five spot. That broke up the game, as that was all the money, except what the man with the valise and I had, and he got cold, for the money he was playing with belonged to the Government. He was a paymaster, and had I won his money I should undoubtedly have got into trouble again. Paymasters in the army were among the best suckers we ever had, and I fear we never shall have such fat plucking again.

"PRANKIN'" WITH A NEW GAME.

I had a partner at one time by the name of Tripp, and he was one of the smartest gamblers I ever worked with. He would play any and all games of chance, and would play them as high as any man in the country, and come as near winning all the time as most of them. He was a good, clever fellow.

He and I were on the Michigan Southern Railroad at one time. Tripp was to do the playing with the three cards, and I was to be on the look-out. I began my part of the business; and in looking around, I saw an old gentleman that I thought might be well fixed in money matters; and if he was, I judged he would be a good subject; so I sat down and opened up conversation. I told him I was a miner from Colorado; that I had some of the richest mines in the country, and that I was on my way to Washington to take out a patent on a crushing machine that I had invented. He became very much interested, and I learned that he was from the State of Michigan, and was very well fixed in this world's goods. I gave him some big talk about the mining business, telling him I often took out $1,000 a day—and much more of the same sort. He did not let me do all the blowing, but gave me to understand that, while he was not taking out of mother earth $1,000 per day, he was—and had been for many years—getting out of the ground quite a number of thousands.

While we were telling each other how much money we had accumulated for a rainy day, a cow-boy came up and took the seat just in front of us, and in a few moments he turned around and said, "Be you gentlemen going to New York?"

The old gentleman said, "I am, but this gentleman is going to Washington City."

"I be going to New York with my steers, for them fellars in Chicago wont pay my price, and some of them beat me out of $2,000 in less than no time," said the cow-boy.

I then told him to turn his seat over and tell us how they got his money.

He got up, turned his seat, and said, "They had some kind of a game that they bet on; I got to pranking with it, and I just lost $2,000 afore you could say Jack Robinson."

"It must have been seven-up, or some game of cards," said I.

"It wasn't no seven-up, for I reckon as how I can play seven-up with any of the boys."

"Well, tell us about the game," said the old gentleman.

The cow-boy then took out an old dirty rag, which I suppose he called a handkerchief, unfolded it, and produced three cards, saying, "Them thar fellows gave me these ar cards, and I'm going to larn that ar game, so as when I get back to Texas I can beat all the boys."

I told him to show us how they could bet on three cards. Then he bent them up and began throwing them on the seat beside him, saying at the same time, "I'm not so good at it as those Chicago chaps, but I'm going to practice, and when I get down in Texas I'll get even on our boys."

I asked him if they got all his money.

"Oh, no, I just got loads of money; and then when I sell them thar steers in New York, I reckon I will have some more. Now you see this card has got an old man on it, and you have to guess this 'er' one or you lose."

We guessed a few times, and then I bent up the corner of the old man card, saying to the Michigan gentleman, "Now we will have some fun." Then I said to the cow-boy, "Will you bet money on the game yourself?"

"I can't play it good enough yet to bet; but as I have two cards to your one, I would just as soon bet on it as on a pony race, and I often put up big money on a pony."

I told the Michigander not to turn up the card with the corner turned so long as we were guessing for fun, so he turned up one of the other cards, and the cow-boy said, "You see you are just as big fools as I was in Chicago."

I then said, "I will bet you $1,000 that I can turn up the old man the first time." I told the old gentleman that we might as well get some of his money, as he would lose it anyway before he got back to Texas.

Finally the cow-boy took out another dirty rag, unrolled it, and displayed a roll of money the size of one's leg. He counted out $1,000, saying, "I'll go you once, for I don't 'low any man to back me out." He mixed the cards up, and I turned up the one with the bent corner and won the money.

The cow-boy laughed and said, " Well, I'll be gol darned if you didn't get me. You must have right smart eyes, for I swan I didn't know which one it was myself."

The old gentleman asked if he would bet with him.

" Oh, yes ; you are old, and can't see like this feller," said he.

" Don't be so sure about me not being able to see well," replied the old gent.

" You couldn't keep the run of them like this fellow ; and then I guess as how you haven't got much money," said the cow-boy. The old gent then got out his leather, and it was chuck full of big bills. He took out $500 and put it up in my hands. The cow-boy told him he would not bet less than $2,000; and said he, " The Indians bet more'n that on a foot-race down where I live." I told the old gent it would serve the fellow just right if he would win all his money ; so he put up the $2,000, turned a card and lost. I snatched up the old man card and turned up the corner again, then said, " How in the name of common sense did you come to make that mistake ?"

" Why, I turned the one with the corner up," says he.

" No, you did not, for here it is," I said, picking up the winner. The old fellow thought he had made a mistake, and the cow-boy told him he couldn't see well, for he was too old. I then told him to mix them up, and I would bet him $1,000. He did so, and I won. Then the man from Michigan got out what he had left, amounting to $1,200, and said, " This is all I have with me, but I will bet it." He turned a card, but again he lost. He then settled back in his seat as though he was going to stay right there, and I don't believe he would have got out if the car had run off the track.

The cow-boy put his cards back into the dirty rag, and remarked, " I be gol darned if I haint larning to play this 'er' game nigh like them Chicago chaps ; and if I hadn't been pranking with you feller with the smart eyes, I reckon I would have been about even." He got up, bid us good-day, and started out.

We sat there talking about the cow-boy's tricks for a short time, when in came my partner, Tripp, all dressed up so that no one would suspicion that he was ever a cow-boy. I introduced him to the old gentleman from Michigan, but he was not near so talkative as he was when we first got acquainted. I did not want to hurt his feelings, so I did not say anything about the game before my partner; and I believe the old fellow was glad of it, for he looked just as if he would rather no one but that d——d cow-boy and myself should know what a sucker he had been. When we changed cars we bid him good-day, and I said, "If you see that fool with the steers in New York, tell him not to go pranking with any more new games, or he will lose all his money." He looked at me in such a way that I believe he did not want to see him, although he did not say so.

CAUGHT A DEFAULTER.

It is a singular fact that most of the men who turn out embezzlers, defaulters, and dishonest clerks, sooner or later lose their money gambling. Oftentimes it is their love of cards that induces them to commit the crimes they do. I very well recollect a number of instances of this kind, and one in particular. I was going up the river on board the *J. M. White*, when I received a card requesting me to call at room No. 14. The name was written in a business hand, so I knew the card was from a gentleman. When I knocked a voice said, "Come in!" Upon entering, I saw a young man that I knew very well, who was a bookkeeper in one of the largest cotton houses in New Orleans. I at once inquired what he was keeping himself locked up in his room for, and he replied, "I am afraid to show up in the cabin, but I will tell you all about it before you get off;" as he knew that I rarely went above Baton Rouge.

Late at night he came out of his state-room so completely disguised that I did not know him. We took several drinks together, until he began to feel jolly; then I asked him what he was up to. "Well," he replied, "I have been playing the bank and poker for some time, and have been several thousand dollars loser, and I knew sooner or later the books would be overhauled, so I collected some money and skipped. Here I am, and what to do I don't know, nor where I shall wind up."

"Oh, there are plenty of people in the same box that you are," I said. "Don't flatter yourself that you are the only one who has taken money; but perhaps they will now go through the books, and, discovering the deficit, arrest you."

"Yes, but I don't intend to be caught. I think I will go to Canada. I am now traveling under an assumed name."

"Are you sure none of the discharging clerks saw you when you came aboard?"

"I was in this disguise, and came over two boats until I reached this one, and having a friend with me, he secured a room for two."

"How much did you get away with?"

"Seventy-two hundred dollars."

Which he had collected the day before he left. He proposed going out and shaking the dice for the drinks. I stuck him again and again, and at last he proposed to shake for five dollars. That suited me; and when he proposed to shake for ten dollars, I was ready.

Then I began to work him, for I thought I might as well have that money as anybody, as I knew he would gamble, and never reach Canada with it. I suggested that we go to my state-room, as the bar-room was too public a place, and he acceded. In half an hour we were throwing for a hundred dollars a throw, and when I quit I was $4,100 ahead, as I knew that it would not do to win it all from him, so I told him that I was sleepy and tired. We took a drink at the bar, and he drank so heavily that I was obliged to tell the porter to see him to his room.

I knew that he must have money to get out of the country, and it would not do to break him, as I would then have to loan him money. We were then twenty-five miles from Baton Rouge, and I slept on a couple of chairs in the cabin, and was awakened by my partner, who wanted to know if I wanted to sleep forever—as I had retired with him, but, unable to sleep, had risen. When I told my partner of the roll I had made, he said that I was the luckiest man he ever saw; but I told him it was no luck to hold out the dice most of the time.

When we reached New Orleans the detectives were hunting him high and low, but they thought he had gone out on one of the trains, and I never made them any the wiser. When they inquired if I had seen him, I replied: "Oh, such fellows wouldn't get on a boat where I was." From that day to this I have never seen him; but I think he went West, as when he was under the influence of liquor he talked a great deal of that part of the country.

HE'S ONE OF US.

Tripp and I at one time played an early train from Chicago down to Michigan City, and there we got off to wait for another train to take us to Detroit. We were in a saloon, and wishing for something to turn up that we might pass the time until the next train arrived. There was an old fellow in the saloon who was very talkative, and I learned from his talk that he was well posted about that part of the country. I did not think he had any money, so I had no idea of playing him, but thought I would talk about the country, crops, and such like. We had not talked long until I found he was waiting for the same train that we were expecting to take. I asked him if he would play euchre to pass the time, and he said he would.

We then sat down and began a game for the drinks.

Once in a while the old fellow would say something about poker hands, so I finally ran him up the old chestnut of four queens and an ace, giving Tripp four kings, and taking nothing myself. I came the old spit racket, and exposed my hand. The old fellow says: "I've a good poker hand."

"How much will you bet on your hand?" I inquired.

He said, "I will bet five dollars."

"Put her up," says I.

He pulled out his money and put up.

Tripp then said, "I believe my hand is worth a call."

I gave them the old "Bush" laugh, and said, "Boys, I believe you are both bluffing, so I will raise you both $25. Then the old one got out his money again and called. Tripp said, "You fellows haven't got anything, and I will make you lay down; I will raise it $100. He was right, so far as I was concerned, for he did make me lay down. The old fellow said, "I'm still on hand, boys." So out came the money again, but this time it took all there was in the roll. He put up, and called the bet. Tripp had hardly time to show his hand when the old fellow, feeling so confident, began to pull her down. Tripp showed down the old four kings, saying, "Hold on! old fellow; not quite so fast." He put up his last hundred dollars to see that hand, and he saw it.

About this time our train was coming, so we grabbed our grips and lit out. I saw the old gent talking to the conductor on the platform, and then go into the smoker. We went into the ladies' car, but in a short time I went over to take a smoke. I saw the old fellow just across from where I was sitting. The conductor came in and passed him without getting any ticket or fare, so when he came back he sat down with a gentleman just in front of me, who was the superintendent of the road. He asked the conductor why he passed the old fellow. "Oh," says he, "He is one of us."

"One of us? That old seedy cuss?" said the superintendent.

"Yes, he has been out West running a freight on a salary," replied the conductor.

POSING AS NIC. LONGWORTH'S SON.

On one occasion while traveling from New Orleans to Baton Rouge, I espied a gentleman who was a Judge at the latter place. He was a man of aristocratic bearing, and somewhat haughty in his manners. I started up my wheel after supper, and soon had a fine game. It was not long before I noticed a slick young man that I knew was from Cincinnati, walking arm in arm with the Judge, and apparently on terms of the utmost intimacy with him. This slick young Cincinnatian had introduced himself as a son of the late Nicholas Longworth, who was well known up and down the river. He claimed that he was traveling for his health.

I had made up my mind that he was playing a dead card, as I did not think the Judge was of much force, though he always appeared to have plenty of money. They soon were playing euchre, and began talking about poker, and presently the Judge came to me and said, "Devol, will you loan me $500? I will pay you when Baton Rouge is reached. I am a sure winner," he continued, and looking at his hand, I saw the old familiar four queens and an ace, with which I had downed so many suckers. I must say that I wanted to see him get it in the neck, and I was not disappointed. I took chances, and loaned him $500, and when I saw Longworth's would-be son putting it in his pocket that was the last time I ever beheld that money. The Judge never recognized me again. This is what an honest man gets when in bad company.

THE GOOD DEACON.

I was playing on the North Missouri Railroad, just out of Kansas City, having a man named Jeffers as a partner. One evening a fine looking, solid appearing gentleman came along, and appeared to take a great interest in the game, which was just for fun. Jeffers came up and insisted on betting, but I quickly replied that I did not care to bet, as I was only showing my friend the game so as to guard him against ever betting on it in case he ever saw it being played. Jeffers was so persistent that I finally yielded, at the same time telling him that the odds were so much in my favor that I would not mind venturing. "Why, I can pick up the right card every time," he said. At last, turning to my friend, I observed, "I have a great mind to let the fool lose his money." Accordingly I remarked, "I'll go you $100 that you can't," and at once pulled out a big roll, which made the solid man look bad. The play was made, and I won, which greatly amused my friend, who was anxious for my success, as the fellow had given me the dare in a blustering sort of a way. Jeffers made no kick, but, picking up the cards, put a spot on one of them, which he showed my friend, threw the cards on the table and said, "Throw again." My friend gave me a hunch, as he did not wish to see me worsted. I paid no attention to him, however, when Jeffers pulled out $200, played it, and won. Then, turning to my friend, he said, "Take $200, play it for me, and I'll pay you for your trouble." He did so, and won. I laughed, and let the old fellow know that I didn't think he had pluck enough to bet at any game.

"Oh, I would bet if the money I have was my own."

Then Jeffers began to work him, telling him that I was rich, and that they might as well have some of my money as not. "Just try it once," said the insinuating Jeffers. "Put the money in my hand, and when you win I will hand it back to you." Jeffers next offered to bet again, but I said

I wouldn't bet with him, "but I will with my friend here, as his eyes are not so keen as yours." At last the old man pulled out $100, and I tried to make him put up more, but he stuck to the $100, when I said, "I will have to raise you $900"—as I had noticed that he had $1,000 in the roll. He wanted to take down his money, but I couldn't see it, so Jeffers told him if he didn't put up the $900 that he would lose what he had put up, so at last he laid it up, turned the card, and lost. Then I looked for fun.

At this moment the porter of the sleeper came in and told me that my wife wanted to see me for a moment. Excusing myself, I started back, with my friend at my heels, but the porter refused him admission to the sleeper. I was ready to get off at the first station, but waited until the train was under way, when I dropped off, only to find that some one else had done the same thing, and was rolling over in the sand. I went to see who it was, and there was my friend, considerably bruised and banged up.

"Do you live here?" I asked.

"Oh, no," he replied, "but I want my money back."

"Well, if that is what you got off for, you are a bigger fool than I took you to be, for not one cent will you ever get of that money."

He hung to me nearly all night, until I was compelled to tell my story to a man at the station, and get him to hitch up a horse for me and leave it standing behind a small hill, and have another horse ready in his barn so that he could follow me and show me the road. A bran new twenty-dollar bill consummated this arrangement.

I fooled around with the sucker for some time; then running, I mounted the horse and galloped off. The game worked to perfection. The old fellow bawled out that I had stolen a horse, and the owner mounted the other horse and pushed hard after me. When I had gone about four miles I slackened up and let him overtake me, and we reached another train going to Kansas City fifteen minutes before starting time. The owner of the horses returned to town and told the story that he had fired at me, and that I was wounded and bleeding, and, he feared, would die. Jeffers came up to Kansas City the next day, and was astonished to see me alive.

Several days after I came face to face on the street with my old friend, who at once had me arrested for stealing $1,000 from him. I went to the chief's office, and explained that I had neither stolen a horse nor robbed any body ; that I had won the money at cards. The old fellow wanted the money back, and declared that he was a deacon in a church. Jeffers, the capper, came in when he heard that I was arrested, and told the chief that he had given the deacon ten dollars to win the bet for him, so the chief, in the face of this evidence, had nothing to do but release me. The next day a prominent member of the church was scouring Kansas City for the good deacon, thinking he had absconded with the church funds. I never gave up a cent, though when they have passed around the hat I have always chipped in, and, during the last forty years, have probably contributed to churches ten times as much as the deacon lost, and never regretted it either.

NARROW ESCAPES.

There are a great many men who, whenever they lose any money, begin to kick, and oftentimes they will resort to very desperate means to recover back the money which they have honestly lost. Coming out of Canton, Miss., one night on the Jackson Railroad, I won some money in the smoking-car, and then retired to the sleeper and was reading a paper, when the conductor coming along said, "Are you the gentleman who won some money a short time ago in the smoker?"

" I am, sir."

" Well, you want to be on the lookout, as the parties are threatening to have it back or there will be blood."

Just then the three entered the car, and as I raised up

my eyes the foremost one, a Pittsburger, said, "We are looking for you." "Well, you have found me at home; what is your business?" "We want our money back; and if we don't get it, you will never get off this train alive."

That was enough for me, and in a second I had my big gun leveled at the one nearest me, and I said, "If you move an inch I'll cook your goose for you sure." He fell back in good order, and in the next second the man behind him made a break at me, when I caught him with my big three-pound pistol, splitting his head open; and next I made a lunge for the third man, cutting him over the forehead so that he fell through a rack of glass, and when he raised up I struck him with my head. The conductor and brakeman interfered and took the ruffians out. There was a quart of blood on the floor; and at the first station they sent out and procured sticking-plaster. I paid the porter $12 to sponge up the blood and get the glass reset.

A man once pulled out his gun on me at Milan, whom I had beaten out of $100. I let on as though I would return it, until he turned his head away, when I hit him a stinging blow on the ear that doubled him up like a jack-knife. I took his pistol, and was arrested for winning his money and assaulting him; but when the Judge heard the testimony, he fined us both $5 and costs, amounting to $6.50. He gave the fellow a lecture for drawing a pistol, and I paid my fine and was off.

Another time in New Orleans, I was crossing the levee late one night with a valise full of money, when two men came from behind a cotton bale and started toward me. I pulled out my big pistol and told them an inch further and I would shoot. They weakened, and after they started I turned her loose, to enjoy the sport of seeing them run.

A CRAZY MAN.

One afternoon I started from Kansas City on the Missouri Pacific Railroad, and while seated waiting for the train to start I fell asleep. We had not gone more than ten miles when a crazy man, armed with a Colt's navy, entered the car. The passengers all fled, leaving me alone. Up rushed the lunatic and cracked me over the head a couple of times with so much force that I speedily awoke, and saw this wild-eyed man standing over me saying, "If you move I will kill you." I didn't move; only said, "You have made a mistake;" at which he backed out of the car. Thereupon the passengers all rushed in with revolvers in hand, wanting to know where that lunatic was. Though I have seen many crazy people since, I can never forget the terrible glare of those eyes, and can compare them to nothing but the fiery glare of a cat's eyes in the dark. I returned to Kansas City and laid up for some time, as the physicians feared that erysipelas would set in. It was not more than a week after this that the lunatic was seen on a house top hurling bricks down on the passers-by. He was at last lassoed with a rope and taken to the station-house. He butted his brains out against the iron bars of his cell and killed himself.

EIGHT HUNDRED DOLLARS AGAINST A PISTOL.

I was playing monte one night on the *Robert E. Lee*, when a fellow stepped up to the table and bet me $800. I knew it was all the money he had, for he tried to make it $1,000 by putting up his watch; but in those days I would not turn for a watch unless it was a Juergensen or very fine make. When he had lost his money and spent a few moments studying, he whipped out a Colt's navy and said, "See here, friend, that is all the money I have got,

and I am going to die right here but I will have it back."
I coolly said, "Did you think I was going to keep the
money?" He replied, "I knew very well you would not
keep it. If you had, I would have filled you full of lead.
I am from Texas, sir;" and the man straightened himself
up Pulling out a roll of money, I said, "I want to whisper to you." He put his head down, and I said "that I
didn't want to give up the money before all these people;
that then they would want their money back; but you offer
to bet me again, and I will bet the $800 against your
pistol."

That pleased him. "All right," he said, and the $800
and pistol went up in my partner's hands. Over went the
wrong card. I grabbed the pistol, and told my partner to
give me the stake money. Pulling the gun on him,
"Now," I said, "you have acted the wet dog about this,
and I will not give you a cent of your money; and if you
cut any more capers, I'll break your nose." I presented
the pistol to the mate of the boat, who kept it for a number of years, and said that it was the best he had ever
owned.

Another time on the same boat I was playing euchre
with a Californian, when we got to betting on poker hands.
He lost $1,600 and his watch, then told the clerk that he
was going to his state-room for his pistol, and going to kill
that gambler on sight. The clerk soon gave me a hint,
and I got out old Betsy Jane; and pretty soon he came
along, holding his pistol under his coat, and just as he
stepped out of the cabin door I pulled down on him, saying, "I have got you, my boy, and if you make one move
I'll turn her loose." He saw I had the drop on him, threw
up both hands; and taking his pistol away, I threw it into
the river.

IT WAS COLD.

There are many occasions when a shrewd man can get in his work on gamblers, it matters not how smart they are, provided his conduct is not suspicious, and his ambition so vaulting that when it leaps it is not lost upon the other side. I shall never forget the trip that I made down the river from Louisville in the good old *ante-bellum* days. When we reached the mouth of the Cumberland River, Anderson Waddell, who is now one of Louisville's wealthiest citizens, and William Cheatham came on board bound for the New Orleans races. Charles Burns and Edward Ryan, better known to the sporting fraternity as "Dad Ryan," were along with me. Both Waddell and Cheatham were gentlemen of good repute in Nashville, and it was not long before they proposed a game of poker. Burns and Ryan both sat in the game, and at the time they were unknown to the gentlemen. The wine flowed freely, and everybody felt very happy, and I resolved that it was about time for me to go to the bar and procure some cards similar to those they were playing with. It did not take me long to run up three good hands, and, sitttng down by Ryan, I laid the cold deck in Ryan's lap. It was not long before the cold deck came up, and then the boys began to bet lively, each getting in a few hundred. Then Waddell commenced to smell a rat, and turning to Cheatham, said, "Hold on, Bill, don't go in any deeper, as I think this deck of cards does not feel as warm as it did a few minutes ago."

"Oh, no," responded Bill, "I hardly believe there is anything wrong."

At last they came to a call; then they knew that they had got the worst of it, yet they never uttered a word or made a kick, and when we reached New Orleans they confessed that the boys had made suckers of them. Poor Bill is now dead, and Waddell, who is still living, would, if asked, laugh and say that he had long ago learned not to hunt up poker games on steamboats.

HOW I WAS BEAT.

Sam Houstin and Harry Monell were in business with me working the Missouri Pacific, and we were very successful, making a great deal of money. During the summer we played the bank, and in the winter operated on the river and Southern roads. Immediately after the big fire we resolved to go to Chicago, but, at the last minute, Houstin was unable to go; but I told him he should be in with the play, and share the profits as if he was along.

Monell and I started, and made a few hundred dollars, and when Houstin joined us he received his share of the spoils. We were all stopping at the Tremont House, on Lake Street. We made a little money, and one Sunday morning I arose early, and resolved to go out on the road about twenty miles. While waiting for breakfast I made the acquaintance of a gentleman from Texas, who had just sold some cattle that he had brought with him. We had a cocktail together, and I sent the porter to awaken my partners, whom I duly introduced to the stranger, letting them know that he had money, and to keep a sharp lookout on him until Monday morning. When I returned at night I found that my partners had beat the Texan, and he had Houstin locked up in jail. I carried him down a good supper from a restaurant, and then hunted up the Texan, who told me that he had started in betting, and at first won, and then lost $7,600, and that his only object in arresting Houstin was to scare him so as to get his money back. The other man he could not find. He said he had gambled when in Texas, but these fellows were too smart for him, and that he could not afford to lose that money.

When the case was called for trial, the Judge dismissed it on the ground that they were all gamblers. Nothing was said about the settlement of the game for a couple of days, when one morning they both arose, paid their bills, and skipped, and I never received a cent of that money. I have since learned that Monell is doing time at Sing Sing, along with "Paper Collar Joe," while Houstin is an old man trying to lead a square life, I understand, down in Florida. The late Sherman Thurston once said to me, "George, those fellows are rotten apples;" but I did not heed his advice, and let them alone.

SETTLED OUR HASH.

Jew Mose and myself were once traveling on the Missouri Railroad, having headquarters at Cheyenne and making a good deal of money, when one evening I picked up a man on the sleeper and beat him out of $1,200. That game settled our hash, for he proved to be one of the directors of the road, and as soon as he reached Omaha he had a lot of handbills printed and hung up in the cars, not only prohibiting gambling, but that conductors permitting the game on their cars would be at once discharged. I was then running a game in Greer Brothers' Gold Room Saloon, and occasionally slipped out and started a game on some of the trains. There were a dozen cow-boys aboard one night, when Mose opened out and took in a couple of them. They began to drink heavily, and then resolved to make the gambler disgorge. I expected fun, so I told Mose to get off and jump on the engine at the first station. He was none too quick, for the boys went through the train and never found him; but they never said a word to me, as they supposed I was a sucker like themselves, for at the time I was very roughly dressed. These cow-boys, while very blustering when on the trains, were peaceable enough when they entered a gambling-house; for the gamblers would stand no foolishness with them, and were always prepared to draw at a second's warning.

I RAISED THE LIMIT.

I recollect playing in a game of poker at one time on the steamer *Natchez*. It was a five-handed game, and the party were all friends of each other. We were playing on the square, with a straight deck of cards and for a small limit. I could enjoy myself in such a game for a limited time ; then the old desire to play my tricks would come over me, and I could not resist the temptation. I did not want to beat my friends only on the square, but I did want to have some fun ; so I excused myself for a few moments and left the table. On my return I sat in again, and the game went on as before. We had been playing a short time, when one of the boys picked up his hand, got a glimpse of it, and then threw it down as quick as lightning, saying, " What's the limit ?" All the others looked at their hands, but none of them seemed to remember what limit we had been playing. One thought it was $10, but was willing to raise it to $20 if the others would agree. I remarked that the limit had been but $5, but I never kicked if anybody wanted to raise her. So they all consented to raise it to $20. The one next to the age put up the limit, the next one saw that and went him twenty better, the next one did the same. I said, " Boys, you are bluffing, so I will just call." The age then raised her the limit, and it went around until most of the boys had put up all their money. Then it came to a draw. Some took one card, some stood pat, and I took three. Then the betting was resumed at a lively rate. Those that had put up all their money borrowed from their friends ; and, to tell the truth, I never did see four men have so much confidence in their hands. I kept calling, and finally it was a call all round, but no one wanted to be the first to show down. I threw down three tens, when they all said, " I've got you beat." I said, " Gentlemen, it's a call all round ; why don't you show down?" They all came down about the same time ;

and you should have been there—for all the passengers on
the boat were looking on. They saw each other's hands,
and I be gol darned if every one of them didn't have fours,
and they were all aces at that. All four of them spoke up
in the same breath, "Who dealt the cards?" I replied,
"I did." We sent for the first and second clerks to bring
a quire of paper and figure out who won the money and
how much each one was entitled to. After the problem
was solved we resumed the play, but first the boys made
me swear I did not have any more cold decks on my person with sixteen aces in them. As I had raised the limit
to $20, I took the oath, and we again settled down to a
square game.

GOT OFF BETWEEN STATIONS.

A man by the name of Charlie Adams, Tripp, and myself, started out from Chicago on the Michigan Central
Railroad one day, to turn a few honest dollars. We took
separate cars and began looking for game. I was in the
ladies' car, and thought I saw plenty of material, but the
most of it was handicapped with female riders. There
was one old gentleman sitting alone, so I took a seat beside
him and began to feel his pulse. He had sold a pair of
horses for $800, and an interest in a patent for $1,600. I
did not want to play him in that car, for I wanted some of
the others a little later on; so I invited him to join me
in a smoke. He declined, and told me that he never
smoked a cigar, chewed tobacco, or drank a drop of
liquor in his life. Then I knew he would be a darling
sucker; so I invited him to go over in the smoking-car
until I could have a little smoke myself. He consented,
and we went over. We took a seat just behind a green
looking countryman who was smoking a cob pipe, and it
was not long until he turned round and asked us the name
of a station we had just passed. We did not know the
name, so he said: "I don't wonder you can't tell the
names, for I never saw so many towns strung 'long a rail-

road.   Why, out where I live we don't have a town only
about once in fifty miles."

I asked him where he lived.   He replied : " When I'm
to hum, I lives on a ranch in Colorado ; but I've been to
Chicago sellin' of my steers, and them thar fellows came
nigh gettin' the best of me with some of their new-fangled
games ; but they gave me some of their tickets, and when
I get home I'll make the boys think I didn't take my critters to Chicago for nothing.   I guess as how théy would
have got more of my money, but I left it up at the tavern
with the feller that had his hair all glued down to his forehead as if he thought it would fall off.   So when they
got all I had with me they thought I was broke and let
me go."

The old gent asked him to show us how they beat him
with the tickets.   He said, " I've not larnt it yet, but I will
try and show you ;" so he got out his three tickets and began
to throw them on the seat, explaining that we must guess the
ticket with the little boy on it.   We guessed, sometimes
right and sometimes wrong.   I bent up the corner of the
little boy ticket, and told the old gent not to turn that one
until we got a bet out of the fool ; so we would miss it
every time after that.   Finally I offered to bet him $500
that I could turn up the boy ticket the first turn.   He said,
"No, I wont bet on her yet, for I can't play her good
'nough."   Then I offered to bet him five to two, so he got
out his big roll, saying, "This is the money I left up to the
tavern, so I'll just try you once."   I put up my $500, and
he put up $200.   I turned the ticket with the corner bent,
and won.

He looked at me a moment, then said to the old gent,
who was holding stakes, "Give him the money, for gol
darned if he didn't get her fair."

Then I offered to bet him $1,000, but he said, " You
got an eye like an Indian, and I don't want to play with
you any more ; but I will play with your pap " (pointing to
the old gent).

The old fellow said, "I am a church member, and never bet; but I expect some one will win all that fellow's money before he gets home."

"Certainly," said I; "and we may as well have it as any one else."

The old gent got out his money and wanted to bet $100, but the fellow would not bet less than $1,000. I then offered to put up the balance, but the fellow would not have it, saying, "Your eyes are too good." Then the old gent put up the money in my hands and turned the card; but it was not the winner, for somehow, in mixing them, the corner of the boy card had got straightened out and the corner of another was turned up. I put a mark on the boy card with my pencil while the fellow was putting away his money, and then told him as he was a little winner he should let me bet once more. He said, "All right," so I put up $1,000, turned the marked card and won.

The old church member could not stand it to see me win all that fool's money, so he put up $1,000 more in order to get even. The fellow told him he would make it $1,500; and as that would get him out ahead, up she went, and he turned the marked card; but, as was the case with the crocked corner, the little mark was on another card. The old gent dropped back in his seat with a groan, and just then a gentleman who had been sitting across the aisle got up and said, "You fellows have been trying to rob this boy out of his money. I have been watching you, and will report you to the officers at the next station." The old gent got up and started back to his car, saying to me in a whisper, "You had better get out of this, or you may get into trouble." I replied, "I think so myself." So I got up and started back with him, but he was in such a hurry that I got lost from him. When the train got up to the next station, there were three less passengers on board than when that fellow said, "I will report you to the officers."

A GOOD NIGHT'S WORK.

There had been quite a number of communications received by the officers of the Michigan Southern, complaining about the gamblers beating the passengers on that road, consequently orders were issued to the conductors not to allow any gambling on their trains. They did try to prevent it, but the boys were too smart for them, and got away with many a good dollar while the conductor was collecting fare or out on the platform at a station. The result was, the complaints continued to go to the officers of the road, and some of them went so far as to claim that the conductors were in with the gamblers. The poor conductors insisted that they could not watch the rascals and their train at one and the same time; but the superintendent thought they could, and threatened to discharge any one who was complained of again. He found out one day that the conductors were right and he was wrong. I will tell you how he was convinced.

Tripp, Adams, and myself got on a train going out of Chicago on the Michigan Southern one evening, and took seats in different parts of the car. In a few moments after the train started, the conductor and a fine looking old gray-headed gentleman came into the car where we were seated, and something told me that he was one of the officers. I saw them talking together a short distance from where I was sitting alongside of a big fat man. The conductor was evidently pointing us out, for I could see by his actions that they had us spotted. The other boys knew what was in the wind, for we had all been there before and understood our business. The conductor left the car, but the old gentleman took a seat facing us; so we began to think the jig was up for that trip, for there was a pair of eyes constantly upon us. But as we did not make a move, the old fellow got a little careless, took out a package of papers, and began to look over them. When I saw he was very

much interested in his papers and began to use his pencil, I gave Tripp the wink, and he slipped over to my seat.
We went through the old business about the same as if the
old pair of eyes was not in the same car, only we talked
low, and while the car was in motion no one could hear
what was going on.

Just before we reached a station, Tripp beat the big fat
man out of $600, and he had beaten me out of $500 before
we got him to put up. I gave him the office to get off at
the station ; so when the cars stopped, he was on the platform.

There was a Jew sitting just behind us who had been
watching the game, and he saw Tripp out on the platform,
so he laughed and said, "You see that fellow? He gets
off when he wins your moneys."

The old superintendent jumped up, put away his papers,
and said : "What's that ? Some one been *gambling* in
this car ?"

The Jew told him that the fellow with the slouch hat
had won $600 from the big fat man, and $500 from me. I
told my fat friend it was no one's business if we lost our
money ; so when the old gent, who had been watching his
papers just long enough for us to get our work in, came up
to us and asked if we had lost some money, my fat friend
said, "It's none of your business ; the money did not belong to you."

Just then the conductor came in, so the superintendent
said to him : "Those d——d villains have played their
games right under my very nose, beat these d——d fools
out of over $1,000, and got off. Now, if any one comes
into my office and tells me that our conductors are in with
the d——d gamblers, I will take a club and knock his
d——d brains out. You attend to your train hereafter, and
let the d——d suckers take care of themselves."

The conductor said, "All right, sir."

The old fellow was so hot that he went out into another
car to cool off. My fat friend bid me good-bye soon after,

and asked me to call on him, should I ever stop off at his place. I promised to do so, and we separated warm friends. When I told Tripp what the old superintendent said, he replied, "George, it's the best night's work we ever did."

At another time we were playing a train (or at least we had paid our passage for the purpose of turning a few dollars), but I noticed that the conductor was watching us very closely; and I knew that about the time we had our man ready, he would drop down on us and tell the sucker that we were gamblers, and then we would have all our trouble for nothing. So I told my partners to work up the business, and when I saw everything was O. K., I would go to the conductor and entertain him until the job was finished. Well, the boys had a fellow all ready to blow himself, when I saw the knight of the punch bearing down upon them. I jumped up and met him, but he was in a hurry, and did not want to stop; so I caught him, and held on until all was over. He kicked like a government mule, but it was too late; so he said I would not catch him again. I gave him a cigar, and told him I would try a new scheme next time, as a burnt child dreaded the fire. He laughed, and so did I, and that ended it.

HE'S NOT THAT OLD.

About forty years ago I was a pioneer in the great Northwest (or Lake and Central States), and was pretty largely interested in the different branches of business that paid a large profit on the amount of capital invested. I was running keno in St. Paul; playing poker with the Indians, and running the risk of losing my scalp, in Minnesota; building frame shanties out of green lumber for lodgers, at a dollar a head, at Winona; and running a restaurant, saloon, billiard and keno room at Dubuque, Iowa. I was kept pretty busy looking after and attending to my different branches of business, and I divided my time between them.

At one time while I was in Dubuque looking after my restaurant, saloon, billiard and keno rooms, I met a robust, rosy-cheeked young man, who had come out West seeking his fortune in the show business. He came into my place and introduced himself, as he was a total stranger in those parts. I took quite a liking to the good-looking young man, and I told him to make my place his home while he remained in our town. He thanked me for my kindness (for in those days I was kind), and said he would be pleased if I would assist him in advertising his show. They did not have such large, handsome show-bills to draw the crowds (to the bill-boards, I mean) in those days, as they have now; but this young showman knew a thing or two, so he adopted the plan that is largely practiced by our minstrel troupes at this late day. He got some of us ordinary-looking chaps to show him the town—I don't mean like it is done in these days. He wanted us to walk around all the nice streets, so he could see the people, and so the girls could see him. We did it; and the result was, all the girls in that place were at the show the first night. I got all the boys to go over and give the young fellow a lift; and when he left the town, he was much better fixed financially than when he landed. All the girls (and some of the boys) were sorry to see him leave. He thanked me for the favors (more especially for the one of showing him the town), and he has not forgotten them to this day, for we often speak of the old times out West; but he insists that it is not near forty years ago. But I know why he don't want me to give dates. He need not fear, for I will not tell who the good looking, rosy-cheeked boy was that I met in Dubuque about forty years ago; and no one would ever guess, for at that time he was not running a Grand Opera House—and, " by Joe " (Bijou), I don't believe he ever expected to.

CANADA BILL.

Canada Bill was a character one might travel the length and breadth of the land and never find his match, or run across his equal. Imagine a medium-sized, chicken-headed, tow-haired sort of a man with mild blue eyes, and a mouth nearly from ear to ear, who walked with a shuffling, half-apologetic sort of a gait, and who, when his countenance was in repose, resembled an idiot. For hours he would sit in his chair, twisting his hair in little ringlets. Then I used to say, "Bill is studying up some new devilment." His clothes were always several sizes too large, and his face was as smooth as a woman's and never had a particle of hair on it. Canada was a slick one. He had a squeaking, boyish voice, and awkward, gawky manners, and a way of asking fool questions and putting on a good natured sort of a grin, that led everybody to believe that he was the rankest kind of a sucker—the greenest sort of a country jake. Woe to the man who picked him up, though. Canada was, under all his hypocritical appearance, a regular card shark, and could turn monte with the best of them. He was my partner for a number of years, and many are the suckers we roped in, and many the huge roll of bills we corralled. He was an arrant coward, though, and would not fight a woman if she said boo. His right name was Jones. When Tom Brown and Holly Chappell traveled with me, the four of us made a quartette that could give most any crowd any sort of monte they wanted. Brown got $240,000 for his share of the profit, and Chappell went North with his portion, and is to-day as poor as myself. Bill never weighed over 130 pounds, and was always complaining of pains in his head. I always found him honest to a fault; and when the poor fellow died, I felt that I had lost one of my truest friends.

THE NATCHEZ AND THE LEE.

When the great steamboat race came off between the *Natchez* and the *Robert E. Lee*, the excitement all along the Mississippi River, and at St. Louis, New Orleans, and all the river towns, was at fever heat. Betting ran high, a great deal of money changed hands, and very little else was talked about for a long time. I came to the conclusion that the boats were pretty evenly matched, but thought that the *Natchez* ought to beat in a straight run. I knew the *Lee* could make two landings to the *Natchez* one, the latter boat being somewhat top-heavy, and difficult to handle. However, I put my money on her, and believe she would have won had not Captain Canon out-generaled and out-managed Captain Leathers.

Captain Canon took off every extra pound of freight, including anchors, chains, beds, and bedding, even taking the doors and shutters off the hinges; while the hold and decks he saved to be filled with dry pine knots. Besides, he engaged the steamer *Paragoad* to go up above Baton Rouge, loaded down with the choicest of fuel. The *Paragoad* was a very fast boat; and when Baton Rouge was reached, the *Lee* never stopped her engines, only slackened her speed a little, while the *Paragoad* lay alongside and dumped the fuel on to the *Lee*. The *Natchez* had to land and take a coal-boat in tow, and by this management made a difference of over three hours. This gave the *Lee* a start of perhaps five hours, as when she did land it was for a moment only. The *Natchez* kept everything on board, and caught all the winds, while they whistled through the *Lee*.

On the day of the race the excitement was so great in New Orleans that when the *Mayflower* advertised to take people up about twenty miles to see the fun, it was not long before she was loaded to her gunwales with all the young bloods of the Crescent City. A jollier set of fellows never got together; and as money was plenty, they made the wine fly with a whirl. I hunted up old Bill and Dad Ryan, and made up my mind we would tackle the gentry and give them something to spend their money for. Bill opened up, and the young sprigs of the aristocracy began to pile up the bills, which Bill was not slow to rake in. There was nothing mean about Bill, and he didn't refuse to take gold watches and sparklers; and after the game closed, some of the fellows resembled picked ducks. They wanted to redeem their watches and diamonds, so Bill agreed to meet them at a certain well known saloon the next day, as all he wanted was the stuff. Nearly all of them wished to make me a nice present, and none of them ever met me afterwards without asking me up to smile. Just as Bill was closing up, an old fellow, who knew me well, came up and said:

"Devol, who is that old fool trying to play that game?" My friend had been up on the hurricane roof, and had not noticed the game going on; so I remarked to him:

"Hold on. I have been watching him, and am going to take him in pretty soon." I then gave Bill the wink to keep on, and turning to the old fellow, I observed, "Don't leave here, as I may want you to hold stakes for me."

"All right," was the answer; and then I turned to Bill and said, "Let me see your cards;" so I picked up the one with the old woman on it and put a pencil mark on it, which I showed the old man (who, by-the-by, was a large wholesale grocery merchant, whom I had known for twenty-five years, and he had seen me play monte many a time). I asked the old fellow that was turning the cards, "if he would bet on the game."

"Yes," he replied; "I'll bet you can't find any card you may mention, after I mix 'em up."

Then I said, "Hide the old woman." So he mixed them up again, and I said, "I know it's hard to find, but I'll bet you $1,000 I can pick her up the first time." He laid up the money on the table, and I continued, "This gentleman will hold the stakes." "All right," said Bill,

"He got out his wallet and put up $1,700," etc.   [Page 193.]

and he put the money in the grocery-man's hand, and I turned the card. Bill said, "All right; fairly won. Give him the money;" and I pocketed the stuff. Then I offered to bet him $2,000, but Bill declined to bet with me any more; so my friend the grocery-man spoke up: "I'll bet you I can turn the card." Bill replied, "I have just lost $1,000, and if I bet any more it will not be less than $2,000." So I handed my friend the money to put up; but Bill wouldn't stand it, and spoke up: "I wont do that. If you don't play your own money, I wont bet;" so I told him to just lay it up and turn the card, and I would hand it to him. He got out his wallet and put up $1,700, and I loaned him $300 to make it up; so he turned the card. The old fellow could not believe himself. He stood still for a few minutes, looked at Bill, then at me, and finally said, "Devol, lend me a five-dollar bill, and I will go home and stay there until I get some sense." He did what he said he would, and I never saw him for a couple of months, when one day, as I was passing his house, he hailed me, and calling me in he counted me out $305 in five-dollar bills, and said, "Here is what I owe you. Now I want to know if you have found any more old fellows who don't know how to play that game of monte." Of course I laughed at the joke, and we were always good friends.

DICKY ROACH AND I.

While playing one night in St. Louis at old Mr. Peritts' game of faro, and Dick Roach was dealing, luck ran dead against me, and at every play I turned up loser, when in came a drunken man who was quarrelsome, and insisted on annoying me. I told him that I was in no condition to have anybody clawing me around. Then he got mad and wanted to fight. I said nothing, and stood it as long as I could, when I got up out of my chair, and hit him a slug in the ear that curled him up on the floor like a possum. Then

I cashed my checks and went out for a walk. I knocked around for about half an hour, and got to thinking about how much money I had lost, and resolved to try my luck again. There was no other bank open, so I went back to Peritts' game, and there, sprawled out on the floor, lay the big lubber that I had knocked over, and Roach was kneeling down by him and rubbing him with ice water and a towel, so I resolved to take another walk, when Roach, catching sight of me, said: "Devol, I guess you owe me something for taking care of your patient, and if that's the way you hit, I don't want you to hit me. I've been rubbing this fellow ever since you left."

Dick was fond of fun, and had a man who went by the name of Shell Fairchild, who he thought could throw down or whip anybody, and he was willing to put up his money on him. One night we were all in Loops' saloon, when Fairchild and Dick Roach came in. Thurston and Roach got into an argument about wrestling, and Thurston said, "I have got a man that can put your man on his back for this fifty-dollar bill," pulling out the money. Roach covered it in a minute, and then Thurston asked me if I would wrestle him. "Yes," I said.

We picked out a place, tossed off our coats, and I put him on his back in a minute. That wasn't satisfactory, and I did it again.

"Satisfied," said Roach, as he handed Thurston the money.

Sherman, poor fellow, bucked the fifty dollars right against the bank, and then, of course, Roach got it all back again, and Sherman only regretted that he hadn't stuck Roach for more.

KNOCKED DOWN $300.

Canada Bill and I were on board the steamer *Doubloon*, going up the Red River on one occasion. Bill was doing the playing, and I was driving and baiting. We had caught a nice string of fish, and had about come to the conclusion that there were no more of our kind left worth fishing for, when a nice looking young man came swimming up. We thought at first he was too small to angle for; but you can't sometimes always tell, for we found out that this one was larger than anything we had caught that evening.

He came right up, and, before we had time to put on fresh bait, wanted to bet $500 that he could turn the winner.

Bill said, "All right; I'll go you just once," and began counting out the money.

I caught a glimpse of the sucker's leather, and gave Bill the office to raise him about $4,000.

Bill then said, "I'll just raise you $3,000 if it breaks me."

The young one then turned to me and asked if I would hold the money.

I told him that I did not like to hold stakes, for one or the other must lose when two men bet, but if they had a thorough understanding, and would promise not to quarrel, I would hold the money.

The sucker replied: "I guess I understand what I'm about, and all you have to do is to give the money to the one who wins it."

"All right," says I; "but I know the loser is not as well satisfied as the winner, and I want you gentlemen to have a fair understanding. Put up your money, and I will hand it over to the one who is the lucky man."

He counted out what he thought was $3,500, but I saw it was $3,800, for I was not a bit excited, although I did not like to hold stakes.

Bill put up $3,500, for he heard me tell the young man he had up that amount. After Bill had mixed them up and said he was ready, the sucker made a dive and nabbed the card with the mark on it, but it was not the winner. I asked him if I should give up the money (just as if I did not know anything about the game).

He replied, "I made a mistake. Give him the money."

I handed it over to Bill, and said to the young man as he was walking away, " I am sorry for your loss, but some one must lose when two men bet."

He replied, " It's all right, but I thought I had a sure thing."

After we closed up, and were taking our night-cap, I said to Bill, " What do you think of our last catch?"

" Well, George, when that chap came right up and offered to bet $500, without any coaxing, I thought he was a smart one, and may be he would get the right card. I don't believe I would have raised that $3,000 if it had not been he wanted you to hold the stakes. Then I knew he was a sucker sure enough."

We had another night-cap and then went to bed. The next day we settled up, and when Bill divided the $3,800 we had won on the last shuffle, he only accounted for $3,500.

" I said, " Bill, that fellow put up $3,800."

" I guess not, George," he replied ; but I could see that he had knocked down $300 on me.

MY VISIT TO OLD BILL.

A short time after the occurrence narrated in the preceding story, Canada Bill said to me, " George, don't you think we could make big money on the wharf-boat at the mouth of the Red River, out of those Texas boys that get off there to take the Red River boats?"

I replied, " Yes, there is plenty of money there, Bill. When do you want to go up?"

I thought he wanted to stop off for a few days, as we had often done before ; but he said, " George, I am in poor health, and I want to quit the river and settle down, and I want you to be with me."

I did not blame the old fellow, for many a time we would have some pretty hard knocks and duckings in our business on the rivers and railroads ; but I was well and hearty—and then I was of a roving disposition, and enjoyed the life I was leading—so I said: "Bill, you go up there and take a rest just as long as you like; but for me, I could not think of settling down on a wharf-boat, with nothing but cow-boys to break the monotony. I'll stick to the old thing as long as they will let me, or until I get married."

I did not think just then there was any possibility of my doing the latter thing; but men don't always know just what they will do, for I am married now, and have a dear old mother-in-law, too.

"Well, George, I don't like to leave you, but I will try her just once, anyhow."

We separated. Bill went to the wharf-boat, and I began looking for another partner. A few months after dissolving partnership with my old friend Bill, I met a man from Red River who told me that Bill was making big money up there. He said, "Why, that crazy looking old fellow is running a corner grocery, livery stable, and winning all the money and horses about the landing." I was not sorry he was doing well—in fact, I was glad of it; and I resolved that I would stop off on my next trip and see him. So in a few days I was on my way up to the mouth of the Red River. When the boat landed I started off, and there stood the old fellow, just as natural as life. I would have known him among ten thousand. He caught sight of me, and then he began to stretch those long thin legs of his, and in an instant he had me by the hand, saying, "Why, George! I'll be gol darned if I haint downright glad to see you, old boy. Come right up and let's take something."

We had a few drinks, talked over old times, and to tell the truth, I was just as glad to see the old boy as he appeared to be to see me. After we had drank enough to make us feel pretty good, Bill said, "George, I've got some of the best critters in my barn that there is in this part of the country, and I won most of 'em playing the baby ticket.''

As we had been together for about an hour and had got no further than the bar, I proposed that we go to his stables and see the horses, for I was always fond of good stock. As we went into the stable, we saw a fellow sitting on a box just inside of the open doors. He looked like a bull-driver, with his large whip, slouch hat, pants in boots all covered with mud, and an old pipe in his mouth. I did not take much notice of him, as I supposed he belonged around there; and then I had come to look at Bill's fine horses.

While we were looking at the stock, some one called Bill, and he excused himself for a few moments. In a short time Bill came back, and I began asking him some questions about a horse I had been looking at; but Bill did not appear to hear me, but said, "George, did you notice that bull-driver sitting by the door as we came in the stable?''

"Yes, I saw a fellow sitting there, but I supposed he belonged around here, and I did not pay any attention to him."

"Why George! What do you think? That fellow is is out there on the box counting his money, and I'll be gol darned if he hasn't got nigh on to $10,000, for I saw him counting over the big bills until I couldn't stand it any longer, and I just came back here to get you, for I know, George, that you can get it if any man can."

I replied, "Bill, I didn't think that old tramp had any money; but if you saw it, all right. We will give him a whirl. How will we play him?"

Bill then said, "Well, George, you go and get in with him, and when you are all ready just give me the old sign, and I will come up and try the old monte on him."

"All right," said I. So I found the fellow, and began my part of the business. I inquired where he came from and all that, told him I was a planter waiting for a boat, and invited him to take a drink. While we were drinking, old Bill came up, rigged out just as I had seen him so many times before; so if the fellow had noticed him and I together when we went in the stable, he would not suspicion that Bill was the same person.

We were just taking another drink when the old crazy looking fool came up, so I said to the bull-driver, "What do you think of that fellow coming up there? Let's have some fun with him."

"All right," said he.

So I said, "Come up and join us in a drink; we are just taking one."

Bill walked up and began his talk about where he had been, where he was going, and how he had lost his money. He got out his tickets and showed us how the game was played. We bet the drinks and cigars. I lost $100, then I put a spot on the baby and won $500. The bull-driver began to get nervous, and finally offered to bet $500 he could turn over the baby.

Bill thought his time had come, so he said, " I'll just go you $5,000 that you can't turn the baby."

The driver got out his big roll and counted out $5,000. Bill counted out $4,200, but I called it $5,000.

Mr. "Bull-driver" then said to me, "If I win that money, I'm going to have it; if I lose it, all right; but I wont stand any foolishness."

Old Bill gave one of those peculiar chuckles, saying, "All right; if you win her, you shall have it." He then mixed them up as well as I ever saw him do it in my life, and when he was ready the driver made a grab and we both thought he was going for the one with the spot on it; but I be darned if he didn't grab up the one with the baby on it, just as he said he would. Then he turned to me and said, " Hand over that money, for I won it."

Bill said, " Hold on; that's one rub on me. Try it again."

Mr. Bull just yanked out a gun as long as your arm,

and drew her down on me, saying, "See here; I want that money d——d quick, for I won it fair." He then turned the big gun on Bill, and said, "Tell him to hand it over, or I be d——d if I don't blow h—l out of you d——d quick."

Poor old Bill was shaking all over, but he managed to say, "Give her up, George," He forgot himself when he called my name; but the old fellow was excited, and did not know that he was giving us both away.

I handed the fellow the money, and he walked away, saying, "I don't want any more to do with you d——d fellows, for you are in with each other."

Bill and I stood looking after the fellow until he got on the wharf-boat, then he turned to me and said, "George, I've been thinking, and I be darned if I can make out how it was he turned the baby. And, George, another thing I can't understand. I've seen more than ten guns cocked up against your head, and that's the first time I ever saw you weaken."

"Well, Bill, I tell you there was blood in that fellow's eyes, and I could see he meant business; besides, Bill, he won the money fair, and you know a fellow will fight like thunder for his own."

"All right, George; but I've always said no man living could make you give up. But I guess you was right this time, for I be darned if I didn't think he was going to let her go at me before you could hand over."

We took a drink, and then Bill went to his room to take off his make-up. While he was thus engaged, I walked down on the wharf-boat, and there was the bull-driver, waiting for a boat that was just coming in to the landing. I waited for Bill to come down; but I guess he was feeling bad; so I went up to the stable, and there he sat, on the same box where he saw the bull-driver counting his money. I went up to him and said, "Bill, I won $500 and lost $100 while we were playing that fellow, so I owe you $400"

He said, " That's right, George."

Then I said, " Bill, you only put up $4,200 against his $5,000, but I called it $5,000."

" That's right, George."

" Well, Bill, do you remember the fellow that put up $3,800 against the $3,500, and you thought I didn't know it?"

He looked all around the stable as if he was looking for the bull-driver, but he didn't say a word.

I counted out $4,200 and handed it to him, saying, " Bill, here is all your money but $300. I wanted to come up and see you ; but you know I like to have some fun at the expense of my friends, and it cost me just about $300 to rig out the ' bull-driver ' to play you for a sucker."

Bill looked at me a moment, and then said, " George, I am a sucker, for I might have known you was up to some of your old tricks."

BEFORE BREAKFAST.

After settling up with Canada Bill for the " bull-driver " racket, I said to him, " Well, old boy, you see now that we are all suckers, and can be caught if the bait is nicely handled."

" You're right, George," he replied.

Then I said, " The faro banks are my diet, and short cards have landed you many a time, but I must confess that I was a little fearful that the bait I had fixed up for you would not land a sucker ; but it did, all the same. didn't it Bill?"

" Yes, George," was all he would say.

" Well now, Bill, that we have had our fun, let's shake hands and be good friends."

He looked at me for an instant, gave one of those old chuckles, held out his hand and said, " All right, George."

We went over to the bar, and sealed the compact with a ——. He arranged his business. and we started on the war-path once more, and were together for two years after that, and made a world of money; but we were both suckers when our kind of diet was spread out before us.

At one time, after forming our new partnership, we made our headquarters at Canton, Miss., and worked the trains up and down the railroad. We made big money during the week, but on Saturday night we would run down to New Orleans, and get away with the most of it before Monday morning. We were at the Canton depot one evening when the train arrived from New Orleans, and among the passengers that got off was my old friend Jack Hardy, from Brookhaven, Miss. He was one of the best men that the sun ever shone upon, and loved to play poker better than to eat when he was hungry.

After supper we got up a game with some of the Canton boys to amuse my friend Hardy. We played along until about four o'clock, when some of the Canton boys thought I had bested them, so I quit and went to bed. Bill was not in the game, but had gone to bed early, as we were to take the up train at about six o'clock in the morning. I overslept myself, and the train had left when I reached the depot. I did not see old Bill, so I went back to the hotel. About eight o'clock I went in to breakfast.

While I was enjoying my morning meal, old Bill walked in and sat down with me, saying, "George, where was you this morning when the up train came in?"

I replied, "I was up late last night playing poker with Hardy and the Canton boys, and overslept myself; but what in the d—l have you been doing with yourself? for I walked down to the depot to find you, for I knew you would not go out without me."

"Well, George, I did go up about six miles, but could not find you on the train, so I got off and walked back."

"The h—l you did!" says I.

"Yes, George, I went up, and if you had been with me, we would have made over $3,000, for the train was full of the best suckers I ever saw."

"I'm d—d sorry, but I wanted to entertain my old friend Hardy, and that's what I get for neglecting business."

Bill then said, "George, we got $1,700 out of the trip, anyway, and here is your half."

I laughed, and told Bill he had done well to make so much, and walk six miles before breakfast. He did not need to tell me of his winnings, for I could hardly believe him when he did; but the "bull-driver" racket at the mouth of Red River had taught him a good lesson, and I believe did him good; at least it did me to the amount of $850—before breakfast.

FOOT RACE.

One day, after Bill and I had worked the morning train on the Jackson Road with that degree of success which was warranted by our prudence and perseverance, we took an afternoon train into the city, and as I was glancing through the cars I spied both of the superintendents aboard, so of course I made up my mind that there would be no playing on that train. To make the matter doubly sure, one of them came to me and said, "George, do not play any on our trains."

"Certainly not, gentlemen, and you can rest assured of that" (while you are aboard), I said to myself.

We had not traveled far when the news came that a freight train was ditched a short distance up the road. Our train stopped, and the superintendents went to the wreck on the engine. Then I saw my chance and got up a foot race among the passengers. Meanwhile Billy opened up on a log as the contestants were getting ready to run. A crowd soon collected around Billy's booth, and he garnered in 1,200 good dollars and some fine gold watches. Up came the engine, and when the superintendents heard of it, they said, "We might have known that Devol would fix up some plan to get these suckers' money."

Thus it was that I was always blamed for all the devilment that was done. I really believe if a horse had been stolen the verdict would have been: Devol did it.

FORTY MILES AN HOUR.

The train was going out of Louisville.

The rate of speed was forty miles an hour.

Ten Owen County yahoos had been beaten at three-card monte.

They pulled at long black bottles. The vacuum made by the loss of their money, they filled with whisky.

"Boys, let's have our money and watches back, or kill that gambler," shouted one of them.

Owen County boys are rough, and tough.

It's a word and a blow, and the blow first.

When in a crowd together, Owen County boys are as brave as a warrior; single-handed and alone, they are as cowardly as a sick kitten.

Canada Bill was not well, so I had been doing the playing.

Bill did the capping; and as he lost, their suspicion did not light on him.

I suddenly had an idea. I rushed back into the hind sleeper, and gave the porter a five-dollar bill. "Tell them the door is locked, and I have the key," were my words.

I was none too quick. The train was going at forty miles an hour, and was sixteen minutes behind time. La Grange was only three miles off, and well I knew that if I got off there I would have to give up.

Did I want to give up my hard-earned money? Never! Lowering my body carefully at a clear spot in the road, I jumped, took chances, broke no bones, rolled over in the dirt, and heard a shower of bullets whizzing past my ears from the fast receding train, that was soon out of sight.

Fortunately the country was not new to me, and skip-

"I jumped, took chances, broke no bones, rolled over in the dirt," etc.   [Page 204.]

ping over a fence, I avoided La Grange, and soon reached the Lexington Junction, some distance above.

"Have you heard the news?" said a switchman.

"No. What is it?"

"The Owen County boys have just killed some gamblers a short distance below La Grange."

"Glad of it," was all the response he got. Meantime I walked in towards Lexington.

At the first station I boarded a train for Lexington, put up at the hotel for a couple of days, and there revived an acquaintance with Clem Payne, clerk of the hotel, whom I had known twenty years or so ago at Kansas City.

One morning I was called for the early train for Louisville, and while waiting for breakfast I made the acquaintance of a large fat man, who was going on a stage journey afar back in the country.

We got into conversation (I was always partial to conversation with strangers), and it was not long before I showed him the big three.

He became intensely interested, and in a few moments I had his twelve fifty-dollar bills.

I did not deem it advisable to wait for breakfast, but, paying my bill, jumped into a hack and drove to the first station in time to make the train.

Before La Grange was reached, I entered the baggage-car and told the baggage-master to pile the trunks all around me. I was thus completely hid, as snug as a bug in a rug.

When La Grange was reached, there were signs of tumult about. Five of the Owen County gang were at the depot, and they boarded every train, and had been doing it for two days.

A newsboy gave me away, and told them where I was secreted. They all then remained on board and kept a regular watch over me until Louisville was reached.

The train moves slowly through the city. I quietly slipped off; not quick enough, however, for one of them espied me, and, pulling his revolver, shot—not me, but himself.

His companions all ran.

He lay upon the ground bellowing like a calf, and said I had shot him.

The police arrested me.

Mr. Shadburne was the Chief of Police. I related to him the true facts of the case.

" Release that man," he said. " I will be responsible for his appearance in the morning."

Morning came, and the Owen County desperadoes were early at the court-house with a lawyer.

They wanted to compromise for $500.

" No, sir, not for a cent."

They dropped to $100. The lawyer wanted $50. I gave them $100, and they went off with their hard-earned stuff.

BILL WOULD GAMBLE.

One of Bill's most striking peculiarities was his love for gambling. He loved gambling for its own sake, just as the moralists love virtue for its own sake. No man that I ever came in contact with ever struck me as being so fond of gambling. I have seen him give parties two points in casino and seven-up, and they would play marked cards on him. On one occasion when we had a settlement there was $375 in small gold coin, which I told him to keep and we would fix it up at some other time. No; he wouldn't have it that way. He wanted to play seven-up for it. This I positively declined, saying that when partners played together it sometimes broke friendship and gave rise to hard feelings. , But he insisted until at last I played him. We cut for deal, and he dealt. Hearts were trumps. I stood, and made three to his nothing. I dealt; he begged; I gave him one, and made three more. Thus I was six to his one. He dealt, and I picked up the queen and stood, which was high. I went out, and refused to play any more. But Bill was bound to play with somebody, so he picked up a man and gave him two points in seven-up, and they kept at it all day, until Bill lost $1,100.

NO GOOD AT SHORT CARDS.

Bill couldn't play any short card game. Monte was his hold, and the gamblers knew it. I never knew Bill to play at a short card game that he did not quit loser, and I have known him to play as long as seventy hours at a sitting. One night we were on a boat that was putting off freight at the wharf boat that lay at the mouth of Red River. Bill was in his element. He had a big pile of money up in front of him, and a large crowd intent on watching the game. Soon I noticed a fellow sitting at Bill's right who was fishing for one of the hundred-dollar bills, trying to coax it over to his side of the house. I waited patiently until he got it, then went around to him and said, "Is that the way you gamble where you live?"

"I don't know what you mean," he said, still holding his hand over the stolen bill. I gave his hand a push, and there lay the bill, which I grabbed. Then turning to Bill, I said, "You would sit here and let these ducks steal all your money. Wont you never drop to anything?"

The fellow was on his feet in a minute, shouting, "That is my money. I took it out of my pocket and was waiting for a chance to bet it."

"You lie; you were trying to steal it."

Three or four of his friends at that arose, and I knew that war was in sight; so I slipped my big gun into my overcoat pocket, and expected h—l. But just then somebody yelled "Monte!" and the mate coming up, the facts of the case were stated to him, and he said, "Everybody must keep quiet." Bill of course cleaned the crowd out, and reached the wharf-boat with a large roll of the good green stuff; but he did not keep it long, for Jack Armstrong, of Louisville, was lying there in wait for him to play casino at $50 a game.

MONUMENTAL GALL.

There are some men who, when they are caught once, like burned children ever after dread the fire. Others there are who have such overweening confidence in their own smartness that their lives are nothing but a series of losses. Canada Bill and myself were nearing Magnolia, about a hundred miles above New Orleans, when Bill opened out his three cards. It was not long before a crowd gathered about to witness the sport. One large man in particular watched the play as a hawk does a chicken. This I was not slow to perceive; so turning to Bill, I said, "What'll you bet I can't turn the baby?"

"$1,000 that no man can turn it."

I pulled out a roll that looked like $1,000, though it was not; for we had been playing bank, and were nearly busted.

Bill won, and I lost. Then he said, in his screechy voice, "By golly! you see I've got two cards to your one, and can win every time."

The big fellow was getting terribly worked up, for he knew that the corner of the baby card was turned up. Then he commenced getting out his money, and I was soon by his side.

"Can you guess it?" I innocently asked. "If you can, tell me, so I can get even."

But he was too selfish, and proposed to win it all. He offered to bet $100, but Bill wouldn't have anything but a thousand-dollar bet. Up went the money quicker than you could say Jack Robinson.

The result is easily foreshadowed. The man turned the wrong card. He made a grab, however, for the money; but I was in a second between him and the stuff, so that Bill got there first.

"There's going to be trouble, Bill," I whispered. "Get off."

He lost no time in obeying. The train was just leaving the station. The fat man followed, and chased Bill around the car. Bill jumped back; so did the fat man. Then Bill slid off again, but the fat man was at his heels. This could not last long. Bill's slim build helped him in the emergency, and again he caught the train. The fat man was unable to, but the conductor backed the cars and took him aboard.

"Where is the tramp cowboy that robbed me?' he excitedly demanded.

"He jumped off as you got on."

"I wouldn't mind the loss of the money," he said, "but the idea of being swindled out of it by such a cowboy looking kind of a tramp breaks me all up."

Where was Bill? In the sleeper was a smooth-faced young man who had taken off a cowboy suit of clothes, put on a bran new suit of black broadcloth, gold eye-glasses, clean-shaved face. This preacher-looking fellow soon came into the car where the big man and myself were talking over the loss, and sat down near us. I was busy pumping the sucker to see if he had any more money.

"Why, anybody can play that game," he said, and of course I remarked: "The dealer though has every advantage, as he has two cards to your one. If I had some cards, I would show you how it is done."

That was enough for the preacher-looking man, and, slipping back into the sleeper, he procured some cards and dropped them down into one of the seats near me. I saw them and picked them up, observing, "I believe these are the same cards."

The sucker looked at them and declared that he believed they were.

I began playing the cards, but the fat fellow said, "You are pretty good, but you can't handle them like the cowboy did."

14

" It wants practice," I said.

I practiced on, when up stepped the preacher-looking, gold-glassed individual, saying : " I'll bet you a dollar I can guess the card."

" Oh, I don't want to bet with any boy preacher," I said.

" I'm no boy preacher. I'm studying to become a priest."

" You'd better keep that dollar ; that's my advice."

I was only waiting for Bill to put a mark on the card, which he soon did while I went back to get a drink. As I came back they all began to laugh at me, and the big fellow said, " Any fool could tell the card the way you throw them."

Then I pretended to get mad ; so I offered to bet $2,000 that no man could turn the right card.

The priest spoke up, " I'll bet you $200 in gold that I can do it."

" Put it up," I replied.

This made the sucker crazy, for he was so anxious to get even that he pulled out and counted down $860. But I would not bet less than $1,000. There was a little man standing near who offered to loan him the $140 to make up the $1,000, when Bill turned and said, " I'll bet you $500 that my friend, the big man, wins."

Talk about monumental gall ; I thought then that calling the fat man his friend, who a few moments before had been chasing him around, ready to kill him, was about the grandest specimen of sublime impudence that I ever saw.

The big fellow turned the card, and lost as usual, and the little man looked at me, then at the fat man, as much as to say, you two rascals are partners. He took the priest aside, who was no other than Canada Bill, and assured him that he was positive of this fact. I won the money, and there was no kick.

CLOSE CALLS.

I never will forget the night that Canada Bill and myself were on the Michigan Southern Road, where we had been working for some time, and finally shaken down a man for $1,200. He telegraphed ahead for a warrant to arrest Canada Bill, and I knew that Bill would have to hustle, as the cars would be searched. I hurried him into the sleeper and found a top berth that was empty, while a lady occupied the lower. Her dress was laying in the top berth, and she was fast asleep in the lower one. "Bill, jump into this," I cried, holding up the garment.

He refused at first, but as the emergency was desperate, at last consented, and, tying a handkerchief around his head, his face being as smooth as a baby's, made as fine a looking woman as you would want to see.

Along came the officers with the conductor and lantern, and searched all the berths in the sleeper; but as soon as they spied the two ladies in the two berths, upper and lower, they apologized and hastily withdrew. When I was asked where Bill was, I informed everybody that he had gotten off, and I feared was seriously injured. Reaching Detroit early in the morning, Bill managed to escape from the cars unnoticed, and I got out at the depot as if nothing had happened.

Another time, on the Missouri Pacific from Kansas City to St. Louis, Bill and I succeeded in beating a Jew out of a few hundred dollars. He was a gamey little hooked-nosed son of Abraham, and, like all the rest of his class, loved money as a duck does water. So when he was on the platform he drew a pistol from his hip pocket, and resolved in an instant to die, thinking, no doubt, it was preferable for a Jew to be dead, rather than penniless.

Placing the muzzle to his mouth, he pulled the trigger. A flash, loud report, when all the passengers rushed out to see what had happened. The Jew lay on the platform bleeding at the mouth. We straightened him up, held over his head to spit out the blood, when out dropped the bullet. Two of his teeth were gone, which must have checked the speed of the bullet, as it had found lodgment in the rear of his mouth. Of course he didn't die, but he had a close call.

Bill and I made a good deal of money one night going up on the cars from Jackson, Miss., to Vicksburg. The suckers began to kick, and I saw trouble ahead, so I told Bill to hustle into the sleeper, but he sat still. I went on into the smoking car. A large man grappled Bill, and, pulling a long bowie-knife, demanded every dollar he had won, and the watches. The conductor hurriedly called me, and grabbing my Betsy Jane, I rushed back just in time to knock one of the men senseless with the butt end of the weapon, which I drew on the rest and held them at bay. This was long enough to allow Bill a chance to reach the platform, pull the bell cord, and jump off. I was not long in following, and that, too, was too close a call to be styled pleasant.

A EUCHRE HAND.

One evening I played a game of euchre on the *Great Republic* with a sucker. I gave him a big hand, and told him I could euchre him. He offered to bet $100, and I bet him $500. Up went the money, when down came the clerk, who I knew would stop the game; but quickly giving my hand to my partner, I rushed up and grabbed the clerk, good naturedly holding him until Bill had all the stuff taken. The clerk made a holy howl and a terrible kick, but I gave him the laugh, telling him that if he made me give up the money it would be taking the bread and meat out of my mouth. This amused him, and no more was said.

I was playing in a game of poker at one time, and one of the party was a friend of mine. I saw I could win some big money if I could get my friend out of the game. I tried every way I could to run him out, but he was game and would not run, so I at last ran him up a hand, and then broke him; then he retired in good order. After getting him out I started in and made the balance of the party sick in less than no time. After the game broke up, I found my friend and asked him how much he lost. He told me. I handed him the amount, saying, "I tried to get you out of the game without winning your money, but you would not go, so all I could do was to break you; but I never try to beat a friend, so I want you to have all your money back."

He thanked me very kindly, and said, "George, if you ever want a favor that is in my power to grant, do not hesitate to ask it of me, for I will be happy to grant it."

The above is one of the many similar circumstances that I have experienced during my forty years as a gambler. I always loved to play a social game with my friends, for a small limit, and I never took any advantage, unless it was for a joke, or to run a friend out, and then I would return all I had won.

BILL'S PRESENT.

My old friend and partner, Canada Bill, presented me with a very fine double-barreled shotgun, which I would often take with me when we were out on our trips. We were on the L. & N. Railroad one morning, and I had the gun with me. We had left our baggage in the ladies' car and were over in the smoker, when we saw a sucker. We went to work on him in the usual way, and it was not long until Bill had $400 of his money. I expected he would kick, from the way he was squirming around; so I gave Bill the office to get off, and I went back in the ladies' car where we had left our baggage. Old Bill was some- times slow in getting off after he had won the money, and on this occasion he was again behind time.

I had not been seated but a moment, when a brakeman came running in and told me my partner was in trouble.

I jumped up, grabbed my shotgun, and started for the smoking-car; and I did not get there any too soon, for the four-hundred-dollar sucker had Bill crouching in a seat, and was standing over him with a big gun covering him. He had given Bill but two minutes to give up the money, and Bill had out his roll counting her out. I rushed up, struck the big fellow with the new gun on the side of the head and knocked him senseless. His big gun dropped on the floor. I picked it up and stuck it in my pocket. Bill lit out as soon as he could get out of his seat, and left me to look after the big fellow on the floor. With the assistance of some of the passengers I got him up, and found he was pretty badly hurt. I told him I was sorry I had hit him, but I thought he was going to kill the old fellow.

He said, "I was only trying to scare him so he would give me back my money, as it was all I had. I could not have shot him if I had wanted to, as the pistol was not loaded."

I pulled out the old thing, and sure enough there was not a load in it. I asked the fellow what business he was engaged in, and he told me he was a ship-carpenter. As that was my father's business, I felt very sorry for him, so I gave him $100 and left the train at the next station. I learned from the brakeman that Bill had dropped off a few miles back, and I knew he would show up soon; so I left the baggage at the depot, took my gun, and made for the woods. Robbins were plentiful, and in a short time I had eight nice birds for our breakfast. I went back to the station, where I found old Bill waiting for me. He was glad to see me and the birds, so he said, "George, I'm glad I bought that gun for you, for it saved my life to-day; besides, we will have birds for breakfast."

I replied, "Yes, Bill, that was the worst fellow you ever met. He would have killed you, sure, with that big gun."

GOOD LUCK.

Canada Bill and I went over from Canton, Miss., to
Vicksburg at one time, to catch a boat for New Orleans.
We met all the boys, and had a good time while waiting
for a boat.   The Meader boys (Jesse and Aud) had fitted
up very fine faro rooms but a short time before our visit,
and they were very glad to see us.   Jesse wanted to buy
all the wine in Vicksburg for me, for he knew I was a good
producer.   After he had expended about $50 for wine, he
invited me to go down and see their rooms.   He did not
ask me to play.   He said, "Just come down, George, and
see our new place."   I went down and took a survey of
the house, and then I was introduced to the faro-table,
where "Aud" was doing the honors.   They knew well I
could not see a bank in full blast without changing in.   I
told "Aud" to give me $100 worth of checks and I would
try my luck in the new house.   I got the checks, and they
gave me a front seat so that I could bet all over the lay-out
if I so desired.   On the first deal I won out about $400.
"Aud" shuffled up again with a great deal of care, and I
started in again.   I played three deals, and then looked
up at Aud, saying, "This is too much of a see-saw, and I
guess I will quit, for I don't want to miss that boat."   I
cashed in my checks, and I had won just $1,900.   Some
of the boys laughed, but Jesse and Aud looked as sober as
Mose Wilson used to look when he was on the police bench
saying "Thirty, fifty."   The Meader boys were game to
the backbone, and although they could not laugh with the
other boys when I made my first play in their new house,
they did ask me to have some wine, and gave me a very
pressing invitation to come and see them again; for well
they knew my luck would change, and then they could
laugh as heartily as any of the boys.   They were right, for
if I had to-day the money I have lost in Vicksburg alone,
I could go into the furniture business and carry as large a

stock, on a cash basis, as any house in this country. Bill and I caught the boat for New Orleans, and I was $1,900 ahead. We made good money going down, but it was nearly all deposited in the faro bank before we left the city.

GOVERNOR PINCHBACK.

Great oaks from little acorns grow; and you can never tell the eminent position to which the little bare-footed, ragged boy may climb if he has good luck. There is Governor Pinchback, of Louisiana. He was my boy. I raised him, and trained him. I took him out of a steamboat barber shop. I instructed him in the mysteries of card-playing, and he was an apt pupil. Never shall I forget the night we left New Orleans on the steamer *Doubloon*. There was a strong team of us—Tom Brown, Holly Chappell, and the boy Pinch. We sent Pinch and staked him to open a game of chuck-a-luck with the niggers on deck, while we opened up monte in the cabin. The run of luck that evening was something grand to behold. I do not think there was a solitary man on the boat that did not drop around in the course of the evening and lose his bundle. When about thirty miles from New Orleans a heavy fog overtook us, and it was our purpose to get off and walk about six miles to Kennersville, where we could take the cars to the city.

Pinchback got our valises together, and a start was made. A drizzling rain was falling, and the darkness was so great that one could not see his hand before his face. Each of us grabbed a valise except Pinch, who carried along the faro tools. The walking was so slippery that we were in the mud about every ten steps, and poor Pinch he groaned under the load that he carried. At last he broke out:

"Tell you what it is, Master Devol, I'll be dumbed if this aint rough on Pinch. Ise going to do better than this toting along old faro tools."

"What's that, Pinch? What you going to do?"

"Ise going to get into that good old Legislature; and I'll make Rome howl if I get there."

Of course I thought at the time that this was all bravado and brag; but the boy was in earnest, and sure enough he got into the Legislature, became Lieutenant-Governor, and by the death of the Governor he slipped into the gubernatorial chair, and at last crawled into the United States Senate.

He did me a good turn when he got up in the world, and true and high honor did not dim the kindly feeling he had for me. I had been playing on the Jackson Railroad, and my luck had been good; but I was satisfied, from certain ominous signs, that a big kick was brewing. To avoid trouble I got off the train a few miles before reaching the city, and had been in town a day or two when the Chief of Police sent for me.

Of course I responded, when he told me, "Devol, you have beat one of the Police Commissioners out of $800, and he says you shant live in the city."

"I have lived in the city too many years to be run out by any one man."

Thinking it best to have this matter settled, I went to my old friend Bush, and we took a hack and drove to the executive mansion. Pinchback, my old boy, was Governor then; and though it was late at night, he insisted on calling us in, woke up all the servants, and set out a royal lunch, with all sorts of liquors, and we had a high old time. "Go to bed, George," he said, "and don't give yourself any uneasiness. I'll settle that fellow in the morning."

That was the end of the $800 Police Commissioner.

A GOOD STAKEHOLDER.

Sherman Thurston, my old friend, is dead. He has passed in his checks, shuffled his last cards, dealt his final lay-out, and been gathered to the gods. He was an honorable, great-hearted man, and I can recall the time when no living man could do him up in a rough-and-tumble fight. Cow-boy Tripp was once doing the playing for me on the Missouri Pacific Railroad; and as I saw Sherman, I said to him:

"See that conductor? I've got a little game going on here, and a first-class sucker in tow. Now the conductor is watching us very closely, and as soon as he sees him put up his money, he will walk up and stop the game. What I want you to do is to go and sit alongside of him, and entertain him until the lawful proceedings are over."

Tripp opened up the game, and the sucker put up his stuff; and sure enough the conductor made a rush to stop the game. But Sherman grabbed him by the waist and held him as you would a baby, and kept on talking all the time, telling him not to have any fuss, that he didn't want to see any trouble, etc.

Sherman Thurston was the best stakeholder in America. He was death to coat-tail pullers. He had a way of acting as if he was in a terrible passion, and coming down on their feet with a stamp that made them lie quiet.

Sherman was a man of hard sense and native resources that rendered him ready for any emergency. Once when we had won some money from a man, he began to raise a fuss and carry on like one bereft of reason. Sherman humored him. He locked him up in the car, and told everybody that he was a lunatic that he was removing to the asylum—to keep away from him, as he was dangerous and entirely irresponsible. Then when the fellow got too noisy, Sherman went and said, "See here, old fellow, you had better keep still, for gambling is a penitentiary offense in this State, and you are just as much implicated as the man who won your money."

That settled it, and the man quieted down as mild as a pet lamb.

SHE KISSED ME.

A woman's heart-rending shriek rang through the cabin of the steamer *Huntsville* one afternoon, as she lay taking in wood. I was standing on the guards watching the jolly, happy negroes as they seized the huge sticks and ran to the music of their camp-meeting hymns and piled it near the engine. Rushing back, I saw that a little girl had fallen overboard into the water. Losing no time, I jumped overboard and got ashore with the little one. When I carried her, dripping and wet, to her parents, who stood on the gang-plank, the mother caught the baby in her arms and nearly smothered her with kisses; and my turn came next, for she began to hug and kiss me, pouring forth her gratitude; but I pushed her away, as I did not want her husband to see her kiss me. The little one was taken into the ladies' cabin and dry clothes put on her, and the father came down and wanted to recompense me, but I would not have it, for I said, "I have only done what I would for any child that was drowning." Years afterwards I met the young lady and her father traveling on one of the New Orleans packets. She had grown to be a beautiful young lady, but her mother had been dead many years.

THE TRICK KNIFE.

There are a great many devices, some of which are very old, some a little more modern, and some new ones are being manufactured every day, to catch the uninitiated, all of which are more or less successful—for there are just as many suckers to-day as there were forty years ago.

I remember seeing a knife that was so constructed that the blade could not be opened without pressing upon springs. It had one spring that if pressed would allow the blade to open; and there was another spring that would lock the first one so that it would not work, and when the second spring was used, no one could open the blade with the first spring alone. Like most tricks, this knife racket took two persons to work it successfully. The one with the knife would be dressed up like a countryman, and he would go up to a person who he thought could be played for a sucker, and enter into conversation with him. Finally he would show the knife, and explain how to open the blade when locked with but one spring.

About this time the capper (a well dressed man) would come up, and the country looking fellow that owned the knife would say to the sucker, "There comes a fellow; say nothing to him about the spring, and we will win some money."

The capper would take the knife and try to open it, then he would say, "That is a dummy; it was not made to open."

The owner of the knife would then say, "Yes, it can be opened."

Then the nice man would try it again, and finally he would offer to bet that no man could open the knife in ten or fifteen minutes. The sucker would take him up; and as he did not know anything about the second spring, of course he lost his money.

I did not have any use for such contrivances, as old monte was good enough for me; but I always tried to keep posted on all the tricks and schemes, so as to be able to down the schemers at their own games.

Bill and I went on board the steamer *Bart Able*, bound for New Orleans, late one night. I was tired and sleepy, so I told Bill I would go to bed. He said he would take a smoke, and then join me. I had not been in bed but a few moments, when a black boy called me and said that my partner was in trouble in the barber shop. I was up and into my pants in a moment. I grabbed old Betsy Jane and started. When I arrived at the shop door, I saw two fellows standing over Bill; one had a big pocket-knife, the other had a poker. I did not stop to inquire what the trouble was about, but rushed in, struck the fellow with the knife, and as the fellow with the poker started to run I let him have one, and they both measured their lengths on the floor. I turned to ask Bill what the d—l the fellows were after him for, when they both jumped up and lit out. Bill said:

"Well, George, I'll tell you. Them fellows took me for a sucker, and bet me $10 that I couldn't open a big knife that they had; but, George, I knew how to open her just as well as they did, and I won their money. They wanted me to give it up; but when I saw the black boy start after you, I thought I would hold on until you came, then I knew they would get left—didn't I, George?"

"Yes, Bill; you bet you wont have to give up when I'm around."

"George, them fellows took me for a sucker. Do I look like a sucker?"

"No, Bill; you look like a nice, smart counter-hopper," I replied.

Bill laughed and said, "George, I'm $10 better off than I would have been if you had not got here just in time; let's take something and then go to bed."

The fellow dropped his big knife, which we found on the floor; so that he was out $10 and his knife by tackling—not a sucker, but one of the oldest and best sucker-catchers in the country.

TWO-FORTY ON THE SHELL ROAD.

During the war, after Ben Butler took possession of New Orleans, the city was always full of Union officers and soldiers. Money was very plentiful, and of course everything was lively. I was running the race-course and gambling games out at the lake, and was making big money. I had nineteen good horses. Some were trotters, some pacers, and some runners. I would drive out and in over the shell road, which at that time was one of the finest drives in this country. I did not allow any one to have a faster horse than myself, and generally drove a pacer, as the road was very hard, and would stove up a trotter in a short time. I had a very pretty bay mare that could pace in 2 : 30 every day in the week, and she had beaten fourteen other horses at the State Fair in 2 : 26½. I drove "Emma Devol" (the bay mare) most of the time. I had a big black horse called the "Duke of Orleans," which was faster than "Emma Devol," but I hardly ever drove him on the shell road, as I kept him for the race-track.

I was driving the "Duke" out the road one evening, when I overtook a big fellow by the name of Jim Dueane, who was a lieutenant of police at that time. He was a good, clever fellow when sober, but very quarrelsome when drunk. He was driving a good horse, and I could see he was under the influence of liquor. He asked me where I got the plug I was driving, for he did not recognize the "Duke." I told him it was an old fellow I had bought for $50 to drive on the road, as I did not want to stove up my race-horses. We were about two miles from the lake, when he offered to bet me a bottle of wine he could beat me to the lake. I took him up, and we started. I let him get a little ahead, so I could see how his horse moved.

We were going along in this way for the first mile, when he looked back and said, "Come on, Devol, or you will have to pay for the wine."

I replied, "All right, I will do it, as I do not want to lose the bet."

I gave "Duke" the word, and he got right down to business and passed Dueane so quick that he did not know what to make of the old plug. After I got about 100 feet ahead of him, I looked back and told him to come on or he would have to pay for the wine. He tried very hard to catch me, but it was no use, as "Duke" was not that kind of a horse.

I was at the lake, out of my wagon, and had the blanket on the "Duke of Orleans," when Dueane drove up. I could see that he was not in good humor. He got out and hitched his horse, and then we walked over to the hotel to get the bottle of wine. I began laughing at him, and wanted to know what he thought of the "Duke" as a $50 plug, when he let drive at me. I ducked my head, and he hit it a pretty hard lick. I started for him, but some of the officers jumped in between us and put a stop to the fight, and in a little while he apologized and we were drinking together. I could have whipped him, for I was in my prime at that time; but I was glad they separated us, as I did not want to have any trouble with the police.

While we were drinking and talking about the race, a great big colonel of a New York regiment, who was pretty drunk, spoke up and said, " I can whip any man that will do anything to Dueane."

I knew he had reference to me; but the room was full of shoulder-strapped fellows, and I did not want any of his chicken pie just then, so I paid no attention to his remarks. He kept on with his abuse, and I was just itching to get at him, but knew I would not stand a fair show unless some of my friends should drop in, which I expected they would do before long, as it was a little early for the town boys.

In a short time a friend of mine, by the name of Joe Summers, and a crowd of New Orleans boys came in. Then I knew I would have a fair show, so I walked up to the big colonel and said, " You are a big lubber, and can't fight just a little bit."

Up went his hands, but before he could lead off I gave him one under the chin, and he measured his length on the floor. My friends were all around us in an instant, and Joe Summers said that it should be a fair fight. I was ready to give him my head when he got up, but the big lubber said, " That will do."

In ten minutes after I knocked him down we were drinking wine together, and no one would have thought we ever had a difficulty. He was so big that he thought

he could bluff me; but he did not know that I was about
the worst man in that part of the country at that time to
bluff at any game, more especially at the game of fight—
for I would rather have fought than not, and I did not think
there was a man living in those days that could whip me in
a rough-and-tumble.

We had several bottles of wine on the strength of our
little misunderstanding. The result was, we were all feeling pretty good and liberal, and I do believe we opened
200 bottles of wine before 2 o'clock.

There were about seventy-five teams hitched around the
hotel, and I knew when their owners started home they
would get to racing on the shell road, and some of the
horses and buggies would get hurt; so I told a stable-boy
to put my horse up, and I would wait until morning. A
few of the others did the same thing, but the balance
started, and some of them were so drunk that they could
not see the road, although it was as white as marble. The
next morning after I had eaten my breakfast I had my team
brought out, and started for the city. The wine of the
night previous had done its work, for I saw seven buggies,
or parts of them, strewn along the road. Dueane had
run into the toll-gate, and came near killing himself and
his horse.

Wine is a great worker when one gets too much of it
inside. It gave employment to the buggy-makers, and put
me to bed on that occasion; and I was glad of it when I
saw the wrecks it had made of my boon companions of the
night before.

A MILE DASH.

About the time referred to in the preceding story, the
livery business was very good in New Orleans, and some
of the livery-men kept quite fast horses, which they would
let out to persons they knew would not abuse them. My
old friend Dick Barnum was running a stable in those

days, and is in the same business to-day; but he is getting old now, like myself, and I suppose he goes to church regularly ever Sunday instead of going out to the race-track, as he and I did twenty-five years ago.

I was at Dick's stable one day when he was feeling pretty good, and he began bragging on a horse that he had, and which he called "Tom Parker." I let him blow for some time, when I said to him:

"Dick, you don't weigh more than 140 pounds, and I weigh over 200. I'll tell you what I will do. I will hitch my black horse to a skeleton wagon and put on a bag of sand weighing 150 pounds. You can hitch Tom to a sulky and we will drive our own horses, and I will bet you $250 that I can beat you one dash of a mile around the track."

He said, "Put her up."

We put up the money in Johnnie Hawkins' hands, and agreed to pace that afternoon. The news of the race spread rapidly, and there was a large crowd at the course to see the sport. Henry Foley was in the judge's stand, and we were all ready. The bets were about even, although my horse was handicapped with four wheels to Dick's two-wheeled sulky, and besides I had 350 pounds to his 140. We tossed up for the pole, and Dick won. We went up the stretch and came down for the tap, but Dick wanted the best of it, and was about ten lengths ahead when he went under the wire. I nodded to Henry, so he let us go. Dick went flying from the start, and I eased my horse around the first turn, so that when I got straightened up on the back stretch Dick was 100 yards ahead. The betting was then $100 to $5 in favor of Dick, as they all thought that I could never close up that big gap. I gave old "Duke" one cut across the back, and he went down that stretch like a race-horse, sure enough. We came around the next turn, and when I got square into the home stretch I gave the horse a war-whoop, and we went past Dick so fast that he thought he was tied to the fence. I went under the wire about ten lengths ahead of Dick, and the fellows that had taken some of the $100 to $5 bets raised the yell and kept it up until you would have thought they were a pack of wild Indians. My friend Johnnie Hawkins took all the bets that he could get in that short time.

Dick did not blow about "Tom Parker" any more after that, and when I would ask him if he wanted another race, he would say, "No, George; I would rather take a drink;" and that was about all I was ever able to get out of him. I hope to see the old fellow alive and happy the next time I visit New Orleans; for he is a good, clever fellow, and I hope he will live as long as I do—and I expect to live forever.

MULE THIEVES.

During the time I was running the race-course and my games at the lake I was taken down with the yellow fever, and was confined to my bed for about twenty days. I was about well, and had been sitting up for a few days, when my horse-trainer, and a friend of mine by the name of George Leonard, called to see me; and as I was feeling so much better, they wanted me to go out to the track and time one of my pacing horses with a running mate. So I muffled myself up in a big overcoat and went out. I sat in the buggy and held the watch, but when they came to ask me what time had been made, I was lying in the bottom of the buggy. They took me back to my room, and I was just as sick as I had been any time during the fever. I had the best physician in New Orleans, and he said, after I was out of danger, that if it had not been for my iron constitution he could not have pulled me through. I felt the effects of my last attack with yellow-jack for two years afterward, and I am not afraid of it to-day.

A short time after getting well of the fever, I was at the livery stable early one morning where I kept some of my horses. The stable was owned by my friends William and George Leonard, and they were large dealers in horses and mules. When I arrived the boys were red-hot, for they had sold twenty head of good mules to some fellows the evening before, and had allowed them to put the mules on board of a little boat lying at the landing, on the promise that they would pay the money as soon as the bank opened the next day. The boys had been down to the landing, and had found that the boat and mules were gone. They wanted me to go with them and catch the thieves, so we armed ourselves with pistols and double-barreled shotguns, took a fast packet, and started. About forty miles above the city we saw the little boat lying at the levee, but as we passed, it could be seen that there were no mules on board. We went up about a mile, and then got off and started back a-foot. When we got near the little boat, we saw the mules in a pasture. We "let" down the fence and started to drive them out, when the fellows saw us and came off to stop us. I told the boys to take the mules and I would take care of the d——d thieves. They were coming with their guns out. I pulled my shotgun down on them and told them to halt, which they did. When the boys got the mules on the run up the levee, I followed them, and the thieves followed me. They ran us up into a little town, when they got out a replevy and took the mules. We had a trial and won the case, so we put our mules on a boat and were soon back in New Orleans. The Leonard boys get the money now before they let the stock go aboard a boat.

AN HONORABLE MAN.

Some men are the soul of honor, and if they lose a bet will walk right up to the captain's office and settle; while others are fast enough to make bets, take chances, and all that sort of thing, but when it comes to paying their losses, if there is a hole to crawl out of, they are the very men to do it.

Coming out of New Orleans one time on the steamer

Peerless, I was open for business, waiting for somebody to try his luck, when, looking around, I espied one of the leading dry goods merchants of the Crescent City, whose place of business was on Canal Street. He asked me the kind of game I was running, and I explained it to him, when my capper came along, and, looking on, made a bet for the drinks that he could turn the jack. The capper won, and we had the drinks all around, when he took the jack and turned up a corner, taking care to let the merchant see what he had done. Then he began bantering me to bet with him. I persisted that I had the best of it, as I had two chances to his one, and was dead sure to win two out of three times. The merchant had often seen me playing short cards and rouge et noir. We kept up a running conversation for some time, till at last I told him that I had never run a game I would not bet on, except this one. Then the capper offered to wager $100 that he could turn the right card.

"Put up your money," was all I said, and I handed mine to the merchant.

Sure enough, he turned the right card, and I unconcernedly remarked, " Well, you got her."

Then the merchant wanted to bet me $100 that he could turn the right card, when I replied:

"I will make just one bet with you for $500."

He began going through his pockets, and only found $425; so I said:

"I'll back out, as I do not know much about the game, anyhow; but if there is any other game you want to bet on, why, I am your man." Continuing, I said: "Any other game but this one, I will bet $10,000 on. I pride myself on betting as big as anybody."

"This is the first time I ever knew of your backing out," replied the merchant.

The capper then offered to bet $500, and began to abuse me. He put up his money, guessed the right card, and of course won.

Things were now getting exciting, and my merchant friend was very warm under the collar, and wanted to bet me the $425; but I wouldn't have it, and said in a majestic manner:

"No, sir; nothing less than a cool thousand, as I am now a big loser."

The capper offered to loan the merchant some money to make up the balance, but I would not allow it. At last he put up his watch and diamond pin, and went to turn the jack. Of course he lost. Afterwards he came to me and gave me a check for $1,000, and I returned him his jewelry and money. We stopped for half an hour at one of the landings, and he slipped off and countermanded the payment of the check by telegraph. When I presented the check at the bank I was shown the dispatch, and to this day the check has never been paid, though the merchant still does business on Canal Street. He was an honorable, high-toned merchant.

MY PARTNER WON.

Dunlap and I got on the steamer *Paragoad* one evening at Baton Rouge, and seeing no one on board that I though was of any particular service to me, I got a bottle of wine and a good cigar and was sitting in the hall, when a coal merchant whom I knew very well in Baton Rouge came along, and seeing me said:

"Devol, this is rather a slim trip for your business."

Laughingly I replied, "Yes."

"But that don't hinder us from taking a drink together, does it?"

"I have just had one, thank you."

He insisted, and I did not hang back; so, after smoking, we sat down near the bar, when he remarked that this was the first boat he ever was on where they didn't have a game of poker. I thought myself it was something strange, as in those days everybody played cards. At last

we got to throwing for the drinks, when he finally remarked that if there were one or two more around we
might have a game of poker. Though I said I didn't care
to play, as I was sleepy, yet he persisted. Along came
Dunlap, whom he did not know, and I asked him if he
ever played poker. He replied a little, when he was at
home in Illinois.

"Come on, then, and take a drink," said the coal man.

I gave Dunlap the wink, and excusing himself for a
moment he went to his room, and procuring a pack of
marked cards gave them to the barkeeper. When he came
in, the coal man at once began:

"Sit down, and we'll make up a game."

Then Dunlap asked the barkeeper for some cards, and
of course the marked pack was handed out. It was then
half-past 12 o'clock. We started in at a $20 limit, and
played until the table was needed for breakfast. The coal
man and myself were both losers. He said he lost $2,300.
I lost $900, but as I lost it to my partner, I was not broken-
hearted.

HAUNTED.

One night, anxious to reach New Orleans, I took a
stern-wheel boat out of Wichita; and as it was late, the
clerk said the only berth he could give me was in a state-
room with another man. I crawled into the top berth, and
towards morning I was awakened by a noise beneath me.
Carefully looking over the berth, I spied the occupant of
the lower berth with a long Colt's navy revolver in his
hand. His hair was disheveled, and his eye was wild,
while his actions indicated that he was hunting for somebody. I lay very quiet, however, thinking that he was
either a victim of delirium tremens or a lunatic. At last
he arose and opened the door and went into the cabin,
the only occupants of which were the porter and the
watchman. They lost no time in leaving, when they saw

a man clad only in a night-shirt and drawers, with a drawn revolver in his hand.

I arose and dressed, as I had had enough of such a room-mate; and on telling the clerk of the facts, he said:

"That's strange, for I knew the man very well. He never drinks, but he has killed three men."

That settled it with me. He was haunted by the ghosts of his murdered victims.

McCOOLE AND COBURN.

When the McCoole and Coburn fight came on, I left New Orleans for the purpose of witnessing the sport. On reaching Cincinnati, John Franklin invited me to go over to Latonia Springs and see Coburn. I did so, and spent a pleasant afternoon with him. He invited me to come over and keep him company; and as I thought I could turn an honest penny as well as have a little recreation, I packed up my faro tools and went into the dark and bloody ground back of Covington. When any strangers came along, I opened up and caught all that was in sight.

As the time for the fight drew near, a number of Coburn's friends came on from New York. They were glad to see him in such good heart and spirits. They came with a good deal of money to back him up; and as the boys had to do something to while away the weary hours, Joe introduced them to my partner, saying that he was a New Orleans gentleman who had come on to aid me in money matters. Joe called him a planter, and the New Yorkers were so pleased with him that they invited him into a game of poker. The result was that he did them up for a few hundred, and one of the party, who was an old faro dealer, secured a few of the cards, examined them in another room, and coming back, observed:

"Count me out of this game. I don't want any more of it."

That broke things all up; and the next day they began

on Coburn and gave him a terrible cursing for steering them against such a game as that, when they came out with good intentions to back him in the fight. They never said anything, however, to Hoy, as they knew he was always looking for the best of every game, and was as ready to fleece a friend as a foe.

When we were going down to Cold Spring, I opened up on the cars and won a little money. Just then a man stepped up and began to get out his money, when Elliott and his gang rushed in, picked up the fellow, and threw him up against the top of the car. When he came down he didn't have a cent. I was amused to see him hunt around for his money.

When we reached the ground I opened out, having a negro to hold the stand for me. At last, as the crowd began to rush for the ring, I told Hoy that I would go and see the fun; so I handed Hoy all my money except a lot of broken bank-notes that I had. This I rolled in a large wad and placed conspicuously in a side coat pocket. I noticed, as I edged close up to the ring, that I was closely eyed by the thieves, and it was not long before the pocket-book disappeared. Then I made a terrible squeal, and when the reporters came around I gave out that I had been robbed of $3,500. The next day the papers all had an account of the robbery of Mr. Devol, of New Orleans. Hazen at last found my pocket-book, which was worth more than the money it contained, and had a good advertisement free.

SALTED DOWN.

If the old saying, "Every man has his price," be true, then every man can be caught on some scheme or trick. There are persons who have never made a bet of any kind in their lives, that would do so if they saw something that they knew to be a sure winner. Then there are others who will bet on many things, but they pride themselves on being too smart to bet on any man's trick; and the more they see others doing so, the more sanguine they are that no one could ever catch them with chaff. I have met many of the latter class, and always tried to down them. They, of course, would not bite at the monte bait, for it was too stale for them; so I would study sometimes for hours how to take the conceit out of them.

I remember being on board the steamer *Grand Duke*, coming out of New Orleans, at one time just after the Mardi Gras Festival. The boat was crowded with passengers, and we were having a very lively game of monte, when a fellow from the Red River country, named Picket, came up to the table and began pulling coat-tails. He was one of those smart Alecks who knew all the tricks (or at least he thought he did), and he imagined that it was his especial duty to warn others of their danger. If he could not stop them with a tail pull, he would tell them not to bet, as I was a regular gambler and would win their money sure when they thought the sure thing was in their favor; and some of them would not heed his warning, but put down their money, and of course lose it.

I put up with Picket's interference for some time, and then I put up my cards, resolving to down the Red River man if it lay in my power. I invited all hands to join me in a drink, and then excused myself, saying:

"I'm suffering with the toothache, and will go to my room."

In a short time I returned and took a seat in the hall near the stove, as it was quite chilly. Mr. Picket and a number of other gentlemen were seated around, and we soon got to telling stories. My tooth ached so badly that I could not enjoy the stories, and was constantly complaining of the pain. A great many remedies were suggested, but they could not be had on the boat. Finally the barkeeper recommended hot salt held on the side of the face. I asked him if he had any. He said no, but I could get it in the pantry. I got up and went for the salt.

I returned in a short time with a package of salt about the size of a goose egg, which was twisted up in a piece of paper. I put it on the stove, and when it got hot I held it to my face until it cooled off, then I put it back on the stove.

While the salt was getting hot a second time, I went to my room to get something. The barkeeper said to the crowd:

"Let's have some fun with Devol."

So saying, he opened the package, threw out the salt, and filled up the paper with ashes. I came back, picked up my salt, and held it to my face. Picket asked me if it was doing my tooth any good. I told him I thought it was. Then they all laughed at the idea of hot salt being good for the toothache, and Picket said:

"Devol, do you know that when salt gets hot it will turn into ashes?"

"No, I don't. What do you take me for? You must have been drinking," I replied.

They all laughed again, and Picket spoke up, saying:

"I don't believe you have any salt in that paper."

I set the package on the stove again, and replied:

"You must take me for a d——d fool, sure enough; but you don't look like you had any more sense than the law allows. I got that salt out of the salt-bag, and I tasted it before I wrapped it up, and I know it is salt, and that settles it."

"But, Devol, salt does turn to ashes when it is hot; and I will bet you the drinks for the crowd that there is no salt in that paper on the stove."

Then they had another big laugh at my expense, and I got mad. I jumped up and said:

"I will bet you $500 that there is nothing in that paper but salt."

Picket jumped up also, saying:

"I will just go you once, anyway."

I put up my $500 with the barkeeper; but Picket did

not have but $350, and he wanted to bet that. I told him he could back out, but I would not bet less than what I had up. Then he put up his watch and chain for the other $150. One of the men that had been enjoying the fun, said:

"I will bet you $100 that Mr. Picket wins the money."

I replied, "I will not bet less than $500."

Then Picket said, "He wants to bluff you out; but he can't bluff me worth a cent."

So the man put up his $500, and I covered it. Everybody was excited, and some of my friends who had seen the trick that was being played on me told me not to bet; but I was mad, and would not listen to them.

When all was ready, the package was taken off the stove and handed to the barkeeper. He untwisted the paper and spread it out on the counter, and in it was as nice fine white—salt as you ever saw in your life.

The barkeeper tasted some of it, just as I did when I put up the *two* papers *just* alike, and then handed me over the money and Mr. Picket's watch and chain.

Mr. "Red River" took a large pinch of the bait, and it (or the loss of his money and watch) came near strangling him. He did not entirely recover from the effect while he remained on the boat; for every time he was well enough to come out of his room, some one would say "Salt," and that would make him sick again.

I have caught a great many suckers in my time, but Mr. Picket was the first one I ever salted down.

THE ARKANSAS KILLERS.

For many years I almost lived on board the packets. I felt more at home on any of the Mississippi steamboats than I did on land in any city or town in the United States. I had friends wherever I went, and I knew every officer and many of the crew on nearly every boat that ran the river. While on water, I did not fear any man or set of men; but there were localities on land along the Mississippi

River that no man could hold his own with the rough element that lived around them. So I always gave such places a wide berth.

Helena and Napoleon, Ark., were two towns where it was not safe for any man to do the bluff act, for they would kill him just to see him kick. I won some money from one of Helena's killers at one time on board a steamer, and he set up a big kick; but as he was alone, he was like all men of his class—a coward. I well knew if he caught me on his ground I would get the worst of it, so I resolved never to give him a chance; but one evening I was compelled to get off at Helena, as things had gotten a little too warm for me on board the boat, and I thought I would run the risk of the killers rather than give up the money I had won at that time. I went up to the hotel to get my supper and wait for another boat, and one of the first men I met was the fellow I had beaten out of his money. I knew there would be trouble, so I put Betsy Jane in a handy place, resolving to use her for what she was worth if the killers got after me. I did not leave the hotel until the boat arrived; and just about the time I was starting out, the clerk told me that some of the gamblers had beaten one of the worst men in the country on a boat, and he was down at the landing with a crowd of his roughs, waiting to do him up.

There was a lot of persons waiting for the same boat, among them some gamblers. I told the clerk to send for a carriage, and I would not go down until just as the boat was about to leave. All the others left the hotel and started for the landing before the boat came in. The killers jumped on to the poor gamblers, supposing of course that I was among them. They beat them up fearfully, and came near killing one of them. During the excitement I was driven to the plank and jumped out, and was on board before any one recognized me. When the killers learned that I had given them the slip, they were determined to board the boat and get me; but the mate got his crew on the guards and would not let any of them on board. The boat backed out at once, and I was again at home among my friends; and you can bet I was glad of it, for I think that was one of my close calls.

CHEAP JEWELRY.

Before the war, there was hardly a boat of any size that plied up and down the Mississippi and its tributaries that did not count among its travelers or passengers some peddler with his pack. For the most part, his stock in trade consisted of cheap jewelry, gilded sleeve-buttons, galvanized watches, plated chains, various notions and unassortable knick-knacks. Sometimes these peddlers carried along a wheel, and had the things marked with numbers corresponding to those on the wheel. The charge was a dollar a spin, and at whatever number the wheel stopped, the article corresponding belonged to the investor in the game.

Captain Dix was then in command of the *Hiawatha*, a packet running from New Orleans to St. Louis. One evening Captain Dix said:

"George, I have got one of those infernal wheel peddling chaps aboard, and he has been annoying the life out of me. I've driven him out of the cabin, and he has taken refuge in the barber shop. I wish you could take him in."

Strolling down towards the barber shop, I caught a glimpse of the fellow; and being satisfied that he did not know me, I watched his game for some time, and then ran against it $5 worth.

"That's a heap fairer game than I lost $1,000 at," I said to the owner.

"What game was that?" he curiously asked.

"The fellow called it Rocky Mountain euchre. I'll go and get you some of the tickets, and show everybody how the fellow chiseled me out of my money."

"Oh, that's three-card monte," said the wheel man.

Alexander was along with me; so I began throwing the

cards around awkwardly, when my partner stepped up to the table and began guessing for fun. Finally he bent one of the corners and showed it to the wheelman, whispering to him.

"Let's have a little fun out of the old fellow."

Aleck told me to mix 'em up, and offered to bet the drinks that he could turn up the old woman.

"I've got two chances to your one," I replied; "but I'll go yer."

He turned the wrong one, and I laughed, as did the wheel man. Aleck then began blackguarding me, saying that I dare not bet on it; that he did not believe I had any money; till at last I pulled out a bundle that made the wheel man look wild. Aleck kept on daring me, so at last I bet him $100 that he couldn't find it the first time after I had done mixing them. Then he made the bet, putting the money up in the wheelman's hands; and sure enough, he turned the old woman. Then I offered to bet him again for $200, and he turned it a second time. Then I pretended to drop on him, and refused to bet, saying "that his eyesight was too fine;" but he offered to bet me "that the wheel man could do it." I replied that I'd bet any amount that he couldn't, unless he told him how. This settled the wheelman, who said that he could turn the right card for $100.

"But I am already a loser for more than that, and I wont bet now for less than $500."

He began counting out his roll, but could only make out $430. He was wearing a $100 watch and chain, and Aleck whispered to him to put up that for the remaining $70. This he did, and I soon raked them in, as of course he got the wrong card. The fellow looked a little blue, but Aleck made him believe that he had in his hurry picked up the wrong card. So the fellow was bound to have revenge, and he put up his jewelry and wheel, all of which I soon won.

When Captain Dix came around, he was so overjoyed

that he set up the wine and had a hearty laugh over it. I gave the fellow $50 and paid his passage back to St. Louis, while his jewelry I gave to a lame fellow that I knew in New Orleans, and it was a start in life for him.

The next morning, before the story of the jewelry man had gotten out among the passengers, we took in two or three suckers, and were intending to get off at Baton Rouge; but noticing several good men getting aboard, determined to try our hands on them. The fates were propitious, for we won $1,400 and a watch from one of them, and the other was plucked for $700 and a $200 diamond pin. I afterwards learned that they were both wealthy men who had been up to see the Governor, so the trifling loss of their pocket money did not affect them.

WON AND LOST.

We had been playing monte at one time in the bar-room of the old Prentis House at Vicksburg, Miss., and had just closed up, when in came four fellows that lived back in the country. We thought they had some money, so we opened up again to take it in. It was not long until we had all of their cash stuff. Then one of them pointed out a fine horse that was hitched with three others out at the rack, and wanted to bet me the horse against $200. The others then said they would do the same thing, so I put up $800 against their four horses, and they selected one of their party to turn the card. He turned and lost. I sent a black boy to put my horses into the stable, and he started with two of them, when two of the fellows rushed out, jumped onto the other two horses, and went up the hill as if the d—l was after them. I sent word to them by the other two that if they ever came back to Vicksburg I would have them arrested for stealing the horses. I did not wait to see if they ever did come back, but sold the two horses I had left for $300, and took the next boat for New Orleans.

There was a poor woman with six children on board the

boat, and she did not have any money to pay her passage, so we passed the hat around, and every person on the boat that was told about the poor woman chipped in something, except one stingy fellow. We took the money to Captain Leathers, as we were on his boat; but he refused to accept one cent for her passage, and told us to give the money to the woman. He gave her a state-room, and treated her as if she was paying full price for her passage. After the poor woman and her children had been taken care of, we opened up monte, and one of the first fellows we caught was the man who would not chip in to help the poor woman and her little children. We downed him for $800, and he kicked like a government mule. He went to the Captain, who had been told how mean he had been, so he got no sympathy from him or any one else. The passengers called him "Old Stingy," and asked him if he was not sorry he had not given something to the woman before he lost his money. It always did me a great deal of good to down a stingy man, for I knew he would soon have more, even if he had to starve himself to get it.

DETECTIVES AND WATCHES.

Tripp and I were playing the trains on the **Missouri Pacific** Railroad at one time. We had been out on the road, and were on our way back to St. Louis, and had got away with all the suckers on the train. I was enjoying a smoke in the sleeper, when a nice looking gentleman came in. I offered him a cigar, telling him I was in the tobacco business at New Orleans. We talked cigars, tobacco, etc. I learned he was a United States detective from Arkansas, on his way to Washington City. While we were talking and smoking, in came Tripp dressed up like a cow-boy. He told his story, and finally caught the fellow for $1,000. The detective did not do any kicking until we got to St. Louis, then he went to the chief of detectives, who was at that time a Mr. Horrigan. He told the chief how we had robbed him, and wanted us arrested. Mr. Horrigan was a sensible man, and knew that the sucker expected to win our money, or he would not have lost his. So he told him that his experience was worth what he had lost, and that he had no time to hunt up gamblers. The detective went on to Washington City a sadder but a wiser man. I always enjoyed taking in detectives, for they think themselves too smart to be caught. They are but human, and like other mortals can be landed for suckers if the bait is good and nicely handled.

At another time on the same road we met a new conductor, or at least we supposed he was a new one, as he did not know us, or we him. When we started to play our game he broke back to the sleeper, and I found out from the porter that he went to the superintendent and told him here was a lot of gamblers in the smoker, and asked him what he should do. The superintendent was something like Mr. Horrigan, the Chief of Detectives of St. Louis, for he told the conductor to look after his train and let the gamblers look after the suckers, as he did not care if they lost all their money, for they would not bet if they did not expect to win. I inquired the name of the superintendent, for I thought he must be a brother of Mr. Horrigan, but his name was different. We downed several fellows. The conductor looked on, but did not say a word. I learned that he was a freight conductor, and had never run a passenger train before, so I excused him for wanting to interfere; and as I had now a few good watches, I let him have one very cheap, and he appreciated my kindness. Speaking of watches, I had orders from a great many persons to win them certain kinds of watches. So when I got one to suit the order I would take it to my customer in place of the pawn shops. My old friend, Simon McCarthy, of Indianapolis, had given me an order to win him a good watch. So one day, going into the city, I downed a gentleman for some money and his watch. When I got to Indianapolis I went to see Simon, and told him I had a watch I thought

16

would suit him. He looked at it, and when he opened the back case he threw up both hands and said:

"Why, George, this is our Mayor's watch. Where did you get it?"

I told him I won it coming in on the train, and described the man. He told me it was the Mayor, and advised me to return it to him. I learned where he lived, went to his house, rang the bell, and asked to see the Mayor. He came out to the door, and I handed him his ticker. He asked me to come in, and told me to say nothing about it, and if he could ever do me a favor he would do so. I did a good thing for myself that night, for it was but a short time after that until I was arrested and taken before his Honor. He let me off with a big fine, and after my prosecutors were gone he remitted the fine, and we then had a drink together. I wanted to return what little money I had won from him, but he would not receive it, saying it was well invested.

FIGHTS.

Before the time of railroads in the West, the steamboats on the Ohio, Mississippi, Missouri, and other rivers carried a great many passengers, as it was the most pleasant and rapid mode of travel in those early days. I was on board of some water craft nearly all the time for forty years of my life, and during that period met with a great many rough characters. I believe that I can truthfully say I have had more fights in the cabin and bar of steamboats than any other man in this country. I never tried to pick a fuss with any man; but in my business it was very hard to avoid them without showing the white feather—and in those days there was no such tint in my plumage. The officers did not like a fuss on their boats, but most of them had rather see a fellow fight than to take an insult; and I can not call to mind just now a single case, in all my many fights, where the captain of a boat blamed me for licking my man; but I do remember some good old captains who would rather see a fight than eat when they were hungry.

I always carried the very best pistol that could be bought for money, and had one that I called "Betsy Jane," for which I paid $100. I never wanted to turn her loose, for I did not want ever to kill a man. I only used her as a bluffer, and she has often responded to my wants successfully.

I was on board the steamer *Kate Kinney* coming down the Missouri River at one time, and had won a great deal of money. One big fellow lost $700, and I could see he was very mad about it. He would go to the bar and take a big drink, and then come back to the table. Finally he got himself nerved up pretty well, so he said to the bystanders:

"I have a d——d notion to kick that table over and break up his game."

I replied, "It will do you no good to kick the table over, as I have caught all the suckers, and am now going to quit and take a drink."

I started to the bar, and invited all hands to join me. The big fellow followed, but would not take a drink. I could see he was sizing me up, and I knew he wanted some of my mutton, so I said to him:

"We have all had a drink but you; wont you join me?"

He replied, "I can buy my own drinks, and you can go to h——l."

I did not reply to him, but walked out into the cabin. He followed me out, for he knew he had me afraid of him by my not resenting the insult. He got up pretty close and said:

"If you did get my money, I can lick you."

I told him he had better find an easier fight, when he let fly at me. I was on my guard, caught his lick on my arm, and then I lit into him, and we had it rough-and-tumble all around the hall. We came near upsetting the stove; but I had him whipped in about two minutes, and he squealed like a pig under a gate.

At another time I was coming down the Missouri River from St. Joseph to St. Louis, and had beaten a fellow out of $40. He was a rolling-mill man from St. Louis, and I found out he could hit a pretty hard lick. I was playing a game of euchre in the hall after closing up monte, when this fellow slipped up and hit me a lick on the side of the neck that came near flooring me. I rallied and was on my guard in an instant. He came at me again, and we had it up and down and around the cabin for some little time before I could get a crack at him with my head. When the old head did get a chance, it was not long until he cried quit. The Captain and every one who saw the fellow hit me from behind said they were glad to see him get licked, and so was I.

At another time I was in a game of poker on the steamer *Telegraph* coming up from Madison, Ind., and there was a big blacksmith in the game who was very quarrelsome. He wanted to fight every time he would lose a dollar, so I ran him up a hand and then broke him. He left the game and went into the bar. My old friend Jake Bloom had the bar at the time. The big fellow told Jake he was going to whip that fellow they called Colonel when the game was over. Jake told him he could get a much easier fight, if he wanted to lick some one. He replied:

" Why, I can lick that fellow in a minute."

I was sitting where I could hear what he said; so, as there was very little more money in the party I was playing, I left the game and went into the bar-room, and said to the blacksmith.

"Come, old top, and join me in a drink, for I beat you on that last hand."

He replied, " I don't drink with such fellows as you."

He had hardly got the words out of his mouth before he was lying on the floor, for I gave him a lick under the chin that straightened him out. As he was getting up, I let the

old head go, and down he went again. He said, " That
will do ;" so I let up on him. He went to his room, and
did not leave it until the next morning, when he had to be
led off the boat, as he could not see. He swore out a warrant for my arrest ; but when the policeman came to get
me, the clerk told him I had left the boat. That was the
last I ever heard of my big blacksmith.

THE ENGLISHMAN AND HIS GUN.

Every nationality has its suckers, and it would be pretty
hard for me to decide which has the most, for I have, in my
time, downed them all. I was on board the steamer *Great
Republic* at one time when there was a number of English
lads among the passengers. They had come over to this
country to hunt the buffalo, and had brought their guns
with them. I got acquainted with them, as they were often
in the bar-room after the bloody, blarsted wine, and they
liked to talk about Old h'England and their fine guns, you
know. I got one of them to show me his gun, and I think
it was the finest piece I ever saw. Each gun had two sets
of barrels, and had the owner's name engraved on it, inlaid
with gold, and not one of them cost less than $500. I tried
to buy one but it could not be done. One night after my
partner had gone to bed I was in the bar-room, when one
of the English lads came in. He had been in bed, but got
up to get a blarsted drink, and he invited me to join him,
which I did, and then I insisted on him joining me in a
small bottle. We drank three bottles, then I excused myself, and sent for my partner to get up and come to the bar-
room. I then began telling the English lad about a new
game, and finally I got out the tickets and was showing
them, when my partner came in about half asleep. He,
like the English lad, had been in bed and had got up to get
a drink. He invited us to join him, as he did not like to
drink alone. We accepted, and as the lad was feeling
pretty good by this time, he could not let a gentleman treat

without returning the compliment, you know. My partner and the lad got to guessing for fun, and then proposed to wager the wine. I lost a bottle, and so did my partner. While we were drinking my partner put a crimp in the baby ticket, but took good care that the English lad saw him do it. Then he wanted me to bet money on the game, and I said:

"I have two chances to your one, and could win all your money if we would bet."

The Englishman laughed, and said:

"Why, lad, you 'aven't a bloody bit of a chance; you would lose every blarsted cent you 'ave if you bet."

My partner kept bantering me, when I pulled out a roll of greenbacks that made them open their eyes, saying:

"I would not be one bit afraid to wager all that."

The Englishman gave me a nudge and said:

"Lad, don't you do it."

My partner then said:

"I haven't got one-half so much money, but I will bet you $500 I can pick up the baby ticket."

We put our money in the Englishman's hand, and I turned to him and offered to bet him a bottle of wine that I would win the money. He took me up. My partner turned the card, and I lost the money and the wine.

He wanted to bet me $1,000, but I told him he was a little too lucky for me. I saw Johnnie Bull was crazy to bet, so I said to him:

"Do you think you could guess the baby ticket?"

"Indeed I do," he replied.

"I will wager you that you can't."

He got out his leather bag and counted out twenty sovereigns. I saw he had plenty more, so I would not bet him less than one hundred sovereigns. He put them up, and I put up $500 in greenbacks. He turned the card and lost. My partner made him believe that he had made a mistake, by showing him that the corner of the baby ticket was still turned up.

He wanted to bet with me, so I took him for $500, and he won. That made Johnine Bull hot, as he did not have any more ready money except maybe $50. I saw he was ready for anything, so I told him I would bet him $1,000 against his gun if it was on the table. He jumped up, went to his room, and soon returned with his case. He unlocked it and showed me the gun. I put $1,000 in the barkeeper's hands, as I wanted to get the gun where he could not snatch it and run, as I expected he would do, if I gave him a chance. I mixed the cards, and he went for the baby, but he must have been excited, for he missed it. It was fun to see him. He looked at the cards, at me and my partner, then at his gun case, but it was behind the bar, and he could not get it. As soon as he could speak he said :

"Oh! my gun; I've lost my gun."

He walked up and down the guards, coming in every moment to look at his gun. I finally told him if he would raise the money I would let him have his gun for $500. Then he was happy, but he would not go to bed or leave the bar for fear I would get off with his fine English gun. The next morning he told his companions, and they raised the $500 in less than no time. I heard them talking. One would say to another :

" The lad has lost his gun, lads, and we must get the bloody thing for 'im."

I could have got $1,000 for it just as quick as the $500. I tried to show the other Johnnie Bulls how the lad lost his gun, but they would not come within a mile of the table. I bid them all good-bye and left the boat at Vicksburg, but I was always sorry I did not keep that gun.

TRAVELING KENO.

Away back in the fifties, when there was but few rail-roads in the Northwest, I went by stage from LaCrosse to Portage City, Wis. It was during the winter season, and a bitter cold day. I came very near freezing on the road, but I expected to make money, and I guess that was what saved me. I had a keno outfit with me, and it was my intention to play the surrounding towns after the manner of a traveling show. The first thing to be done after my arrival was to get thawed out, then to see the Mayor and get his permission (or license) to advertise and run my game. I called upon his Honor and stated my business. He did not know much about keno, so I explained the little innocent game to him. The result was, I got authority to open my game. I secured a room that had been used as a school-room, and advertised that I would open the next night, and in a short time after the door was opened the room was full of pupils. Some of them had never been to such a school, so I had to teach them the first principles; but it did not take me very long, as all those that had taken lessons rendered me all the assistance in their power, and I was very thankful for it, as I was anxious to get to work. After distributing the books, I began to call the numbers, and I must say I never saw a more quiet and attentive set of pupils in a school-room. We were getting along so nicely that I began to think it a pleasure to teach such nice boys, when a great big, rough-looking fellow came in, stalked all around the school-room, and made so much noise that I had to call some of the numbers over again. Some of the boys told him to sit down, take a book and study his lesson, but he would not do it. I saw he was a bad boy, and would not let the other boys alone; so I spoke to him very kindly, telling him to sit down, and see if he could not learn something; but he was one of the worst boys I ever saw, for he told me to go to h—l, and he would do just as he pleased. I remembered when I went to school how my teacher used to serve me when I was a bad boy and would annoy the other boys. So I told the scholars we would take a recess for about twenty minutes. They all threw down their books, and most of them went out to play. During recess I walked up to the bad boy and said:

"You are a very bad boy to come in here and annoy my pupils, and you deserve a whipping."

He replied: "You are not man enough to whip me."

"That was all I wanted him to say; so I let fly and gave him a good one on the jaw, and then I kept it up, until he cried worse than I ever did when I went to school. He got out of that school room faster than he came in, and then I called order and went on with my duties just as if nothing had happened out of the regular order.

I remained in Portage City for some time. My pupils liked me and paid their tuition promptly. Some of them paid much more than they could well afford, but they did it voluntarily. I went from Portage to Madison, where I had a good game, but I had to whip a fellow the second day, and in fact I had one or more fights in every town I went to; for there is nearly always some big bully in a town or city that has whipped some one, and he thinks that every one is afraid of him, and he can do just as he pleases; but they found out that they could not run me on my keno business.

A BULL FIGHT.

The steamer *John Walsh* was on an upward trip, two days out from New Orleans. A crowd of gentlemen were gathered about the bar, punishing wine at $5 a bottle. With flushed faces, jocund laughter, and the incessant pop of the champagne corks, the time flew unheeded past. The barkeeper smiled when at the little window of the bar the ebony head of a stalwart negro appeared.

"Say, boss, gimme some whisky."

Everybody turned, and laughter that was about to burst forth, or the jest that was ready, was hushed; for the negro's head was split open and the blood pouring down his cheeks in rivulets, crimsoning his swarthy, shiny skin and clothing.

"Been fighting?" said the barkeeper.

" Yes ; de fireman he butted me."

Up came the mate, who observed :

" We've got a fireman down below who has killed two or three niggers by butting them to death with his head."

" Send him up," I said, " and I'll butt him till he is sick of butting."

We had all been drinking wine, and everybody laughed, supposing that it was the liquor talking, and not me.

" Why, Devol, I wouldn't give five cents for your head if that nigger gets a lick at it," spoke up a young planter who was in the party.

Then I got mad, and exclaimed :

" I'll bet $500 I can make the nigger squeal."

The mate roared out with laughter ; but I put up my money, and so did the young planter, thinking that I would back out.   He only had $175 in his roll, and he offered to bet that.

" All right ; I don't back out.   I'll butt the nigger for $175."

The money was soon up in the barkeeper's hands ; and then the mate knew that I meant business, and he put up $25 to make bet the even $200.

At this juncture the mate called a halt.   " Wait till I see if the nigger will butt with a white man ;" and rushing down stairs, the " image of God cut in ebony " was inter- viewed.

" I doant like for to butt a white man," he said, " for I'm afraid I'll kill him, and den dey hang de ole nigger."

But the mate said, "I've just put up $25 on you, and I want to win it."

" All right ; if yer means it, boss, I'll go yer."

At the bar I procured a long string and a ribbon from a cigar bunch, and started down stairs.   Instantly the wildest excitement reigned on the boat.   Two of the deck- hands stood guard at the foot of the stairs to keep the crowd back, and the hurricane roof and boiler deck were thronged with an eager and excited crowd. Fastening one end of the string to the jack-staff and the other to the steps at about the proper height, the ribbon was tied in the centre of the string, and the black man and myself stood back five feet on either side, and at a given signal were to come forward and strike at the ribbon. Then the passengers said it was a shame to let that nasty nigger butt that nice white man to death; but as there were no S. P. C. A. officers aboard, the game went on.

The deck-hands all rolled up their eyes and looked at me as they would at a corpse. Just before the word ready was given, I asked the nigger if he had any money to put up on the result, and running his hand down in his watch-pocket he pulled out a ten-dollar bill. I covered it, and the planter told the nigger he would give him $10 more if he downed me. I cocked my eye on the nigger's head, and saw that it was one of those wedge-shaped cocoanuts so peculiar to people of African descent; so I inwardly resolved to hit him on one side of his wedge-shaped cranium. The nigger had his face to the sun, so that I felt confident that I could hit him pretty near where I wanted to.

The word was given, and at the ribbon we both rushed like a couple of frenzied bulls. I gave him a glancing blow that skinned his head for about three inches. The next time there was a crash, a jar that shook the boat and drew a shriek of terror from the passengers, for the nigger fell with a dull thud on the deck. He lay as stiff and cold as a dead man.

"Dat nigger is done gone dead! Dat nigger is no good any more!" shouted the alarmed roustabouts.

The mate lifted him up, and he began bleeding from the nose, eyes, and ears. The mate kindly asked him if he wanted to butt any more. He did not reply, only shook his head sadly and murmured inaudibly, "No." They applied whisky and water to his head, and at last removed him into the deck to cool off.

Many years have rolled by, and I have never heard the

last of that butting adventure. The papers wrote it up, and in less than ten days every planter on the coast had heard of it. The planter who lost the $175 tells the story to this day; and Bill Patterson, the mate (he is dead now), used to tell it to every new crew that he shipped.

Towards night the old nigger came crawling up stairs and said:

"Massa, you have done for this poor nigger, for I must go to the hospital and get cured up."

I returned him his $10, and for the rest of the trip the passengers paid for everything I wanted to drink.

IT SHOOK THE CHECKS.

It never pays a man to be too officious and volunteer information or advice when it is not asked, for he very often makes enemies and courts a disturbance that he could easily have avoided if he had simply minded his own business.

Some seven years ago I attended a fair at Cynthiana, Ky., and opened out a gentleman's game in the Smith Hotel bar-room. There were a number of sports from Louisville and Cincinnati present, and everything was moving along lively, and as decorous as a funeral, when some of the Paris and Louisville boys indulged in a scrimmage and were arrested. Everybody left the hotel and went to see the result of the trial. I sat near the judge, and when the evidence was all in I whispered to him to fine them $10 each. This he did, and as we were leaving the court room, I noticed that a big fellow from Paris, Ky., regarded me with very sour looks.

After supper I opened up my game, and in he came, and going to the bar-keeper, whispered in a tone of voice loud enough for me to hear: "I am going to whip that dealer."

Pretty soon I closed up the game, and then Sam Aliways and myself took a turn around the town, and running into a saloon, met the big bully. He had his coat off and a six-shooter a foot long hanging to his side; so, edging up to where he stood, I tapped him on the shoulder, observing:

"You are the gentleman that is looking for a fight."

As soon as he saw who it was, he grabbed for his shooting-iron; but just as he got hold of the handle, I dealt him a blow in the neck and he fell over against the counter, but I soon grabbed him and hit him a butt with my head. That ended the fight. He had sense enough to say, "That will do;" and seeing a policeman coming in one door, I went out another, hastened to the hotel and paid my bill, and caught the train for Covington. I was none too quick, however; for the next day when Aliways came along with my tools, he said that the fellow had a host of friends in the town, and that at least fifty fellows came around armed with case-knives, axes, double-barreled shotguns, revolvers, and rocks; and that if they had caught me, I would have met a fate worse than the martyr Stephen or the Chicago anarchists.

The fellow went by the name of Bill Legrets. When he was asked why he didn't shoot me, he said:

"Shoot h—l. The first lick he hit me, I thought my neck was disjointed; and when he ran that head into me, I thought it was a cannon-ball."

Bob Linn was dealing up stairs at the time, and he afterwards said that when the bloody duffer fell to the floor, that all the checks on the table trembled like aspen leaves. Poor fellow! He is dead now, having been shot in Paris a few years since.

WITH A POKER.

Once when traveling in the West, and winning some money from a man from Kansas City, some smart Aleck told him that I had cheated him, so he made up his mind to kill me on sight. I made some inquiries, and ascer tained that he was a desperate man and had already killed his two men. Accordingly I put my gun in my pocket and staid about the town, just keeping my eyes on the lookout, and at last went up to Omaha.

I was sitting one evening playing the bank, having forgotten all about the Kansas City man, when a friend of mine came to me and said that the man was in the adjoining room, and would soon be in to play faro. I lost no time in making my preparations to meet the gentleman. My friend had no pistol, nor had I; but seeing a poker lying on the floor near the stove, I rushed for it; and as I knew I could not go out without going through the room where he was, I simply put the poker under my coat and got close up to the door that led into the faro room and awaited his arrival. It was not long; and as soon as I saw him and was sure, I let drive and caught him square in the mouth, knocking him stiff. Then I rushed forward, and, grabbing him, secured his pistol, as I thought he would in all probability turn it loose on me. Then I attended to his head for a few minutes, endeavoring to kick the fight out of him.

I learned afterwards that he had a very bad reputation, having killed three men and been warned off the plains by a vigilant committee. He was confined to his bed for a couple of weeks, and I was congratulated on all sides for having walloped the fellow.

LEFT IN TIME.

Thirty-five or forty years ago the Cincinnati boats used to carry a great many passengers, and the New Orleans boats were always well filled. I once got aboard the *Yorktown* at Vicksburg. There was a full passenger list, and when I opened up there was at once a crowd around my frugal board. They seemed to enjoy the fair, and I won a good pile of money. At last we reached Bayou Plaquemine, at which point there was a strong current sweeping down the bayou, so that flat-boats were frequently driven in there and stranded. The *Yorktown* undertook to land at the mouth of the bayou, but the current which flowed like a mill-dam was too strong, and she started down the bayou. They headed her at once for the bank, and her stern swung around, and, lodging against the opposite bank, formed a perfect bridge across the mouth of the bayou. The boat was loaded to the guards, and the water ran through her deck rooms so rapidly that I thought every minute she would sink or fill with water, but they put weight on the hatches, then dug around the stern, so as to let her swing around. Just then two boats came along, one upward bound and the other down. One of them pushed and the other pulled the boat off, and then I began to look around, only to see that all the passengers had gone ashore. After wandering about the town the suckers decided that it was time to kick and have me arrested, but I divined what was in the wind, and, like Lord Byron's Arab, silently folded my tent and crept away. I reached New Orleans first.

ON THE CIRCUIT.

During the summer of the Centennial year I followed the races; gambling on horses, running faro bank, red and black, old monte, and anything else that came up. I had a partner at the beginning by the name of John Bull, of Chicago, and he was a good, clever boy. He dealt faro, and I the red and black. We separated at Jackson, Mich., he going to Chicago and I to Cleveland, where I witnessed the great race between " Goldsmith Maid " and the horse " Smuggler," on which I lost some money; but I had a good game of red and black, so I was about even. I then concluded I would follow the trotters through the circuit. While sitting at the hotel one day in Cleveland I saw on the opposite side of the street a face and form that I thought I recognized. I ran over, and sure enough it was my old partner, Canada Bill, and with him another great capper by the name of Dutch Charlie. I was more than glad to see Bill, and he was very glad to see me. He wanted me to tell him where I had been, what I had been doing, and where I was going, and wound up by saying:

"George, let's go and get something."

We soon found a bar-room, and began telling each other all that had happened since we were last together. I told Bill I had about made up my mind to follow the horses through the circuit. He told me that he and Charlie were going to do the same thing, and insisted that I should join, allowing as "how we three would make a good, strong team." I agreed. So it was settled we would all work together. While we were talking a slick-looking fellow, who I took to be a store clerk, walked in, and Bill invited him to take a drink, which he did, and I was introduced to Mason Long, who now styles himself "the converted gambler." Bill, Charlie, and I left Cleveland and went to Buffalo, but the night we left we had downed a sucker for $1,300, and thought best not to wait for morning.

We caught some good ones on the trip over, and they set up a great big kick. They telegraphed a description of Bill to Buffalo, so we got him to get off before we reached the city, telling him where to meet Charlie and myself the next day. We went on to the city and waited for Bill to show up, which he did the next night. He was too smart to come in by rail, so he got a man to drive him in.

We kept him in his hotel for a few days, until we thought the kickers that we had beat out of $2,100 had left the city. Then we made him dress up in store clothes, which he did not like a bit, saying:

"I don't feel good in these tarnal stiff things, nohow."

We thought best not to try our old games in Buffalo for fear the police would be looking for Bill, so we played the faro banks, bet on horses, and quit big losers at the end of the week. Dutch Charlie saved his money. He did not play the bank or horses, and it was well for us that he did not, for we always had a roll to use in making a bluff, which sometimes we would not have had if it had not been for him. We went from Buffalo to Rochester, and as we did not catch any kicking sucker on the way down, we had clear sailing during the week. We won a pile of money at monte, but Bill and I lost heavily at the races and faro banks. From Rochester we went to Utica, where I remained but a day or two, then concluded to run down to Philadelphia and see the Exposition. I bid the boys good-bye, promising to return before they left Utica. I did not take but little money with me, as I did not expect to do any bluffing while I was away. I took in the faro banks the first night, and the next day did not have a dollar. I started out on the street and soon met a man that I knew by the name of John Wilson. I saw by his actions he was like myself, "running light," for he did not ask me to take something, which I knew was his custom, for he was a clever fellow. We understood each other very soon, and parted. I had not gone very far until I heard some one call my name. I looked up, and saw two old friends of mine from New Orleans in a carriage that had just passed me. Then I knew I had struck oil. I lost no time in getting alongside of that rig and shaking hands with Samuel DeBow and Wm. Graham from my adopted home. They invited me to accompany them to the Exposition grounds, which I was very glad to do. They soon saw by my actions that something was out of tune, so they pressed me to know what it was. I told them, and I soon had all the money I wanted. After taking in the Exposition and a very large quantity of wine, I bid my friends good-bye, promising to meet them in Saratoga within a week. I went back to Utica and found that the boys, Bill and Charlie, had won $3,800, and they insisted that I was in with it. From Utica we went to Poughkeepsie, and in a few days I again left the boys to meet my New Orleans friends at Saratoga. I put up at the same hotel where they were stopping. The next day we took in the races, where I met another friend by the name of Rufus Hunt. He was well posted and gave us some good pointers. We bought pools and won $900. Then we all tried to see how much wine we could take in, and I do believe we got in $900 worth.

Canada Bill came over, and we spent a week with my friends. Then we promised to meet them in New York, and left for Poughkeepsie, where we found Dutch Charlie, and we all took a Hudson river boat, called the *Mary Powell*, for New York. On our way down we got into a friendly game of euchre with an old gent, and we relieved him of $700. After dinner I went up on the roof and saw my old friend Captain Leathers, of the steamer *Natchez*, in the pilot-house. He was insisting that his boat could beat the *Mary Powell*, and when he saw me he said:

"I can prove it by that man coming up here now."

I was glad to see the old fellow so far from home, so I told the pilot that the *Natchez* was the fastest boat on the Mississippi; and Captain Leathers went down to see the boys and the barkeeper.

Bill, Charlie, and I remained in New York for some time, and we proved what old Bill said in Cleveland: "We three would make a good, strong team."

The time came when I was compelled to leave the boys and go to Chicago, and that was the last I saw of old Canada Bill and Dutch Charlie until the following winter, when they both came down to New Orleans, and then we again made the suckers think we three were a good team.

STRATAGEM.

We went on board of Captain William Eads' boat at St. Charles, Mo., late one night, and found that all the state-rooms were taken and we could get no bed. There was no one up about the cabin except the officers of the boat, and as we never tried to win their money, things looked a little blue for any business before morning, unless some of the passengers could be got up. Young Bill Eads, a son of the Captain, was one of the pilots on the boat. He was off watch and at the bar drunk when we got on board. His father had married a young wife that day, and was taking his wedding trip on that boat. Young Bill was mad because his father had secured a young step-mother for him, and was just raising "Ned" about it.

A short time after going on board, the boat made a landing, and while we were tied up, the other pilot came down to the bar to see Bill and also to get something. His name was John Consall—an old friend of mine. I invited him and Bill to join me, and while we were drinking I said:

"I wish we could get up a little excitement, so some of the suckers would come out of their holes."

Young Bill replied: "I'll get them out for you, and that d——d quick."

John Consall went back to the pilot-house, and soon had the boat on her way. Bill went out, and in about twenty minutes there was the darndest racket on that boat you ever heard. Everybody was sneezing at one and the same time, and you would have thought they were trying to blow the roof off, from the amount of noise they made. Bill came up to us out on the guards, and said:

"Didn't I tell you I would drive them out of their holes?"

I looked into the cabin, and, sure enough, everybody was out of their rooms, rushing up and down the cabin and finally out on the guards. Old Captain Bill and young Bill's new step-mother were among the crowd, and it was fun to see the young bride rushing around after her old hubby, trying to keep him from blowing up the boat with his sneezing and cursing. He would pull away from her every time he would make a big sneeze, and then he would curse until another one would overtake him. He and young Bill knew what was the cause of all the racket, and the old one soon learned who had put the red pepper on the hot stove. He tried to find his bad boy, but he was up on the roof, so his step-mother did not get to see her hubby throw him overboard, as he swore he would do if he caught him.

They opened all the doors, and soon the red pepper was all out of the cabin and state-rooms. The old Captain and all the passengers, except a few good suckers, went back to bed. Young Bill came out of his hiding-place, and we all took something to wash down the pepper. We went to work on the fellows who remained up, and won $1,200, besides several good watches—which we would not have had a chance to do if the passengers had not been sneezed out. I appreciated the part Bill and John had played, and presented each with a good watch.

At another time I got on a boat after all the passengers had gone to bed, and did not want to wait until morning without doing some business; so I inquired after the passengers, and learned that there was one on board who had been drinking and flashing his money. I sent the porter to his room and told him to knock and tell him to get up at once, then whisper to him that the boat was on fire, but for him not to make any noise. In an instant the fellow was into a part of his clothes and out into the cabin. He rushed up to where we were sitting and wanted to know where the fire was. We told him down stairs under the boiler. Then he told us that some one came to his room and told him the boat was on fire. We laughed, and told him he must have been dreaming—and he thought he must have been, if we had heard nothing about it. We all took something at his expense, and then my partner began to throw the tickets. We beat him out of $500, and as he started to his room, he said: " I wish the d——d boat had been on fire."

MOBILE.

General Canby captured Mobile, taking 1,000 prisoners, 150 cannon, and 3,000 bales of cotton on the 12th day of April, 1865, and this about closed the war of the rebellion. I was in New Orleans at the time running the race-course and my games. I knew there would be plenty of money at Mobile after the Union Army took possession, and I resolved to get over there just as soon as possible. So in a short time after the surrender I was in Mobile trying to get permission to open up my games. It was not long until I had a faro bank in full blast in the city, and a rouge-et-noir and wheel game at a resort on the shell road, about seven miles out from the city. I had a partner in the faro bank by the name of Pettypan. He was a Creole, and not the best fellow in the world by any means when in liquor. He looked after the city trade, while I ran the game out on the shell road, in which he had no interest.

The Union officers, and all the citizens that could afford it, would drive out to the road-house where I was holding forth, and I was making a barrel of money out of them. My old friend and former partner, Charlie Bush, was running faro in New Orleans, and when he heard how much money I was making at Mobile he came over to run opposition. I gave him a call and he downed me for a big roll. He made big money, and then wanted to go back to New Orleans without leaving any of it, but the Grand Jury indicted him and made him come down pretty heavy. They got an indictment against me at the same time, but somehow it got into a pigeon-hole, and I guess it is there yet, for I never heard anything of it after Bush left. My partner in the faro bank was a little jealous of me, for I was making more money out on the shell road than he was in the city. One day when we were settling up our bank account he got mad, as he was drunk, and pulled his gun and said he would shoot me. He knew I did not have any gun with me, so he took this advantage. I saw he had me, so I just opened my vest and told him to shoot. That made him ashamed of himself, and he put up his gun and apologized.

I was dealing red and black at the resort one night, when an officer came up and said:

"I'll bet $25 on the red."

I replied: "Which $25 do you mean?"

Then he said: "It don't make any difference which. I say I will bet you $25 on the red."

"No bet goes on this layout unless the money is up," I said.

He then straightened himself to over six feet, and said:

"You are a d——d rascal."

"That is the conclusion I have come to about you," I remarked.

Then he made a rush for me, and at it we went. We had a lively time for a few moments, but I soon got a chance to give him my old head, and he hollowed enough. He went away and washed himself, and I did not see any more of him. His fellow officers heard how he had acted, and as he was a very quarrelsome man, they told me I served him just right, and they were all glad of it, and I had a better game after that than before.

I remained at Mobile for some time, then sold out and went back to good old New Orleans, for it was hard in those days to stay away any great length of time, and even now I feel more at home there than any other place in this country.

Sometime after my return to New Orleans I was taken down with the yellow fever (of which I have spoken in a preceding story). I remained for a few months, when I took a notion to go North. So I sold out, and again I was on board one of the packets going up the old Mississippi. I played all the old games up to St. Louis, and then I took a Missouri River packet and went to Omaha, still keeping up my games. I then started out on the Union Pacific Railroad, and went as far as Julesburg, which was at that time the terminus. I remained there, playing the contractors and every one else I could get a hold of, until the road was finished to Cheyenne City.

I won a great deal of money, but as the good old game of faro followed in the track of civilization and the railroad, I lost nearly as fast as I won. I remained in the West for five months, when the old desire to get back home on the Mississippi took possession of me, and I could not resist the temptation, so I turned my face to the east, and in a short time I was in St. Joseph, Mo., where I met my old friend Ben Allman, who was running a fine large billiard hall. I concluded to stop and open a keno room, so I went to Chicago, bought a very fine outfit, and opened up over Allman's place. I advertised my business in all the papers, just as a dry goods merchant would advertise his business. My keno netted me from $150 to $200 per day, and I set a lunch each night at a cost of $25. Most men would have been content, but I was not, as I still longed for the life I had led for so many years on the river. So I sold out, and was soon in St. Louis ready for a down river packet. On my way down I won considerable money, and that, together with the fact that I was on my way back to the place I loved so well, made me happy.

One night I went on board a boat that was so crowded with passengers that I could not get a room; so I opened up monte, and as I was winning money, I did not realize that I was sleepy until they began to make up cots in the cabin, and most all the passengers had gone to bed. Then I would have given almost any price for a place to sleep, but all the cots were engaged, and I was left. Nothing remained for me but to patronize the bar, which I was doing, when a man came in to get a drink that had been asleep on one of the cots. I told him as he had been resting if he would let me have his cot for the balance of the night I would give him $5. He accepted my proposition, and I went to bed. I had been lying down but a few moments, when there was a fuss started near me. I raised up to see what was the cause, when I saw two Jews that had come aboard at Baton Rouge, and they were fighting for the possession of a cot. I got up and told them to stop their fighting and join me in a drink. They accepted the invitation. While we were drinking I learned that they had been playing cards at Baton Rouge before they had got on the boat, and had had a falling out over the game. I told them I saw a fellow playing a game that beat anything I ever had seen. They wanted to know what it was, so I showed them the three cards, and in a short time I had won $200 from them. I forgot all about being sleepy while I was working up the Jew boys, and by the time I had won their money the steward was clearing the cabin to set the tables for breakfast. I had lost the sleep for which I had paid $5, but I did not mind it much, as I had won $200.

A DUCK HUNT.

During the winter season, wild ducks are so plentiful around New Orleans that a good wing shot can bag a hundred of them in a few hours. I have often seen men coming in on the boats and trains with hundreds of nice wild ducks, and at such times I would promise myself to lay off and have a hunt; so one morning I took my gun and about a hundred rounds of ammunition and went out on the L. & N. Railroad to Lake Pontchartrain. I killed at least twenty five ducks, but only got six of them, as they fell in the water and I had no dog to fetch them. I went back to the station with my six ducks, and there I saw five Frenchmen and some dogs, and they had about 200 ducks. I felt ashamed of myself, so I tried to buy some of their ducks, but they would not sell. Then I thought I would interest them in old monte until the train arrived; so I opened up on an old fish box and soon had them guessing for the baby ticket. One fellow wanted to bet a dollar, so I put up and he won. Another put up, and he won. Then I pulled out a roll and offered to bet them $50 against their entire lot of ducks that they could not turn the baby ticket. They all talked French to each other for a while, and then told me they would take me up. I told them to put their ducks all up beside the box and I would put up the $50. They did so, and all pointed to the same card, so I told them to turn it over. One of them did so, but it was not the card they wanted or thought it was, so they lost their ducks.

The train arrived; I got my ducks into the baggage-car and went to the city. I had the game hauled up to a restaurant, and sent for a lot of my friends, and I gave them all the ducks they wanted. I sold some, and had some cooked for myself and friends.

All the boys heard of my good luck. Some of them wanted to borrow my gun, while others wanted to go out with me the next time I went hunting; and there were some of the boys who knew me very well, who said: "Devol did not shoot a single one of those ducks—he either bought or won them." I insisted that I shot every one; and as the Frenchmen did not know me, none of my friends ever knew that I won them on the baby ticket.

QUICK WORK.

I went fishing one day out on Lake Pontchartrain, and caught a large string of fine fish. When I got back to the hotel, I sent an invitation to some of my city friends to drive out that evening and join me in a fish supper. They accepted the invitation, and were all on hand at the appointed time. We were seated around a table enjoying ourselves drinking wine and telling stories, while waiting for supper, when we heard quite a noise down stairs in the direction of the bar-room. I told my friends to remain seated and have some more wine, while I went down and inquired into the cause of the racket. They did so, and I ran down to the bar-room. Looking in, I saw ten or twelve steamboat cooks, who were on a big drunk. They were breaking glasses, fussing with the barkeeper, and raising old Ned generally.

I knew some of them, but as they were all pretty drunk, I concluded I could do no good, and was just turning away to go back to my friends, when four or five Union officers and a man by the name of Dave Curtis came up and started into the bar-room. They saw and recognized me, and insisted on me joining them. We all went in and were taking a drink, when the cooks began their racket again. One fellow was just spoiling for a fight. He was a bully, and had whipped some of his associates, so no one seemed to want anything to do with him. Like most drunken men, he wanted everybody to know what a great man he was, so he began on us. We requested him to go away and join his friends, but he would not do it, so finally I said:

"That fellow must have a fight, or he will get sick."

Then I told him I would let him try his hand on me, if he was sure he could lick any man in the room. He came at me, made a feint with his left and then let drive with his right. I dropped down, ran under, and had him on his back before he knew what I was doing. Then I gave him just one with "that old head of mine," and I broke every bone in his nose. He yelled like an Indian, then I let him up. His friends or companions did not offer to interfere in his behalf, so I expect they were very glad to see him get licked so easy and so very quick—for it was all over in much less time than it takes me to tell the story.

I took another drink with the Union officers and then hurried up stairs to my friends whom I had left waiting for the fish supper. They asked me what was the cause of the noise down stairs, and I told them it was a lot of drunken cooks. I said nothing about having had a fight, and they did not know anything about it until we all went down stairs, when some one spoke to me about the fellow's nose being all broken, etc. Then they asked me when I had a fight. I told them while we were waiting for supper.

They thought it was pretty quick work to raise a fuss and whip a good cook while another cook was frying some fish.

A HARD HEAD.

In most all of the many fights that I have been engaged in, I made use of what I have called "that old head of mine." I don't know (and I guess I never will while I'm alive) just how thick my old skull is; but I do know it must be pretty thick, or it would have been cracked many years ago, for I have been struck some terrible blows on my head with iron dray-pins, pokers, clubs, stone-coal, and bowlders, which would have split any man's skull wide open unless it was pretty thick. Doctors have often told me that my skull was nearly an inch in thickness over my forehead. They were only guessing at it then, of course, but if my dear old mother-in-law don't guard my grave, they will know after I am dead, sure enough, for I have heard them say so.

For ten or fifteen years during my early life, the sporting men of the South tried to find a man to whip me, but they couldn't do it, and finally gave it up as a bad job. After they gave up trying to have me whipped, and they knew more about my old head, they would all go broke that I could whip or kill any man living, white or black, by butting him. I have had to do some hard butting in my early days, on account of the reputation I had made for my head.

I am now nearly sixty years of age, and have quit fighting, but I can to-day batter down any ordinary door or stave in a liquor barrel with "that old head of mine;" and I don't believe there is a man living (of near my own age) who càn whip me in a rough-and-tumble fight. I never have my hair clipped short, for if I did I would be ashamed to take my hat off, as the lines on my old scalp look about like the railroad map of the State in which I was born.

During the winter of '67 or '68, John Robinson's circus was showing in New Orleans, and they had with them a man by the name of William Carroll, whom they advertised as "The man with the thick skull, or the great butter." He could out-butt anything in the show, except the elephant. One night after the show, Al. and Gill Robinson were up town, and their man Carroll was with them. We all met in a saloon and began drinking wine. While we were enjoying ourselves, something was said about butting, when Gill spoke up and said Carroll could kill any man in the world with his head. "Dutch Jake," one of the big sporting men of New Orleans, was in the party, and he was up in an instant, and said:

"What's that? I'll bet $1,000 or $10,000 that I can find a man he can't kill or whip either."

I knew what was up; and as we were all friends, I did not want to change the social to a butting match, so I said:

"Boys, don't bet, and Mr. Carroll and I will come together just once for fun."

The Robinson boys had great confidence in Carroll, and so did "Dutch Jake" have in me. I was at least fifty pounds heavier than Carroll, and I knew that was a great advantage, even if his head was as hard as my own. It was finally agreed that there would be no betting, so we came together. I did not strike my very best, for I was a little afraid of hurting the little fellow; but then he traveled on his head, so I thought I could give him a pretty good one. After we struck, Carroll walked up to me, laid his hand on my head, and said:

"Gentlemen, I have found my papa at last."

He had the hardest head I ever ran against; and if he had been as heavy as I was, I can't say what the result would have been if we had come together in earnest.

Poor fellow! He is dead now, and I know of no other man with as hard a head, except it is myself. My old head is hard and thick, and maybe that is the reason I never had sense enough to save my money. It is said of me that I have won more money than any sporting man in this country. I will say that I hadn't sense enough to keep it; but if I had never seen a faro bank, I would be a wealthy man to-day.

SAVED BY HIS WIFE.

I shall never forget a trip that I took many years ago on the steamer *Tagleona*, a Pittsburg boat. It was her first trip out, and Adam Clark, who has now been dead for many years, was with me as a partner. He was doing the playing, and money was plenty. Clark was an Englishman, and when he spread his board in the hall-way and made his introductory speech, a great crowd gathered about; for as he dropped his h's, like all Cockneys, it was very amusing to hear him talk. In those days the big fish had the first choice, and the small fry, or poor fish, had to wait around some time before they got a chance to lose their money. I noticed an old man hanging around, and as I sized him up as a pretty solid fellow, and giving my partner the wink, I called up all hands to the bar, and they all came willingly enough except a couple of fellows, who hung back. I sent one of the crowd back to invite them up, as I did not want them to see what the old man lost. They came along, and while we were at the bar Adam downed his man for $4,000 at one bet. When we came back from the bar, Adam kept right on playing as if nothing had happened, using the same cards with the corner turned up. When the poor fish saw this they all wanted to play, so I said:

"Boys, let's make up a pony purse and give him a good bet."

This was readily agreed to, and when I asked Adam what was the least he would turn for, he said $2,000. I was pretty sure there was not that amount of money in the party, but I remarked that I would go half of it. Then a little wizen-faced, dried-up old man said he would put up

$400. The rest chipped in, and $900 was raised. I put
up the balance, and we were all ready to turn, when down
the cabin rushed a woman squealing like a stuck pig.
Adam looked up, and the little woman grabbed the dried-
up old man and shouted:

"Where's my money? Give me my money?"

Of course such a commotion aroused all the passengers
on the boat, who were anxious to see what the trouble was.
I got the old lady to one side, and when she cooled off a
little, she said that she had $400 in her dress pocket and
had lain down to sleep; that when she awoke she found her
money gone, and knew no one had taken it but her husband, as he had done such a trick before.

"I knew he was gambling," she said.

Adam counted out the $400 and handed it back to the
old man, and said:

"That settles it. I won't take the bet."

Somebody turned the card for the balance, and, of
course, Adam won.

At another time a man lost a few hundred dollars and
then went back and got the keys of his wife's trunk, and,
securing some jewelry and a fine shawl, sold them to a passenger, and receiving the money came around and lost it.
After the game was all over I learned of the occurrence,
and going to the party who had purchased the goods I
made him disgorge, and paid him what he paid for them.
Taking the goods and wrapping them up in a paper, I
handed them to the lady, at the same time I advised her to
keep her keys from her husband, and have no doubt she
was very grateful to me for it, for she seemed to be. I did
not want the lady to lose her jewelry and shawl, for I have
noticed that a man who will gamble away all his money,
and then steal his wife's money, jewelry, or clothes to raise
a stake, is not the man to replace what he has stolen, in
any great hurry.

COLD STEEL.

We got aboard of Captain Charles Blunt's boat at Omaha, Neb., bound for St. Louis, Mo. We played our games during the trip, without anything of notice occurring until we made a landing at a wood station, about twenty miles above St. Joseph, Mo. It was a lonely place in the woods, with nothing but long wood-piles to make it a desirable place to stop over night at. There had been some trouble between the deck-hands, who were mostly Irishmen, and some of the officers of the boat. So the former chose this lonely spot to settle the matter. After loading the wood they all armed themselves with clubs and bowlders, and took possession of the stairway, swearing that no man should come down on deck or let go the line until their wrongs were righted. Captain Blunt was a brave man, and did not like to be forced to do anything against his own free will; but he did not know just how to manage those fellows, for they were a bad crowd, and had the advantage of him in numbers; besides he had no arms on board except a few pistols, and he knew that an Irishman did not fear gunpowder. Finally I said to the Captain:

"If you will take my advice, we can soon run those fellows ashore, and then we can cut the line and leave them."

He asked me what I would do, so I told him to get all the butcher knives in the kitchen, and everything else on board that would cut, or looked like it would, and arm the officers and passengers, and we would charge down the steps on to the fellows.

He thought it a good plan, so we were soon ready. I wanted the largest knife, telling the Captain I would lead if he would let me have it. He wanted the glory of leading the attack himself, so I had hard work to get the largest one; but I did get one about fifteen inches long. We all rushed out of the cabin and down the steps with a war-whoop, and before the deck-hands had time to rally, we were onto them, cutting right and left. We did not want to kill; we only wanted to scare them. I got a lick on the head; it did not hurt, but it made me mad, and I cut two or three fellows across the part that they sit down on, and they began to yell cold steel, and made a rush for the plank. The others followed, and were in such a hurry they did not take time to find the plank, but jumped overboard and waded out. Some one cut the line, and we were soon away from shore. The Captain told the pilot to hold the boat, and then he told the deck-hands if they would come on board and behave themselves he would take them to St. Joseph. They promised they would not raise any more disturbance, so he took them on board and we started on our way.

Soon after starting some one told the Captain that the deck-hands were talking about having me arrested when we got to St. Joseph, so he put me ashore on the opposite side of the river, and when he was through with his business at St. Joseph he came over after me and took me to St. Louis. We landed alongside of the steamer *Emigrant* a short distance below St. Joseph. Captain Blunt went over on board and told the officers all about our gallant charge. My old friend, Henry Mange, who keeps a boat store in New Orleans, was running the bar on the *Emigrant* at the time, and he often asks me about the war on the Missouri River.

"RATTLESNAKE JACK."

" Rattlesnake Jack " was about the last man I worked with as a partner playing three-card monte. His right name was Jackson McGee. He was born and raised in the mountains of Virginia, and spent much of his early life catching snakes, which he would sell to showmen, who gave him the name of " Rattlesnake Jack." He was over fifty years of age, and weighed about 160 pounds, at the time he and I worked together. He was a good talker, and had but few equals at throwing the three cards. He looked like the greenest sort of a backwoodsman when he had his "make-up" on. He was not the bravest man in the world, but he was not afraid of snakes, and could make some good big bluffs with his long six-shooter. He is now living in West Virginia with his family, and no one would think, to see him, that he used to catch rattlesnakes for a living, or played three-card monte with old Devol. He has a beautiful daughter, who is highly accomplished, and Jack is proud of her.

Old Jack and I were on board of the steamer *Natchez* one Saturday night, coming out of New Orleans, and she had a large number of passengers on board. We did not see any good monte suckers, so I opened up a game of rouge-et-noir and did a fair business until 11 o'clock; then I closed up and went to the bar, where I met a gentleman I had often seen on the packets. He knew me and my business, for he had seen me play monte several times. He invited me to join him in a drink, and then laughingly said:

"Devol, how is the old business, anyway?"

I laughed back, saying: "Oh, it's just so-so; but let's take another drink."

He accepted, and while we were drinking, old "Rattlesnake Jack" walked up and said to the barkeeper:

"Mister, how much you ax fur a dram o' liquor?"

The barkeeper told him 15 cents.

"Fifteen cents?" says Jack. "Wall, now! Up whar I live you can get a dram for 5 cents; but let's have her, even if she does cost 15 cents. I reckon as how it must be perty good."

The barkeeper set him out a small glass and a bottle. Jack looked at the glass, picked it up, and stuck his finger in it, then set it down and said:

"Say, mister, do you call a little thing like that a 15 cent dram o' liquor?"

18

The barkeeper told him he did. Jack filled the glass full, saying:

"Up whar 1 live they give you a tin cup when you take a dram."

He pulled out a roll about the size of a "boarding-house pillow" to pay for the drink, and the smallest bill he had was $100. That made my friend open his eyes, and he whispered to me:

"Devol, he would be a good subject for you."

I replied, "Yes; and I am going to have some of that money before I go to bed."

My friend then turned to Jack and said: "Old boy, where do you come from?"

"I used to live in Greenups," replied Jack.

"Where in the world is Greenups?"

"Wall, Greenups is up nigh the Big Sandy."

As I was born in that part of the country, and knew something about the people, I asked Jack if he was one of those fellows who made the counterfeit half-dollars on the Big Sandy. He laughed and said:

"No; but I'd spent more'n a half-bushel of em for dames afore they got on to 'em."

I then asked Jack where he was bound for, and he replied:

"Wall, you see I sold my farm up on 'Sandy' for a perty big pile, and pap writ me to come out whar he lives in Texas and buy another; so I'm just goin' out to see pap, and if I likes it out thar, I reckon as how I'll stay."

My friend then asked him if he would not join us in a drink.

"I'll jine yer in a dram; but I'll be gol darned if you don't look just like a chap what dinkered me out of $1,000 when I got off at Cincinnati to see the town; but he wasn't so big."

That made my friend laugh. He asked Jack how he lost his money.

"Wall, I'll tell yers. I went into a place whar thar

was a big glass full of beer painted on the winder to get a dram, and a nice-looking chap got talking to me, and perty soon he asked me to have a dram along with him. Then another fellar what was thar, he axed us if we ever played Rock-mountain euchre. He had some tickets, and he would jumble 'em up, and then he would bet yer on 'em. This nice-looking chap he bet him, and he win $500. Wall, I just planked down my money, and the fellar win it; but he gave me the tickets for a dram, and I'm goin' to take 'em out whar pap lives—but I won't tell pap I lost anything, fur he don't know how much I got fur my farm."

My friend said, "Why, Devol, he has been playing three-card monte."

I told him not to give me away, and I would get the fellow to play the game for us. Then I said to old Jack:

"What are you going to do with the tickets when you get out to Texas?"

"Wall, I'm goin' to larn 'em, and when I get out to pap's I'll win all the money them gol-darned cow-boys hev got."

"Do you think you can learn them well enough to win their money?"

"Oh, yes; I'm larnen 'em all the time, and sometimes I can mix 'em up so I fool myself."

My friend thought he must help me, so he invited us to join him in another drink.

Old Jack said: "Wall, I don't care if I do."

After getting another dram into old Jack I asked him if he would show us the tickets. He said:

"Yes, but you mustn't spile 'em, fur I want to keep 'em perty till I git out war pap lives."

He then pulled out a leather pouch, opened it, took out a handkerchief, unfolded it very carefully, and produced the three cards. My friend shrugged his shoulders and laughed. I asked old Jack to show us how he played the game, when he said:

" I can't show yer so good without a table."

I told him there was a nice table in the barber shop, and invited him to go back. He consented, so we were soon in the shop seated around the table, and Jack began to throw the cards. My friend was very attentive, for he was sure I would win the old fellow's money, and he did not want to miss any of the fun.

I told Jack I would bet him the drinks I could turn up the ticket with the boy on it.

He said: " Wall, look here. I've got the name of bein' the spunkyest fellar up at Greenups'. I never 'lowed any man to back me down fur a dram, or two drams, either."

He mixed them up; I turned the wrong card and lost. Then Jack laughed so loud and long that it attracted the attention of everybody that was awake on the boat, and quite a number of gentlemen came in to see the fun.

When Jack recovered from his big laugh, he said:

" I knowed yer would miss it."

I called for the drinks, and then told my friend I did not want to turn the right card until I could get a big bet.

After we drank our liquor, I began bantering old Jack to bet me some money, but he did not want anything but drams. I kept on playing him, and finally he said:

" I'll go yer once for $5, anyhow."

I told him to put up. I turned and lost again.

Then old Jack rolled off his chair and roared so loud that I was afraid he would wake up all the passengers on the boat. The room was soon full of people, and every one was crowding around to get a look at the old fool that was making so much noise.

Jack ordered the drinks, saying:

" You fellars think I haint got no sense, but I'll bet yer's long's I's got two kerds to yer's one."

While old Jack was paying the barkeeper for the drams I put a pencil mark on the boy ticket, and my friend saw me do it.

I then offered to make another bet.

Old Jack said : " I'll bet $10 this time."

I told him to put up, and he did. Then I replied :

" I will raise you $500," and I put up the amount in my friend's hands.

" What's that? What yer put up $500 agin my $10 fur?"

My friend told him he would have to put up $500 more, or he would lose his $10.

" Wall, I'll be gol darned ; I haint goin' to be backed out, fur if the boys in Greenups would hear on't they wouldn't speak to me when I go back thar."

He put up $500 more, then mixed the cards, and I turned the winner. Everybody roared with laughter. Old Jack turned around, looked at the crowd for a moment, then said :

" You fellars kin laugh at me just's much as yer like, but I don't 'low no man to back me down."

He then told the barkeeper to bring him a dram.

I said to my friend : " That old fool will lose all his money before he gets to Texas, and I may as well have it as any one else."

He replied : " Yes ; and I'm going to have some of it myself."

He then insisted on making a bet. I told him to make a good big one, as the old fellow was getting too drunk to handle his cards, and he might fall over and stop the game.

My friend then ordered the drinks, thinking, no doubt, that if he would treat, old Jack would bet more liberally with him.

When the bystanders saw Jack take another of those big drams, some of them remarked :

" Those gamblers have that old fellow so drunk they will win all of his money before they let him go. It's a shame, and we ought to stop it."

My friend offered to bet $500, when old Jack said :

" Boy's, I'm drinking, and I don't care, fur my spunk's

up, and I'd just's soon bet her all the first bet; them tarnal fellers guzzled me out of $1,000 in Cincinnater, and I wants ter get even." So saying he pulled out his big roll, slammed it down on the table, and said:

"Thar's my pile, and you fellars darn't cover her."

"I whispered to my friend, telling him that now was the time. Then I asked Jack how much he had in the roll. He said:

"Wall, I don't know; I had $7,000 when I left Greenups, and I lost $1,000 in Cincinnater and what yer win just now, so I reckon I've got nigh onto $6,000."

I requested one of the bystanders to count the money, which he did, and found it to be just $5,500. My friend had $3,400, and I put up the balance.

I told him to turn the card, as he had up the most.

Old Jack mixed them up, but he was so drunk he could hardly pick up a card. My friend could hardly wait for Jack to say ready before he dove in and grabbed the one with the spot on it, but when he turned it over he saw it was not the one with the boy on it.

Old Jack snatched the money from the gentleman that was holding stakes, and shoved it down into his pockets. Then turning to the crowd, he said:

"Wall, why don't yer's laugh now?"

They did laugh, for most of them felt like it. Old Jack joined in, and laughed louder than any of them, and then turning around to the table, he began looking for his precious tickets. He had put them in his pocket without any one seeing him, but pretended he was ruined if he could not find them. I told him the barkeeper had some just like them, and I would go and get them for him. That quieted him down, and he said:

"Wall, if I kin get t'others I don't care, fur I wanted to show 'em to pap when I gets out thar in Texas."

I went to the bar, as though I had gone for the cards and returned with them. Old Jack laughed when he saw them, saying:

"Wall, I be gol-darned if they haint just like t'others."

I gave Jack the new set, but I turned up a corner on the boy card so every one could see it. Then I told him to mix them up, and I would make him a bet of a $1,000. We put up the money; I turned and won. Then the by-standers began to take more interest in the game than ever, and the fun began again. One fat gentleman crowded in and wanted to bet. I said:

"Boys, let us make up a pony purse, and we will all bet on the same card. My friend wanted to get into the same party, but did not have any ready cash, so he asked me for a loan, offering his watch and diamond as security. I let him have $1,000, which he put up. The fat gent put up $1,300, and another man put in $400. I put up $1,000, which made the purse $3,700. Old Jack was very drunk, but he got up his money someway, and then began to mix. We picked on the fat gentleman to do the turning. He took his time, as most fat men do, but when he turned the card it was the wrong one, so we all lost our money. Just then some one yelled out:

"Sold again and got the money."

That broke up the little game, and old Jack said:

"Boys, come and take a dram with me, and then I'll go to bed."

We all went to the bar, and when Jack took his big dram I noticed that he drank out of a different bottle from the rest of us. He then went to his room, and in a short time I went to look for him, but I did not find him in his room. He was up in the texas eating up the officers' lunch.

My friend said he would send me the money to redeem his jewelry by the barkeeper the next trip. As I had downed him for $3,400 in cash I gave him his jewelry on his promise. He did not keep it, and well I knew he would not. The next time I met him he said nothing about the $1,000, so I told him he did not owe me anything, as I got one-half of what he lost, and that I had sent out West and got "Rattlesnake Jack" on purpose to down him at the old game that he knew so well. That made him mad, and he would never speak to me after that, and that nearly broke my heart.

"SHORT STOPS."

McGowley, "Rattlesnake Jack," and myself were on the Morgan Railroad, going out from New Orleans.

I occupied a seat beside an old gent from Iowa, on his way to Texas to buy a farm.

The conductor was on to our racket, and would not give us a show.

We had to wait for a change of conductors before we could open up for business.

I gave old Jack the office to come up, which he did, looking like a Texas ranchman.

The cow-boy had been to New Orleans to sell his critters, and wanted a dram.

The old gent did not drink, nor did I—just then.

The cow-boy had been pranking with a new game, had lost $1,000, but had plenty more left. He showed us how he had lost his money.

I bent up a corner of the winning card and won a few hundred dollars. McGowley, not knowing anything about the corner of the winner being turned up, lost a few hundred dollars.

The old gent knew all about the corner and how I won. He wanted to bet, but his money was sewed up in his shirt.

I had a sharp knife that I loaned him.

He cut his shirt and got out his money.

The cow-boy would bet his pile, amounting to $10,000, against the old gent's pile.

I would bet with him if I was the old gent, for he had but $4,600.

The money was put up. The card was turned. The old gent lost.

The cow-boy bet another man $200 and won, then asked him for a dram out of his bottle.

I had an idea that my wife wanted me to come back and see her in the Texas sleeper. I would return as soon as I learned how her headache was.

A station was reached. I got off. Looking after the receding train, I saw two men drop off; they walked back to the station. McGowley, Rattlesnake Jack, and myself waited for the next train to New Orleans, with $4,800 more than we had a few hours previous.

We were on the train going in to New Orleans. Old Jack occupied a seat just behind a lady and gentleman.

The lady had something lying in her lap about the size of an infant, covered with a shawl. Whatever it was, she was very careful of it.

McCowley and I were seated across the aisle, near by.

Jack was telling the lady and gentleman some very interesting story. He showed them three tickets. He threw them over each other on the seat beside him.

The lady gave the gentleman some money, which he laid over on the seat where Jack was throwing the tickets. He reached over and turned one of the tickets.

Jack put the money in his pocket.

The lady gave the gentleman more money.

He laid it in the same place as before. He turned one of the tickets the same as before.

Jack put the money in his pocket the same as before.

The lady talked to the gentleman in very angry tones. She talked to Jack very pleasantly. She took out more money and offered to lay it on the seat where the gentleman had laid the money before.

Jack would not let a lady put money down.

The lady uncovered the something she had lying in her lap. She showed it to Jack. They talked about it. She got up and called me over to hold it.

Jack gave me $100 to hold. He threw the tickets.

The lady reached over and turned one of them. She

threw up both hands and said: "Mercy on me! What shall I do? I have lost my dear Tommy."

I handed Jack the $100 and the twelve-pound Tommy. The passengers all roared with laughter.

The lady scolded her hubby very badly. She cried, sobbed, and wrung her hands, saying: "I have lost my Tommy! Oh, my dear Tommy, Tommy; I will never see you any more!"

Jack could stand it no longer. He handed his Thomas cat over to the lady.

First she smiled, then she laughed, and then she said: "Hubby, get out your bottle and give this dear, good, nice gentleman a drink."

The passengers all roared again.

Jack took a drink. The train rolled into the depot. We all bid the lady and gentleman and "Tommy" good-bye, and got off. "Selah."

KICKERS.

All men that bet should not be classed as gamblers, for some *things* that style themselves *men* will bet (to win, of course), and kick if they lose, which a gambler will never do, although he may sometimes be sucker enough to bet (to win) against a sure thing, like old monte or a brace game.

A kicker, or squealer, always speaks of the money he has lost, against any game, as his money; while the gambler considers the money he loses, against any game, as lost; and it belongs to the person who won it, and you never hear one of them do any kicking.

"Old Rattlesnake" and I left New Orleans one evening on the steamer *Robert E. Lee.*

We played the good old game in the usual way, and caught quite a number of good sized suckers, among which was one from St. Joseph, La. We got off at Baton Rouge, and took another boat back to New Orleans. The next trip we made on the *Lee* we learned from my old friend Carnahan, the steward, that the St. Joseph sucker, whom we had downed on the last trip, made a big kick when he learned that we had left the boat at Baton Rouge. He said he would get a lot of the St. Joseph boys, go back to where we got off, and make us give up his money, or he would kill us.

The steward told him not to do it, for said he:

"Those fellows are bad men to fool with. I have seen twenty suckers try to make them give up, but I never saw them do it."

As we were not within miles of this kicker, who, I have no doubt, styled himself a man, of course he could do a great deal of blowing; but when a short time afterwards we met him with a lot of St. Joseph boys at his back, we could not get within speaking distance of him. I was glad of it, as they were a bad crowd.

Old Carnahan and I were cabin boys on the same boat before the Mexican war. He is dead now, but I shall always remember him for telling the kicker, "Those fellows are bad men to fool with."

Old Jack and I traveled North during the summer season, playing the boats and railroad trains

We were going out of Detroit, Mich., on the Great Western Railroad, over into Ontario, one night, when there was quite a number of half-breed (French and Irish) Canadians on board. They had six or seven bull-dogs with them that had been fighting against some dogs in Detroit, and from their talk we learned that they had downed Uncle Sam. So we thought (as we were Americans) that we would try and down them; not with bull-dogs, but with the good old game.

Jack was soon among them, and in a short time, with my assistance as capper, he had downed several of the Canucks for a few hundred. They were kickers from the old house. They all got together and began cackling like a lot of old hens when a hawk is after them. No one but themselves could understand a word they said; but they soon made a rush for old Jack and demanded, in English, that he give up their money, or they would kill him. Their bull-dogs wanted to take part in the fight, and I guess they would have done it if it had not been for their owners, for if a dog's master runs he will be sure to run after him. Old Jack whipped out that big, long six-shooter of his, and the instant they saw it they all started and made a regular stampede for the other car. The dogs took after their masters, and it was fun to see the passengers climbing upon the seats The men and the dogs rushed into the ladies' car, and you would have thought it was on fire if you had heard the screams and yells that the passengers set up when the men and bull dogs rushed in among them. The poor dumb brutes were frightened as much as their owners, and they set up the d——d howl I ever heard in all my life. We were just nearing a station, so I told old Jack to drop off, which he did, and then he got onto the hind sleeper. The people at the station had heard the screams, and came running to see what was the matter.

The railroad boys had hard work to get the dogs and men out of the ladies' car, but they could not get one of the dogs back into the cars he had been run out of. I did not blame the brutes much, for they had been badly frightened.

We were coming out of Chicago at one time on the Burlington & Quincy Railroad, and had downed some suckers, when one of them began to kick like a bad mule. He told the conductor that old Jack had robbed him out of his money. The conductor told him he could do nothing except turn the gambler over to the police at the next station. He locked the doors to keep Jack from jumping off, and the sucker quieted down, thinking he would be O. K. when he reached the station. I saw two gentlemen from Quincy in the car that I was acquainted with, so I wrote a note to them, requesting that they tell the kicker he was in the same boat with the gambler, as he would be fined just as much as the man who got his money, and that the fine in Illinois was $100. The result was the fellow hid himself, and when the conductor pointed old Jack out he could not find the kicker. We got off with the officers, and as no one was on hand to testify, of course we only had to treat until the next train arrive

WILLIAM JONES. (CANADA BILL.)

Canada Bill—peace to his ashes—is dead. He died in Reading, Penn., about ten years ago, and, poor fellow, he did not leave enough money of all the many thousands he had won to bury him. The Mayor of Reading had him decently interred, and when his friends in Chicago learned the fact, they raised money enough to pay all the funeral expenses and erect a monument to the memory of one who was, while living, a friend to the poor. I was in New Orleans at the time of his death, and did not hear the sad news for some months after.

I hope the old fellow is happy in a better land. If kind acts and a generous heart can atone for the sin of gambling, and entitle men to a mansion in the skies, Canada Bill surely got one, "where the wicked cease from troubling, and the weary are at rest."

There never lived a better hearted man. He was liberal to a fault. I have known him to turn back when we were on the street and give to some poor object we had passed. Many a time I have seen him walk up to a Sister of Charity and make her a present of as much as $50, and when we would speak of it, he would say:

" Well, George, they do a great deal for the poor, and I think they know better how to use the money than I do."

Once I saw him win $200 from a man, and shortly after his little boy came running down the cabin, Bill called the boy up and handed him the $200 and told him to give it to his mother.

He was a man, take him for all in all, that possessed many laudable traits of character. He often said suckers had no business with money. He had some peculiar traits. While he was a great man at monte, he was a fool at short cards. I have known men who knew this to travel all over the country after Bill, trying to induce him to play cards with them. He would do it, and that is what kept him poor.

Mason Long, the converted gambler, says of William Jones (Canada Bill):

"The confidence men and monte players were in clover. Among them was the most notorious and success· ful *thief* who ever operated in this country, Canada Bill. He was a *large* man, with a nose *highly illuminated* by the joint action of *whisky* and heat. Bill squandered his money very lavishly, and *drank* himself to death in about a year after the incident I have related. He died a pauper."

> " But by all thy nature's weakness,
>   Hidden faults and follies know,
> Be thou, in rebuking evil,
>   Conscious of thine own."

Is Mason Long converted? God and himself only know.

Was he fully converted when he wrote " The Converted Gambler "?

If the Bible be true, and it was left for me to decide, I would answer in the language of St. Paul :

"Though I speak with the tongues of men and of an gels, and have not charity, I am become as sounding brass or a tinkling cymbal."

A true Christian will exercise charity toward all offend ers, granting a boon of pity to the erring, and cast a glance of mercy upon the faults of his fellows. He will cherish a recollection of his virtues, and bury all his im perfections.

Is Mason Long a true Christian? Read his description of Canada Bill. Then read a true description of Bill's per sonal appearance on page 190 in this book. If Mason Long had never seen Canada Bill, I would excuse him, but he said he capped for him once, or at least he tried to do so.

Has he shown any Christian charity in speaking of a man in his grave? Read what he says, and you will see that he or I are mistaken.

Bill was not a thief, he was honest to a fault. He was not a large man, for he never weighed over 130. He did not have a nose highly illuminated by the joint action of whisky and heat. He did not drink himself to death within a year of 1876, for he visited me in New Orleans in 1877. He did not drink whisky at all. His great drink was Christian cider, and it was very seldom I could get him to drink wine. He did die a pauper, and God bless him for it, for he gave more money to the poor than a thousand professed Christians that I know, who make a great parade of their reformation.

The public put all sporting men into one class, called gamblers; likewise they put all church members into classes and call them Christians, etc.

There is as wide a difference between a true gambler and one who styles himself a sport, as there is between a true Christian and one who puts on the cloak of Christianity to serve the devil in.

There is an old saying, " Honor among thieves." I will add a maxim or two: There is honor among gamblers, and dishonor among some business men that stand very high in the community in which they live.

THE TWO JUDGES.

> " He can not e'en essay to walk sedate,
>   But in his very gait one sees a jest
>   That's ready to break out in spite of all
>   His seeming."

Some years ago Judge Smith was upon the bench of the Police Court at New Orleans, and during the time Judge Wilson occupied the same position at Cincinnati.

Judge Smith made a trip to the North one summer, and stopped at Cincinnati for a few days on his way home.

While in the Queen City he formed the acquaintance of

Judge Moses F. Wilson, and as he was in the "thirty-fifty" business like himself, he felt as though they were somewhat akin.

Judge Smith was very fond of a joke, and when he met Mose Wilson, he met a good-humored man, who had a fondness for "gags," and was ever joking.

These kindred spirits were soon well pleased with each other. Wilson felt that the duty of entertaining a fellow Judge from a sister city was incumbent upon him, and he just spread himself to do it.

They had a right royal good time together, but all things must come to an end some time, and the time had come for Judge Smith to tear himself away and return once more to the field of his labor. They bid each other an affectionate good-bye, but not until after Mose had promised Smith to visit him the next winter, and stay forever-more. Judge Smith was at the depot. His baggage was on board, and he was just stepping upon the platform, when two gentlemen stepped up, and one of them said:

"We want you," at the same time displaying his police badge.

"What for?" inquired Smith.

"Suspicion," replied the officer.

"Gentlemen, you are mistaken; I am Judge of the Police Court of New Orleans."

"Oh! you are? Well, we never arrest a fellow like you that he is not a Judge, lawyer, doctor, or some big bug somewhere, to hear him tell it; but you take a walk with us up to the chief's office, and explain to him who and what you are."

Smith saw it was of no use trying to explain. The train was moving off with his baggage on board, and he was left (in the hands of the two officers). They marched him up to the chief's office, and when they arrived everything seemed to be in readiness for an immediate trial; for there was Judge Wilson, the prosecuting attorney, and quite a a number of witnesses.

Smith was found guilty of desertion. The Judge fined him (a bottle), and ordered that he be confined within the city limits for one day. Smith paid the fine, but pleaded to be let off from the imprisonment. Judge Wilson was firm (for once in his life), so poor Smith had to serve out his time; but the Judge was kind enough to see that he did not suffer for the want of anything, and when he was set at liberty he was like some birds born and raised in a cage. They like the confinement, and when the door is open they will not fly away; but frighten the bird, and away it will go. It was so with Smith; he had already stayed too long. He got frightened and flew away to the sunny South.

The cold blasts of winter were sweeping over the North, when Judge Wilson remembered his promise made to Judge Smith to visit him in New Orleans, and he was soon on his way to make his promise good, for he is a man of his word.

He telegraphed Smith that he would arrive on a certain train, expecting, of course, that he would be received with a brass band, etc.

The train on which Mose was being transported from the land of snow to the land of flowers was about ten miles from New Orleans, when it passed a northern-bound freight, and in a few moments two large men, with brass buttons on their coats, came marching into the Cincinnati sleeper. They came down the aisle, closely scanning the faces of all the male passengers. They halted at the seat occupied by Mose. They looked at him and then at a photograph they had with them. Finally one of them put his hand on Mose's shoulder, and said:

" We want you's."

The Judge took in the situation at once, for he had not forgotten the time he played a similar joke; but he did not like the idea of all the passengers (especially as there were a great many ladies on board) thinking that he was under arrest in earnest. So he smiled one of those sweet smiles of his, and said:

19

Officers, this is all a joke. I am Judge of the Police Court of Cincinnati, and I am well acquainted with the Judge of your Court. I expected to be received in New Orleans with a brass band, in place of brass buttons."

"Do yez hear that? He a Judge of the Police Court; expected to be received wid a brass band. Why, he's got more brass than there is in twenty brass bands. He's the biggest thafe in the whole country. Didn't we see the chafe go right straight to the rogue's gallery and get his picture; and did't he tell Pat and meself to come out here and arrest yez, and didn't we's ride on a freight train?"

Mose saw it was no use trying to make the officers or passengers understand that it was a joke, so he said:

"All right, I will go with you."

"Of course yez will. Won't he, Pat?"

"You bet he will," says Pat.

The officers sat down facing him, so they could keep a watch on him, for they were afraid he would try to jump out the window.

When the train arrived at New Orleans the officers got a carriage (at Mose's request), and they were driven to the chief's office.

The chief pretended not to know the Honorable Judge, and told him to send for his friends. He called for an officer to take Mose down and lock him up, when in walked Judge Smith. Mose smiled and said:

"Smith, I owe you one."

Judge Smith told the chief he would be responsible for Mose while in the city, so he let him go. There was a carriage in waiting. They got in and were driven to Leon's restaurant, where they found a large number of Judge Smith's friends and a fine dinner awaiting them.

After dinner, while we were drinking to Mose's health and smoking cigars, Judge Smith requested me to show our honored guest the baby ticket. I did, and downed him for a bottle, but it did not cost him a cent, for his Queen City money was no good in the Crescent City so long as he remained with the Judge, for they were kindred spirits.

TAPPED THE TILL.

It is often said that faro banks are never broke, but I recall one incident that will prove the contrary. It was during the war, and a number of us were playing together at New Orleans at Charlie Bush's, my old partner. They were all high rollers, and when one of them, who was a big loser, went to get his checks cashed for a $1,000, the cashier pulled out the drawer and found that the bottom had been cut out, and all the money was gone. Some snoozer had crawled under the table, and with a sharp knife cut the bottom clear out. Of course the proprietors were very mad, but the joke was such a good one that it wouldn't keep. Still, in spite of all this, I had rather deposit my money in faro banks than the Fidelity, of Cincinnati, and I guess all honest citizens feel the same way.

A SQUARE GAME.

I met a man in a saloon one night at Cincinnati. He was a stranger, and he inquired of me if I knew of a good, big poker game. I told him there no were public games running at that time, that most of the hotels had games, but they were private. We took a drink or two together, and he again remarked he would like a game. I invited him to my room, and we had a nice, square game from that time until morning. I won $900 from him, and as he was about broke I invited him to take breakfast with me. After we had finished breakfast and were smoking our cigars he began to kick. I told him if he was that kind of a man I would never play with him any more. I left him and went to bed. I got up in the afternoon and went out on the street, when I saw my poker friend in company with Detective Steve Mead. Then I knew he was a kicker, sure enough.

Mead told me the chief wanted to see me, so we started for his office. On our way up Central Avenue we stopped to get a drink. I thought I could trust the good-looking bar-keeper, so I just threw a roll over behind the counter, and was then ready to see his Honor. The chief asked me if I won the man's money. I told him I did.

"But," said Chief Woods, "he said you cheated him."

I replied: "Why, chief, how could I, a man that knows but very little about cards, cheat an old gambler like this fellow?"

"I'm no gambler," replied the kicker.

The chief asked Mead what he had learned, and he said:

"They were playing a square game of poker."

"That settles it," said the chief.

So I walked out and down to where I had left my roll. The good-looking young man handed it over, and since then I have always thought Billy Gruber was an honest man and deserved to own two of the finest saloons in the Queen City.

A COWARD.

While in Chicago playing the bank one day I had some angry words with a fellow by the name of John Lawler, and I slapped him in the face. He did not resent it, but went out. About 2 o'clock in the afternoon I cashed in my checks and started to my room. I was walking down Clark Street, and was near the corner of Madison, when this fellow Lawler stepped out and began firing at me. The first shot would have hit me in the breast if I had not thrown up my arm; as it was, it struck me on the wrist-bone and ran up my arm near the shoulder. After the coward fired he began running backward, and kept it up until he had fired all six shots. I had nothing but a little cane, but I started after him, and just as he fired the last shot I struck him with my good arm and downed him. I was onto him, and was just getting that old head of mine ready when the police arrested me. There were thousands of people on the street, but you could not see a cop until the last shot was fired. The fellow was sent up for three years, and I signed a petition to get him out. I was mad when he shot me, and I guess I would have killed him if they had not taken me off; but I do not hold malice to any one, not even if he tries to kill me.

I was laid up for some time with my arm. The bullet was cut out, and was as flat as a half-dollar.

I went from Chicago to St. Paul to see my dear old mother and a sister, who were living there at that time.

My arm is as strong as ever; or, at least, some fellows who have felt it since, say so.

REDUCED THE PRICE.

No one knows the difficulty that a man experiences who, having been a gambler for a long period of years, suddenly resolves to change his course, lead a new life, engage in a different business, and make a new man out of himself. It is all very well for moralists to say that all that is needed is will-power. There is something else. I well remember once that I resolved to leave the business. It was when I was living at Vicksburg. I saw an opportunity to start a beer garden. I rented a house and furnished it up in fine style, and stocked it up with liquors and cigars. My friends were glad to see this course I had taken, and promised to encourage me. They did so, and I could not complain for a lack of patronage. Beer I sold at five cents a glass, and as everybody before had been charging ten cents, I soon secured a large patronage. Securing a band of music I opened in grand style. When the boats landed at the wharf the passengers and crew all came up and paid the garden a visit. Did I succeed in my new undertaking? No, of course I did not. The saloon-keepers all combined and kicked against me because I had reduced the price of beer. Two of them were members of the City Council, and two more of the Board of Aldermen. They sent spies to see if I sold liquor to minors, but being unable to detect me they resolved that I should not have a license. I had taken out my United States revenue license. I was compelled to sell out at a great sacrifice, and all my efforts at reform were unavailing.

GENERAL REMARKS.

When a sucker sees a corner turned up, or a little spot on a card in three-card monte, he does not know that it was done for the purpose of making him think he has the advantage. He thinks, of course, the player does not see it, and he is in such a hurry to get out his money that he often cuts or tears his clothes. He feels like he is going to steal the money from a blind man, but he does not care. He will win it, and say nothing about how he did it. After they have put up their money and turned the card, they see that the mark was put there for a purpose. Then they are mad, because they are beat at their own game. They begin to kick, and want their money back, but they would not have thought of such a thing had they won the money from a blind man, for they did think he must be nearly blind, or he could have seen the mark on the winning card. They expected to rob a blind man, and got left. I never had any sympathy for them, and I would fight before I would give them back one cent. It is a good lesson for a dishonest man to be caught by some trick, and I always did like to teach it. I have had the right card turned on me for big money by suckers, but it was an accident, for they were so much excited that they did not get the card they were after. I have also given a big hand in poker to a sucker, and had him to knock the ginger out of me, but this would make me more careful in the future. I've seen suckers win a small amount, and then run all over the boat, telling how they downed the gambler; but they were almost sure to come back and lose much more than they had won.

I have often given a sucker back his money, and I have seen them lose it with my partner, or at some other game on the same boat. I have won hundreds of thousands from thieves who were making tracks for some other country to keep out of jail and to spend their ill-gotten gains. I enjoyed beating a man that was loaded down with stolen money more than any one else. I always felt as if it was my duty to try and keep the money in our own country.

Young men and boys have often stood around the table and bothered me to bet. I would tell them to go away, that I did not gamble with boys. That would make some of the smart Alecks mad, and they would make a great deal of noise. So, when I was about to close up, I would take in the young chap. He would walk away with a good lesson. But when I had to win money from a boy to keep him quiet, I would always go to him and return the money, after giving him a good talking to.

I meet good business men very often now that take me by the hand and remind me of when I won some money from them when they were boys, and returned it with a good lecture. I have sometimes wished I had one-tenth part of what I have returned to boys and suckers, for then I would have enough to keep me the balance of my life.

I had the niggers all along the coast so trained that they would call me "Massa" when I would get on or off a boat. If I was waiting at a landing I would post some old "nig" what to say when I went on board, so while the passengers were all out on the guards and I was bidding the "coons" good-bye, my "nig" would cry out:

"Good-bye, Massa George; I's goin' to take good care of the old plantation till you comes back."

I would go on board, with one of the niggers carrying my saddle-bags, and those sucker passengers would think I was a planter sure enough; so if a game was proposed I had no trouble to get into it, as all who play cards are looking for suckers that they know have money; and who in those old ante-bellum times had more money than a Southern planter? I have often stepped up to the bar as soon as I would get on board and treat every one within call, and when I would pay for the drinks I would pull out a roll that would make everybody look wild. Then I was sure to get into the first game that would be started, for all wanted a part of the planter's roll.

I have downed planters and many good business men, who would come to me afterwards and want to stand in with my play; and many are the thousands I have divided with them; and yet the truly good people never class such men among gamblers. The world is full of such men. They are not brave enough to take the name, but they are always ready for a part of the game. A gambler's word is as good as his bond, and that is more than I can say of many business men who stand very high in a community. I would rather take a true gambler's word than the bond of many business men who are to-day counted worth thousands. The gambler will pay when he has money, which many good church members will not.

ANCIENT GAMBLING.

Hobbes, the philosopher, says man is the only animal that laughs. He might have appropriately added, he is the only animal that gambles. To gamble or venture on chance, his own property with the hope of winning the property of another is peculiar to him.

Other animals in common with man will fight for meat, drink, and lodging, and will battle for love as fiercely as the old knights of chivalry; but there is no well authenticated account that any of the lower animals ever changed any of their property on "odd-or-even," or drew lots for choice of pasturage. No master has ever yet taught his dog to play with him at casino, and even the learned pig could never learn what was trumps. Hence gambling is a proof of man's intellectual superiority. Certain it is that men, from the earliest ages, have been addicted to some form of gambling, or settling matters by chance. It was by lot that it was determined in Biblical days which of the goats should be offered to Aaron ; by lot the land of Canaan was divided ; by lot Saul was marked out for the Hebrew kingdom ; by lot Jonah was discovered to be the cause of the storm.

Even in legendary days there is a pretty story that Mercury fell in love with Rhea (or the Earth), and wishing to do her a favor, gambled with the Moon, and won from her every seventieth part of the time she illumined the horizon, all of which parts he united together, making up five days, and added them to the Earth's year, which had previously consisted of only 360 days, and was now 365.

There is not an age of the world, nor a people, who have not been gamblers. The Romans, the Greeks, the Asiatics—all have their games of chance. There was, indeed, a period in the history of the world when gambling was the amusement and recreation of kings and queens, professional men and clergymen. Even John Wesley, the founder of Methodism, played cards. The Rev. Caleb C. Colton was one of the luckiest of gamesters. He was a graduate of Cambridge, and the author of "Lacon, or Many Things in a Few Words." At one time in Paris he won $100,000. He left a large fortune, part of which he employed in forming a picture gallery at Paris. General Scott, the father-in-law of George Canning, made one of the largest winnings ever known. He won at White's one million dollars, owing to his sobriety and knowledge of the game of whist.

Who loved his country more than Cato? And yet he was a great gambler. Guido, the painter, and Coquillart, a famous poet, were both inveterate gamblers.

The great philosophers Montaigne and Descartes at an early age were seduced by the allurements of gambling.

The generality of people throughout the world are of

the opinion that gamblers are the worst people on the face of the earth. They are wrong, for I tell you there is ten times more rascality among men outside of the class they call gamblers than there is inside of it.

Persons that the generality of people class as gamblers are only those who play at games of chance with cards. What are the members of the Board of Trade but gamblers? The Board of Trade is just as much a gambling house as a faro bank. Do not the members put up their (and often times other people's) money on puts, calls, margins, and futures? Do not some poor people have to wait a long time in the "future" before they get back the money some rascal has put up and lost? Talk about the morality of gamblers. They are not thieves and swindlers, and I never heard of one who ever served a term in the penitentiary, or was arrested for embezzling money.

GEORGE—"THE BUTTER."

"There goes one of the most remarkable men in this country," said a well-known gentleman standing in front of the Gibson House yesterday. The person referred to was a stoutly-built, sandy-whiskered individual of medium size. He is well known to most men about town, and his exploits on Southern rivers might fill a book. It was George H. Devol. "I have known him for thirty-eight years," the gentleman continued, "my acquaintance with him having been strictly in the South. Do you know that physically he was for years one of the best men we had down there?"

"No. Never heard that George was a fighter," added the reporter somewhat surprised.

"Well, he was, and as good as they made them, too. I never saw him take water in my life, and personally know that for nineteen years they tried to find a man to whip him. They couldn't do it. He was a terrible rough-and-tumble fighter, and many a tough citizen have I seen him do up. George was a great 'butter.' He could use his head with terrible effect. One night at New Orleans a stevedore tackled him. It was a set-up job. The stevedore was a much larger man, but George got the best of it. During the fight the stevedore's friends stood over George with drawn pistols, threatening to kill him should he do any butting. He can kill any man living, white or black, by butting him. Although over fifty years of age, I don't believe there is a man living who can whip him. New Orleans sporting men will go broke on that."

"He made considerable money in the South, didn't he?"

"Yes, he has won more money than any sporting man in the country. He had the privileges for years on all boats on the Southern Mississippi. When Ben Butler took possession of New Orleans he confiscated all of George's horses and sent him to jail. That little affair cost George just $50,000. He retaliated, however, for he had not been released two weeks until he beat one of the General's pay-masters out of $19,000. It was on the Red River. I see he has settled down and quit sporting, and I am glad of it. Had he never seen a faro bank he would have been an immensely wealthy man thirty years ago. One night before the war I saw him lose $23,000 at one sitting. He left the table without enough money with which to buy a cup of coffee."—*The Cincinnati Enquirer*.

Printed in the United States
43151LVS00001B/20